Paupers' Paris

Miles Turner is an impoverished American, living in Oregon. He spent his fourteenth birthday in Paris and never recovered from the experience. Over the years he has spent vacations there whenever possible, living cheaply, exploring the city, and researching this book. He has made numerous Parisian friends and contacts, whom he has persuaded to divulge up-to-the-minute hints, and some well-kept secrets, for the penniless traveller.

Miles Turner

Paupers' Paris

Pan Original
Pan Books London, Sydney and Auckland

First published 1982 by Pan Books Ltd,
Cavaye Place, London SW10 9PG

Revised 1983, 1984, 1986, 1988 and 1990
This new edition published 1990

9 8 7 6 5 4 3 2 1

© Miles Turner 1982, 1983, 1984, 1986, 1988, 1990

ISBN 0 330 313150

Photoset by Parker Typesetting Service, Leicester

Printed and bound in Great Britain by
Richard Clay Ltd, Bungay, Suffolk

Contents

PARIS

Introduction

This book is for paupers – or if not paupers, cheapskates – who would love to spend some time in Paris, but would prefer not to spend much money. It sets out to prove that, while Paris has justly earned its reputation as one of the world's more outrageously expensive places, there are hundreds of ways to avoid the city's grasping hands and still share in its pleasures.

Now that the 1789-1989 celebrations have faded into history, Paris is coming back to itself, Parisians who flocked out of the city to avoid the hype and hysteria are all home again, and once more it's one of the great affordable pleasures of this world.

If we have a single motto, it's 'Sleep cheap and eat well'. It turns out that you can sleep *and* eat for next to nothing, and do both rather well if you set your mind to it. There are cheap routes to Paris; there is limitless cheap transportation all over the city; there are hundreds of low-budget hotels that are clean and friendly and charming; there are incredible meals to be had in the humblest restaurants; there are more – free – spectacles, sights and attractions per square block than anywhere else we can think of. We've tried to fill this book with specifics – a mere scratching of the surface – of all these subjects, and with some pointers on how to use the information.

To make maximum use of our information, you'll need at least some of the following:

A sense of adventure. If tripe is half the price of steak on a menu, and you've never had tripe before but have a queasy idea of what it is, still you're *driven* to order tripe.

A low entertainment threshhold. That quality which makes a person a cheap date. In Paris it means that the clientele of the nearest brasserie are as interesting and amusing and exciting to you as the entire cast of Covent Garden.

Unqualified adoration for the city. Everyone loves Paris in theory.

To relish that slightly Gorgonzola-like aroma in the lower depths of the Métro is a measure of true love.

A sense of self-mockery. If you can't enjoy the spectacle of yourself as a total imbecile when it comes to haggling (or saying 'good morning', for that matter) then you should go to Denmark where they speak English.

A tourist's loathing of other tourists. The best thing that can happen to you is when a Parisian asks *you* for directions.

More taste than money. While you can't actually bring back a Cézanne or two, or the contents of Lanvin's windows, at least you will have paid them a visit.

A good deal of low cunning. The ability to wash (and dry) your entire wardrobe in a hotel sink without leaving a trail of evidence for the chambermaid.

We suggest that you take with you at least a few words of French – even if they're all in a pocket phrase book. Parisians are rather proud of their language, and on their own turf would rather converse in French than try their English out on you. If you need help, or just crave human contact, remember that the French help those who help themselves. The ice begins to break when you make the effort to communicate, but it's up to you.

It's this lack of linguistic hospitality – and also some misunderstandings about customs and manners – that has given the French a reputation for rudeness among travellers. *La politesse* is central to all transactions in France. The French are formal: they'll preface every question with 'Pardon, Monsieur ...' or 'S'il vous plaît, Madame ...' They'll consider *you* rude if you don't do the same.

Remember also that Parisians who habitually deal with tourists, with apparently ill-mannered Americans, Germans and English, who may in fact be less callous than tongue-tied, develop their own callousness for dealing with foreigners. If you stay off the beaten track (and with the help of this book you can) you'll avoid these unfortunates and come into contact with a friendly, garrulous, buoyant race of Parisians you've never met or heard of before.

You will note that certain *arrondissements* – the 5e, 7e, 8e, parts of the 19e and 20e – have been give fairly lengthy descriptions in the Footwork section, while others better-known apparently have been slighted. This is highly personal; the ones that are in are there just because they are places we have enjoyed which may have been missed out in other publications. The 6e, especially around St-Germain-des-Prés, has been written about everywhere; visited by everyone. As a consequence, waiters can be rude, hotels over-crowded and over-priced, meals in the main to be avoided. You'll go there anyway, and find your own pleasures without help from us, so there's no general talk about it here. But it would be a pity to miss, for example, the less-known areas such as the Batignolles (page 51), the hidden and charming parts of the haughty 7e *arrondissement,* and the pleasant rather domestic bits of the forbiddingly elegant 8e. Two neighbourhoods which are changing so fast that it's impossible to include them with accuracy in this edition are the 11e around the Bastille, and the 13e near the rue de Tolbiac – Asia in Paris – you'll have the delight of discovering them yourselves.

Paupers' Paris is the result of the labour and support of all my friends and relatives: many contributions from people I've never met but am most grateful to. Bawn O'Beirne-Ranelagh took over the task of editing, co-ordinating information, and putting it all on disc for this new edition. As well, she diligently checked hotels and shops. A crew of young Paris residents ate their way through restaurants, and in the process turned up many new ones: we thank Gloria Girton, Adam Steinhouse, Tim Allan, Annie Polatsek, Jeanne Corey, Ruth Peters, Joshua Kobb, Jonathan Gilbert, and all their friends. I still owe thanks to my mother Martha Lomask, who researched and rewrote entire sections of the original editions, and my father, Milton, who covered art galleries, museums, and music as well as verifying dozens of addresses. Leonard Yoon helped me plot the book over countless bottles of wine, and Charlie White closed his eyes to my long absences from work. M. Patrick Goyet and Pauline Hallam of the French Government Tourist Office in London have been as always a source of strength. I must also thank Marc Humphries and Richard Viren of that office for their help. Michèle Vengeois Cirak of the Office de Tourisme has been this year – as from the first edition of this book – immensely helpful.

It should be noted that prices in this book were correct in August 1989. We hope they'll still be as accurate as possible when you read these pages, but costs do have a habit of creeping upward when your back is turned. Still, Paris continues to offer, at very good value, hundreds of good hotels, charming restaurants, and its own distinctive attractions for those who know where, and how, to look.

M.T.

Allons-y *(Preliminaries)*

Who?

Before anything else you must decide – who's going? Just you, your nearest and dearest, your bridge club? A few pros and cons:

Travelling alone is the best way to see and do exactly what you want. If you get lost or bungle seriously in a restaurant, feel like sleeping till noon, or decide to spend the rest of your life in Paris, the decisions (and the responsibility) are all yours. If you make mistakes, nobody else gets blamed. You don't have to adjust to anyone else's diet, or standards of hygiene, or attention span. If you can handle being on your own, it's the best way to go.

But if your gregariousness and your French aren't up to it, you can die of loneliness. You'll have to survive on a few encounters a day – in cafés, restaurants and shops. You'll always be treated well, if you make the effort to make yourself understood, but it's unlikely that anyone will adopt you.

Travelling in company guarantees that you'll have someone with whom to share the experience, and a helping hand if things get dicey. The drawback is that your tastes will differ. *You* will want to spend eight hours in one room of the Louvre; *she* will choose to spend the day playing pinball machines in a café behind the Bastille.

Our solution for days when your energy and interests don't coincide is to split up: plan to meet for lunch, and plan to meet again for dinner. (Agree in advance on the restaurants. No last-minute searches on an empty stomach.) If one person doesn't show up within fifteen minutes, the other forges ahead with the meal. We've found this to be a good way to avoid getting bored with each other. Travelling in company can have an odd, isolating effect. You can get on each other's nerves. And it's bad for your French.

Small groups can be worked the same way: you can pack the kids off to the Bois, send Granny to the flea market, and you're on your own. The one thing you must not do is travel in packs. Even a benign dictatorship can end up in communal misery.

When to go?

Of course it's best to go when the spirit moves you. When you can't stand the grind a minute more. When your boss *lets* you go. But if it's not purely a matter of impulse, desperation, budget, or tight scheduling, there are a few matters about timing to consider.

High season, low season, normal season

Naturally, this affects airline fares: get a good travel agent, or do a real study yourself of what the flying people are up to at any given moment. Equally important: there are certain times of the year when it is all but impossible to find a room in central Paris or anywhere near it at short notice. The Office de Tourisme in Paris has this advice:

Most heavily booked periods:
2-6 February
2-10 March
1-2, 4-7 April
5-10 June
4-10, 17-26 September
18-22 October
17-22 November

Do not arrive on any of these dates without a firm booking.

Second most difficult:
All of June, much of September, most of October. Wisest to book in advance if you can.

Normal periods:
Most of March, April, May and November, other than the heavily booked dates above.

Low season:
Surprisingly, July, August, December, and early January are times when you can almost always find a room somewhere, even on short notice. However, it may be a good precaution to have a firm booking for the first few days if arriving in July or August. For real Paris-lovers, December and the first week in January (when the wonderful sales are on) – when Paris is at its silvery best, with the light shining through the bare trees and the life of the city vibrating all around – can be the choicest time to be there.

We once found ourselves, through ridiculously bad timing, in Paris in the first week of March during two major trade fairs and the opening of an important art show. We managed to get a room in a very good, low-priced hotel, in a great neighbourhood we'd never stayed in before, which immediately became our second home. This was done by exerting ourselves somewhat, visiting a number of hotels until we found one that would have us for one night, which stretched to six. We wouldn't care to do this if arriving at midnight after a long flight, tired, drunk, or travelling with small children or an elderly companion.

Climate

The weather can influence your plans, and will certainly influence your wardrobe. To give you a rough idea – the mean temperature in February is 36.5°F (3°C), in July 65.5°F (18°C). East and north-west winds keep Paris cool and fairly dry in winter and spring; there can be stretches in December and January when bitter winds come shrieking across North Europe from Siberia, and you'll be glad of woollies and a warm coat. Prevailing south-west winds bring the heaviest rains in summer and autumn, so pack a folding umbrella and a light waterproof coat then.

What to take

Your wardrobe naturally depends on what you have, and how much you are willing to lug around. 'Travelling light' is a phrase that has an adventurous ring to it – people who drag along only one steamer trunk rather than three, probably consider themselves light travellers – it's a relative term, but a worthwhile goal. We figure you can live comfortably, and indefinitely, on about fourteen kilos of luggage; more if you are strong of arm or not averse to porters; less if you're a wimp, anti-porter, or plan to switch digs every few days by Métro, not taxi. In either case, here are a few suggestions:

1 Dress in layers – for all climates and most seasons. Everything easily washable or dry-cleanable. Everything easily folded, or preferably rolled, which cuts down on creasing. Think twice about heavy items. If your overcoat is going to be a millstone, don't take it. In all but the dead of winter, rely on piling one sweater on top of another under that light waterproof coat.

2 Take nothing you haven't worn before, and nothing that you don't love. Take nothing you can't walk or climb in.

3 Take a couple of pairs of durable, comfortable, well-broken-in shoes. Armies may travel on their stomachs – *you* travel on your feet.

4 *Indispensables*

A cotton kimono

A pair of rubber flip-flops (thongs, zoris, or whatever these Taiwanese sandals are called)

For cold weather, a really warm, soft scarf – lambswool for preference. And two identical pairs of gloves, because you're going to lose one glove the day you arrive

A telescopic umbrella – one that fits easily into the suitcase

A good plush hand-towel – not too small – which will help pad breakables and will supplement the sometimes meagre one common to Paris hotels

Soap

Blow-dryer, heated rollers, electric razor (see Electricity, page 231)

A plastic carrier bag for unwashed clothes. A few plastic bags and twist-ties. A featherweight bag that folds into your luggage, and can double as an overnight case or to carry home all the extras you will buy

Nail scissors and, even more important, toe-nail clippers – real agony-savers

Glasses or contacts if you wear them: take an extra pair and/or a recent prescription

Medicines: an adequate supply, and a refillable prescription

Indispensable for picnics, hotel and otherwise: a cup and an immersion heater if you *must* have tea (see Electricity, page 231)

A saucer-sized plate, a small sharp knife, a fork, a spoon. Be as ingenious as you want about this

Clip-on reading light (220 volts) if you can't live without it and don't trust hotel lighting

Three or four lightweight plastic hangers for drip-drying. A few clip-type clothes pegs. A little detergent in a plastic squeeze bottle (see Hotels, page 63)

A corkscrew

And, not to belabour the obvious, don't forget your toothbrush.

All of this, excluding what you wear on your back, should fit into a fairly small suitcase that could be carry-on luggage, bypassing that awful wait at airport or hoverlanding. Take along a thin, strong, nylon soft-sac for *en route* essentials such as book, flask, camera, tissues, maps, whatever.

Money questions

(For denominations, mechanics and equivalents, see Money, page 240.)

How much to take? Some advance decisions are going to be necessary here. You'll have to decide after considerable thought what's important to *you*, not to us or your next-door neighbour. Budget for your extravagance, and save somewhere else. Do you feel best in a room big enough to spread out wet coats, luggage, bottles, flowers, newspapers? That's what you should budget for. Can't live without *petit déjeuner* served in your room, or your own shower, a private loo, a lift? A hotel within an arm's length of the Louvre, or a quieter, cheaper, possibly more spacious place ten minutes away on the Métro? Budget for it. Save on museum entrance fees by going on Sundays (free or half-price), or have a week of picnic lunches instead of eating in restaurants, and spend your money how you will.

Transport to and from Paris

Maximum: will buy you airfare,
London-Paris and back, open-dated   £148
ticket and ultimate convenience.

Minimum: provides the
cheapest bus/boat/bus service,
and a modicum of discomfort.
See pages 20–21 for details.

£43

Hotel per night

Maximum: a nice, bourgeois
hotel in a 'good', close-in
district, all facilities including
shower and loo.

270F

Minimum: cheap, clean, away
from it all, no frills.
See pages 65–95 for details.

90F

Food per day

Maximum: breakfast in bed; a
lunch that will take up half the
afternoon, and dinner half the
night.

250F

Minimum: coffee at the *zinc* of
the local café, a picnic lunch
indoors or out, a modest but
satisfying dinner.
See pages 99–153 for details.

100F

Getting around

Maximum: includes a few taxis
for quick getaways to station or
airport.

150F
(20F per day)

Minimum: unlimited Métro/
bus/RER travel for seven days.
See pages 38–50 for details.

47F

The sights

Maximum: full-price museum admissions; a movie; innumerable cups of coffee, seated.   120F

Minimum: everything gratis, or very, very cheap.
See pages 163–199 for details.   25F

The shops

Maximum: a matter of taste and income.   ?F

Minimum: don't buy *anything*.
See pages 200–223 for details.   0F

Necessities

Maximum: enough to get your laundry done, your hair cut, your baby sat, your post sent, and your pockets full of change.   250F

Minimum: an afternoon in the laundrette and one postcard.
See pages 224–258 for details.   30F

Emergencies

Maximum and minimum depend entirely on you. If you're accident-prone, provide extra money for crises. If you have an invisible plastic shield, or a lot of sensible insurance, take less. But always keep some money in reserve.

See pages 259–270 for details.

How to carry money

Cash

You'll need some within five minutes of your arrival in Paris: enough to get your *Paris Visite* tourist pass, or *Carte Orange*; enough to get a bite to eat and transport you to your hotel; a few more francs for a left-luggage locker; possibly a phone call home, or to pay the *Hôtesses de Paris* for locating a room for you. Arm yourself before you leave with at least 100 francs in cash to get you into town. Change pounds or dollars before you leave home, at a bank or bureau de change where you know you'll get a good rate.

Traveller's cheques

Your own bank or building society may offer them as a free service (but avoid the lesser known brands which can be difficult to cash in some Paris banks or bureaux). Size of denominations depends on how often you want to sign your name, and how careless you get when you've cashed a big one.

Eurocheques: see page 244.

Visa, Access, Mastercard, Eurocard and such

Be careful with these, use them if you are well-organised, or not spendthrift , or in a real pinch. The exchange rate at which you are billed is calculated by the issuing company on the day they bill you, not the day you used the card, so you can't know in advance how much you are spending. And it's an easy way to run up bills that can curl your hair when you get home. If you're travelling for a long period, remember that after an initial grace period you start paying interest on the unpaid amount at a horrendous 25 per cent per annum and up. Be advised, too, that many smaller hotels, shops, and restaurants you frequent *do not* accept credit cards.

Booking hotels in advance

If you know more or less what you want, where you want to be and
how much you want to pay (see 'Au lit', pages 59–98), it's a good
idea to reserve in advance. It's not in the least difficult if you have a
little time to work it out. It can save you energy and anxiety at the
moment of your lowest ebb – your arrival in the chaos and confusion of the Paris airport, terminal, or railway station.

Once you've picked a hotel, write a letter to the management. In
French. Use, if you like, the form letter – a service of the Office de
Tourisme – reproduced below. Specify the dates of arrival and (if
you can) the date of departure, number of people, and your
requirements – with or without a loo or *salle de bain*, single or double
room, and so on.

Form letter to hotels (freely adapted from that used by the Paris
Office de Tourisme)

Le Directeur
Hotel _____
Address _____

Monsieur le Directeur,

Je vous serais obligé de me communiquer vos conditions
(I would be grateful if you would let me know your terms)
et tarifs pour un séjour de _____ nuits, commençant le _____
(and prices for a stay of _____ nights, beginning _____)
à _____ heures, et se terminant le _____ à _____ heures.*
(at _____ o'clock, and ending _____ at _____ o'clock.)

Nous souhaiterions réserver _____ (chambres à un lit)
(We would like to reserve) _____ (single rooms)
(chambres à grand lit) (chambres à deux lits) (avec WC/bain/douche).
(double rooms) (twin-bedded rooms) (with WC/bath/shower).

Avec mes remerciements,

*Use the 24-hour clock.

Use an International Reply Coupon

Whether you're reserving a room or just asking for information from any French source (other than a government tourist agency). The hotel, shop, or agency, or whatever, can exchange the coupon for return postage. Many of these operations are running on a tight margin, and cannot afford to send free information to rich tourists. The courtesy will be appreciated. A self-addressed airmail envelope is another form of good manners, and can help ensure that you do get a reply.

IRCs cost 65 pence in Britain and are available at post offices.

Postscripts to preliminaries

Life-saving tips from the most experienced travelling paupers we know:

1 Never travel without a good supply of soft toilet paper (not just for obvious purposes, but for blowing noses, mopping brows, even as napkins for picnics).
2 Never travel with more luggage than you yourself can carry in comfort, without porter or taxi.
3 For dire emergencies never travel without a little bit of cognac in a flask.

En route *(Getting there)*

Your choice of routes to Paris will depend on your finances and need for comfort; how much you want to spend *en route*, how long you want to stay, what time of year (or time of day) gives you the best deal.

London to Paris and back

Myriad possibilities, listed from the cheapest to the dearest.

Eurolines

National Express, the giant spiderweb that links all the UK to London, now can take you to Paris – and beyond. Eurolines Coaches leave from Victoria Coach Station, and usually run two daytime and one overnight trips all year round. Return trip to Paris can cost as little as £43, and you can buy one-way tickets for about £25. Prices vary with the seasons, so check with your travel agent or any National Express office in the UK. It's a flat fare, no reductions for students, the very young or the elderly. Here's how you travel:

Coach/Boat/Coach: Day trips are about 8½ hours, depending on road conditions, night trips as comfortable as can be expected – and you do save a night's hotel bill. But you'll roll into Paris with the dawn, and the first day can seem endless, as most hotels won't book you in until noon. The buses are equipped with reclining seats and all the usual facilities, ventilation is reasonably good, and rumour has it that some coaches this year will be non-smoking. Departure:

Victoria Coach Station. Arrival: Porte de la Villette, Eurolines Coach Station, 19e *arrondissement*.

Book through any National Express office in the UK. In Paris, at the Porte de la Villette and 55 rue St Jacques, 5e *arrondissement*, or at SNCF (French railways) offices.

Other coach services: Have a look at *Time Out* or the free-sheets distributed on the street and mainly for young Aussies and New Zealanders, for details of other cheapos . . . we have varying reports which range from 'not too bad considering the rock-bottom fares', to 'beer drinking all night long, smoke you could cut with a knife, and a coach driver who hadn't had his license long.' You make up your own mind.

Hoverspeed

City Sprint: Half an hour faster and the same price as the above. Clean, comfortable coaches which take you from Victoria Coach Station in London to Dover and across on Hovercraft, then on the Autoroute into Paris. About 8 hours travelling time.

From April to the end of June, there are three departures a day. In July, four departures; in August, five a day, dropping back to three a day in September and October. From November to early spring, no departures are scheduled at this writing. The first bus leaves London at 8:00 a.m., the last at 11:30 p.m. or 12:30 a.m. according to the season. Returning, you leave Paris on the first bus at 8:30 a.m., last bus about 12:30 or 1:00 a.m. A useful way to travel if you plan to return from Paris by another route, or are going on to other European stops, as you can buy one-way or round-trip tickets and it's pretty cheap.

Adult, one way	£25
return	£43
Student (under 26) and Senior	
Citizens (over 60), one way	£24
return	£42
Children under 4 go free.	

Round-trip tickets are good for one year, but book your return journey four days before you plan to travel.

Train/Hovercraft/Train: From two to four flights a day depending on season. It's clean, not too expensive, and free from the restrictive conditions which hedge in cheap airline flights. And it's surprisingly fast – can be as little as 5½ hours from the centre of London to the Gare du Nord in Paris.

Trains depart from Victoria and the outward journeys are in quite new and comfortable carriages with few stops. Coming back, trains from Dover to Victoria can be fairly fast or all-stops-between, depending on how prompt or delayed the Hovercraft was.

There's usually plenty of time at each end (Dover and Calais) to collect some duty-frees and have a snack or a beer.

The one big catch to this mode of travel is that at the English end, trains to and from Dover begin and end at Dover Priory,which is *not* at the Hoverport. In between it's a short bus ride, which can be uncomfortable, even if you travel only with hand luggage. There are too few double-decker coaches crammed with back-packers, duty-free plastic bags, and some incredibly huge suitcases, all of which have to be lugged and jammed up the coach steps and into the narrow aisles. One seasoned Hovercraft traveller says his motto is 'Take No Prisoners', which means that he tramples the young, the old and the infirm under foot and grabs a seat.

At the French end, trains are direct from the Calais terminal to the Gare du Nord and vice versa. You can have an on-board meal of croissants, wine, coffee, or soft drinks, served from rolling carts to the airline-type seats.

Between the two countries, the Hovercraft trip is fast, noisy, with a smooth-as-satin ride or a lot of bounce as the weather dictates. People who order drinks are apt to get their come-uppance: what goes down, may come up.

	2nd class single	2nd class return	5-day return
Adult	£46.00	£69.00	£53.00
Child, 4-11 inclusive	£24.10	£36.00	£27.00
Child, 12-15 inclusive	£32.50	£48.00	£36.00
Senior Citizen*	£35.00	£54.50	£42.50

Children under 4 travel free.
Return fares are valid for 2 months.

*For holders of the UK Senior Citizens Railcard (£15) plus the Rail-Europ Card (£5). Senior Citizens now must arm themselves with the Rail-Europ Senior Card, to add to the familiar purple UK card. You can't get the Rail-Europ card alone.

Hovercraft tickets are available from British Rail centres and most travel agents. In Paris, at 135 rue Lafayette, 10e *arrondissement*.

Beware: some travel agents will apply a £5 surcharge on any fare which includes continental rail travel. Others won't handle Senior Citizen rail tickets. If this happens to you, make your displeasure known on the spot and go to a more amenable travel agent.

Sealink

Train/Boat/Train: Slower than the Hovercraft, and conditions can be highly variable from reasonably clean to unreasonably squalid. The boats sail in fog or dicey weather, when Hovercraft or planes may be grounded or delayed. You can jog around the decks. Take your own picnic, unless you want to eat in the restaurants or snack bars. For obvious reasons, you won't choose this way of travel at football match time. Up to five sailings a day, about 8 hours Victoria Gare du Nord. There are overnight sailings and you can book reclining chair accommodation or cabins.

	European saver	*Ordinary fare*	*Senior Citizen*
Adult (return fare)	£51.60	£42.40 (single)	£25.90 (single)

Child fares on request from British Rail
Berths range from £8.80 to £10.50, with Club Class or reclining seats from £2.25 to £5.00

For under-26s and students

Many travel agents specialise in inexpensive rail and coach and air fares for travellers in these special categories: they advertise in school and college magazines, and in *Time Out*, *City Limits*, and free-sheets such as *LAM* and *TNT*. STA Travel, 86 Old Brompton Road, London SW7, and 117, Euston Road, London NW1, Tel. 071-581 8233; and Campus Travel Group, 52 Grosvenor Gardens, SW1, Tel. 071-730 3402, are both long established in this field.

Cheap flights

Magazines like *Time Out* and *City Limits*, *LAM*, *TNT* and *London Girl*, are crammed with ads for cheap airfares. These days you don't have to depend on bucket shops for such good deals, most major travel agents will probably do you just as well and save you some footwork.

The Air Travel Advisory Bureau (in London 071-636 5000; and Manchester 061-832 2000) is a clearing-house for information about agents who offer cheap flights worldwide. We have found them quick, helpful and accurate, and one phone call to them could provide you with the names of the five or six agents who can give you the best deal that day on flights to and from Paris, saving you dozens of fruitless calls.

Major airlines insist that you book your return journey when you sign on for the outward leg, and you can't alter dates or flight times without a bitter penalty (be sure you take out adequate travel insurance to cover costs of cancellation for illness or whatever). At peak holiday times the fares go up. But there are ways around these fixed-price deals. Read on.

From the cheapest to the most expensive round-trip fares:

£60-72: for students and under-26s. British Airtours, Gatwick-Beauvais, then on by coach to Paris. Offered by, among others, Globe Travel, 16 Leicester Square, London W2. Tel: 071-727 6043

£64: Late Savers (standby), British Airways and Air France, Heathrow–Charles de Gaulle. Bookable only the day before you fly, and valid for two weeks only. Cannot be booked by telephone. The catch: if you want to return from Paris on a Monday, you will have to go to Charles de Gaulle Airport early on Sunday morning to book as all airlines offices are closed on Sundays. Book direct through the airline or through any authorised travel agent.

£65.60: Air India. Out only on Fridays, back only on Sundays, but valid for a year. Travel Arcade, Triumph House, 189 Regent Street, London W1. Tel: 071-734 5873. (Non-cancellable, and outward and return flights must be booked.)

£70: Gulf Air, Heathrow–Charles de Gaulle, Tuesdays, Thursdays, Fridays, 10:00 a.m.: from Paris, Tuesdays and Wednesdays, 7:00 a.m. and Wednesdays 4:35 p.m. We have had good luck with Gulf as the in-flight service is superb. But if you're a non-EEC citizen travelling this way, be prepared to queue at British Immigration desks for ever on the way home. Flyair, 15-17 Heddon Street, London W1R 7LF. Tel: 071-287 1954. Open return, tickets good for one year.

£71.60: Dan-Air, Gatwick–Charles de Gaulle, several flights a week between Mondays and Thursdays. Tickets valid for 3 months. Travel Arcade, Triumph House, 189 Regent Street, London W1. Tel: 071-734 5873. (Non-cancellable, and outward and return flights must be booked.)

£89: British Airways or Air France, APEX fare, direct from airlines or through agents. Flights must be booked both ways and cannot be changed.

One-way fares: While the major airlines tie you up with all the restrictions they can devise, others are more flexible. Many airlines flying to the Middle and Far East pass on to you the benefit of something called the Sixth Freedom of the Skies, meaning that they can offer you a one-way-only seat to Paris at a moderate fare, since there will be someone waiting there to occupy the seat on the main leg of the flight. You can pick up a one-way flight home in Paris through such agencies as Nouvelles Frontières. For tickets from London, try these:

£26.50: Students and under-26s only. London Student Travel, 52 Grosvenor Gardens, London SW1. Tel: 071-730 3402.

£28.50: Students and under-26s only. Miracle Bus/Flight, 408 Strand, London WC2. Tel: 071-379 6055. Very hard to reach by phone, best to write well in advance or call in person.

£55: Gulf Air, Flyair, 15-17 Heddon Street, London W1R 7LF. Tel: 071-287 1954

Check other long-haul air carriers – Thai, Malaysia, Kuwait, Singapore – for latest information on one-way bargains.

The agents we mention above are those whose information we have found accurate. Some others will advertise alluring prices which have mysteriously disappeared when you call. The practice is known as 'bait-and-switch', and originated in the used-car lots of Los Angeles, where it belongs.

Package Tours

These come in all shapes and sizes, and, naturally, all prices. They range from the antiseptic (everything through a coach window, with English commentary) to the spartan (transportation, bed and breakfast, no frills).

The advantage of the no-frills package is that it takes the guess-work out of the basic amenities, and leaves you free to explore the city on your own. The means of transportation (air, hover, coach, and the rest) and the types of accommodation (1-star to 4-star) are varied, and you'll want to sort through the possibilities very carefully.

We have had good reports on two UK package tour agencies which specialise in Paris – French Leave and Time Off. There are a number of others which are undoubtedly equally good, but as we never give you information that hasn't come directly from someone who has been there, we can't comment on them.

All colour brochures featuring Paris have almost impenetrable charts – prices, number of nights, type of accommodation, supplements for holidays, and so forth. The chart we give you here is a simplified version from a major tour agency's brochure to give you an idea of the possibilities.

Prices here are for *two nights only*, to make things easier; for longer stays, just add on the extra cost per night.

The tour operator whose brochure we've used offers much glossier stays in 3-star and 4-star hotels, even in luxury-class Hotel Lancaster – but if you travel in such circles, stop reading now and give this book to some deserving pauper.

The prices here are for good, centrally located, well-run *one-* and *two-star* hotels only. One-star places have basins and sometimes bidets in each room, two-star will give you a private bath or shower and possibly a private WC. One-star hotels do *not* have lifts, two-stars often do.

You can often save £££ travelling by night by Euroline coach on the Dover-Calais service, at the lowest package tour prices, if you don't mind sitting up, drowsing in fairly comfortable surroundings. Most costly, of course, is travel by scheduled services from Heathrow to Charles de Gaulle, and coach direct from the airport to the city centre.

	City Sprint	Hovercraft or Rail/Ship/ Rail	Off-peak flights	Gatwick Paris	Heathrow Paris
Low season (1 January-15 March, 1 November-31 December)					
1-star	£65	£74	£106	£111	£136
2-star	£81	£91	£123	£128	£153
High season (16 March-31 October)					
1-star	£73	£76	£110	£115	£139
2-star	£91	£94	£128	£133	£157

Prices are based on *two people* sharing *for two nights*. Continental breakfast included. Travel from your city arrival point to your Paris hotel *extra*. For single rooms, add £7 per night for a 1-star hotel, £15 for a 2-star hotel. Extra nights, of course, are available at additional cost: check the tour operator's brochure.

Many package tour operators offer special terms for Winter Bargain Breaks, Weekends and Long Weekends, and some good cheapies like a 3 or 5 night holiday by coach, ship and coach – one such 'mini-week' holiday offered five nights in a pleasant one-star hotel for £199, and a British Rail 'Supersave' fare cut the cost even more. The only drawback to this 'mini-week' was the nine-hour travelling time each way. And Time Off now flies from London City Airport – a very uncrowded, comfortable, hassle-free airport – to Charles de Gaulle in Paris, for the same price as their off-peak tours.

Personal note from one of our well-travelled friends: 'Some package tours tout their Paris excursions, which range from Bateau Mouche cruises to trips to Chartres and Fontainebleu, and Moulin Rouge and Lido Cabaret Shows (£43 for the evening). We say – skip them, go on your own, with this book in hand. Others say "Great to have everything organised for you, worth the money." Best to make this decision on the spot, not by pre-booking and pre-paying.'

Entreé/sortie
(Arrivals and departures)

Passports, visas, customs

You ought to have a valid passport to enter France (although strictly speaking it isn't necessary for EEC residents). Non-EEC citizens need a visa for France. Apply to the nearest French Consulate in plenty of time, or try the Visa Shop Ltd, Charing Cross Shopping Arcade, WC2; Tel. 071-379 0419 and 071-379 0376.

In Britain, standard passports are good for ten years, and cost £15 (for 30 pages) or £30 (for 94 pages). Get forms from your local post office. Two photographs needed. Return the application, with fee and photos, countersigned by someone impressive who knows you – vicar, solicitor, doctor, or JP – either to the passport office or to the nearest main post office in your city. Expect to wait about ten days for the passport in winter, or up to a month in heavy periods. Don't leave it until the last minute.

A British Visitors Passport is good for one year only. The fee is £7.50. Apply for forms at the post office. Two photos. No counter-signature needed. Valid only for Europe. This seems an expensive way to travel, but the waiting time for issue is less than for the standard one.

A British Excursion Document, for travel to France only – and for a duration of only 60 hours! – is available from post offices at £2.00: good for one month from date of issue only.

Length of stay

For up to three months, a resident of the EEC countries needs no visa. For longer stays, apply at the Préfecture de Police nearest to where you are living. Take along your passport and a good reason why you want to remain in Paris. They will issue a *Permis de Séjour*. Keep this with your passport and produce it when necessary (in time of trouble or when leaving France). If you are going to study in France, take to the Préfecture some kind of proof of enrolment in a school or college.

On leaving Britain, you must for some reason show your passport to an immigration official. On entering France (airport, or at boat or hovercraft landing) a French official looks at it but probably won't bother to stamp it. Likewise on the return journey. As a foreigner entering either country, you could be asked the reason for your stay (business, tourism, family matters), how long you'll be around. With the advent of the EEC, this has become – in France, at least – the merest formality.

Douanes/Customs

Again, these days, it's mostly a matter of waving you on. If they're looking for you they'll stop you, or they may hold you up briefly, by pure chance, rifle your luggage, and leave you to repack. Contraband is illegal drugs, firearms (except hunting guns with permits), explosives, pornography. A respectful demeanour and a blank face will probably keep you from getting hung up in Customs at either end. Do not attempt to charm or chat up a customs officer anywhere. They are not susceptible to charm.

Duty-free allowances

For those returning to Britain from an EEC country (including France) – you may bring back these amounts bought in France: 300 cigarettes, 75 cigars or 400 grams of pipe tobacco, 3 litres of wine, 1½ litres of spirits, and other goods up to the value of £35.

If you buy in duty-free shops (for instance, at airports, ship- and hoverports) customs allowances are less. Check on the spot. If you're travelling late at night these shops may be closed. And duty-free prices are NOT the bargains you may be led to expect – compare them for yourself.

Arriving

First impressions can make or break your trip. If you step off the train or plane confused and disoriented, you can expect to stay that way for days. It helps to know what to expect: instead of floundering around in the chaos of the Gare du Nord you can begin immediately to develop a Paris expertise which will see you through your visit.

The airports are smoothly organised, well signposted and furnished with bureaux de change, information services and so forth. But like airports everywhere, Charles de Gaulle/Roissy and Orly are sterile, unamusing places, pervaded by a kind of travel *angst*, and you'll want to be on your way at once.

To reach central Paris from Charles de Gaulle or Orly, you have several choices:

Charles de Gaulle/Roissy

Bus: cheapest and reasonably fast: take the free bus from your arrival point to the SNCF station, buy a *carnet* of ten tickets, walk about 15 yards and find the service bus stop to Paris – No. 350 takes you to the Gare du Nord, No. 351 to Gare de l'Est. If you have bought a *Paris Visite* card in London, the ride costs you nothing – but don't put the little ticket into the ticket-stamping machine as this will invalidate it. Otherwise, it's six tickets from your *carnet*, or 27F in cash. The advantage of these buses is that you climb directly on and off, without having to cope with the railway turnstiles, escalators, stairs and platforms. The buses are blessedly uncrowded, and when you arrive in Paris you're at ground-level ready to take another bus or the Métro. About 45 minutes travelling time depending on traffic.

Roissy/Rail: very fast direct train service to the Gare du Nord. Take that free bus to the SNCF station for trains every 15 minutes from 5:05 a.m. to 11:50 p.m. Ticket to Gare du Nord is 27F, or 29F50 if you are changing there to the ordinary Métro. The only problem with this superb service has been manoeuvering luggage through turnstiles, and picking our way out at the Gare du Nord end. 25 minutes travelling time.

Air France bus: swift and luxurious, to the Étoile and Porte Maillot in the 17e *arrondissement*. (For an explanation of the *arrondissement* system, see page 38 and the map on pages 272–3.) Buses run every 12-15 minutes, and your luggage is taken off your hands. 36F, and about 25-45 minutes long.

Orly

Orly/Rail: fast train to nine stations on the Left Bank, every 15 minutes from 5:50 a.m. to 9:05 p.m., then every 30 minutes to 11:00 p.m. 30F.

Express bus: high-speed, low-fare bus directly to Denfert-Rochereau Métro station, 14e *arrondissement*. A smartly-designed coach with plenty of luggage space, every 15 minutes from 6:00 a.m. to 11:30 p.m. 35F, and the trip is about 30 minutes.

Air France bus: to the Gare des Invalides, Left Bank, 7th *arrondissement*. Runs about every 12 minutes, your luggage is dealt with for you, and about 30 minutes travelling time. 36F.

Railway Stations

Boat and hovercraft are linked to the Gare du Nord by fast train – about 2½ hours from Calais or Boulogne, and included in the cost of your ticket.

Railway stations are large, chaotic, and always crowded, even early in the morning. It takes five minutes and three wrong answers to find anything but there are centrally located information booths, usually with English-speaking personnel, who can provide authoritative answers.

If you're burdened with luggage, look for the free, energy-saving luggage carts. Avoid porters: the fixed charge per bag is 7F50.

If you haven't provided yourself with some francs in cash before arrival, seek out the bureau de change and pick up some survival money. Not much: you'll probably get a better rate of exchange at one of the large commercial banks in Paris.

Help

If you haven't already reserved a room, and need help . . .
If you need a simple but comprehensible map of Paris, the Métro, buses . . .
If you need to know how to use the telephone, figure out the transportation system . . .
Or if you are merely tired and totally disoriented . . .

Look for the Hôtesses de Paris: These run a service provided by the Office de Tourisme de Paris, they speak all useful languages and they know almost everything. For the first-time traveller arriving in Paris without a place to lay the head, for someone arriving after dark, the Hôtesses can be invaluable. They have a list of hotels in each price range where they know there are vacancies at that moment. They will not call a specific hotel of your choice (they figure that if you know that much, you can fend for yourself), but they will find you a room no matter how many phone calls it takes. The charge is 5F for an Auberge de Jeunesse (Youth Hostel), 15F for a one-star hotel, 20F for a two-star, 35F for a three-star, and when you're on your last legs, worth it.

It has been our experience that they will not necessarily find the cheapest room in the best-value hotel. A sign displayed gives minimum prices for the kinds of hotels they use: 160F for a single, 250F for a double in a 1-star hotel, 260-380F in a 2-star, 450-600F in a 3-star. This may be broadly true, but in practice you can do better for yourself (see 'Au Lit,' pages 59–98.) The Hôtesses can only book for you on the day you want a hotel, not in advance. They can be invaluable if you don't speak much French, can't face the telephone system, or haven't the energy to start the search on the Métro with your luggage. Let the Hôtesses book you a room for your first night, and strike out on your own the next day.

Try to get to them, either at the railway stations or at the main office, as early as possible, as from late morning until closing time, in summer, the queues build up to bursting point.

If the Hôtesses de Paris at the railway station where you arrive look slightly weary and sceptical, especially at the end of a long hot day, don't be too surprised. Considering the number of idiot travellers who fall into their offices at all hours, often armed with nothing more than touching faith and a copy of an out-of-date or fanciful guidebook, expecting to find a double room near Pigalle for 40F, their slightly disillusioned air may be justified. And they will indeed make umpteen phone calls, until they place you in a room.

Gare d'Austerlitz (arrival hall)	Mon–Sat 9 a.m.–8 p.m.
	(10 p.m. in summer*)
Gare de l'Est (departure hall)	Mon–Sat 8 a.m.–1 p.m.
	5 p.m.–8 p.m. (10 p.m. in summer*)
Gare de Lyon (arrival hall)	Mon–Sat 8 a.m.–1 p.m.
	5 p.m.–8 p.m. (10 p.m. in summer*)
Gare du Nord (mainline hall)	Mon–Sat 8 a.m.–8 p.m.
	(10 p.m. in summer*)
Main tourist office (Bureau de	Mon–Sat 9 a.m.–8 p.m.
Tourisme de Paris)	(10 p.m. in summer*)
127 Champs-Élysées, 8e	Sundays and holidays 9 a.m.–6 p.m.
Métro: George-V	(8 p.m. in summer*)

Tel: 47 20 88 98 for announcements in English of almost everything you need to know, 24 hours a day.

The tourist offices are a mine of information and a great source for free maps and other handouts. Most useful of these are several varieties of Métro and bus folders; individual pamphlets on certain sight-seeing bus routes; a comprehensive list of hotels and restaurants listed by *arrondissement* (see map pages 272–3), alphabetically, and classified by price and amenities. In addition, the main tourist office in the Champs-Élysées has posters displaying current cultural events; they give information about other parts of France; and there is a travel bureau in the basement run by SNCF. Across the street is a bureau de change open seven days a week (see Money, page 240).

If you're just a little knocked out, but don't need the immediate assistance of the Hôtesses for hotel booking or map help, take time to get your breath. We strongly advise you to spend the next half hour getting acclimatised to Paris (what could be more pleasant?) before jumping on a bus or Mêtro.

First: find somewhere to leave your luggage. In all the railway stations there is a left-luggage place, the *consigne*. Cart your bags there in your trolley, and check them in. Cost 9F per bag. If you are travelling light, a storage locker (3F50 for a small one, up to 9F for a big one) will do nicely, if you can find one that's empty when you need it.

*Summer indicates Easter to 1 November.

Then: get a bite to eat, a glass of wine, or a cup of coffee. A brasserie is perfect, but don't head for one in the terminal (too hectic), or directly opposite (double the cost, as they know how to soak the tourist). Walk one street away, in any direction, find a bar-tabac or a brasserie. Here you can sit down, catch your breath, relax for a bit before you go on. Try out your first five words of French. Begin to figure out how the money system really works. Don't be shy about laying the coins on the table, getting used to the colour and feel. Plan the route to your hotel, with the aid of the *Plan de Paris* (see page 37).

For a little basic brasserie vocabulary, see under 'La nourriture', pages 102. Smile. And finish with 'Merci, au revoir, monsieur (or mademoiselle)', which will surprise them so much they'll smile back.

If you haven't already booked a hotel, and have (as you should have) absolute confidence in this book, consult the chapter 'Au Lit', pages 59–98, for information, and page 253 to find out how to use the phone.

Getting to your hotel

If you are really weighed down, take a taxi. If necessary, write down the address and show it to the driver. There are taxi ranks outside all the stations and terminals. See the information on page 255 for tipping.

If you are ready to brave the Métro or the bus, see pages 39–50, in 'Getting around'. At railway stations, airports, and major Métro stations you can pick up a *Paris Visite* or *Carte Orange* (see pages 42–44 for how to do it), and start using it to travel for almost nothing right away. The process for *Carte Orange*, including getting a picture taken in a photomatic booth, takes about five minutes; for *Paris Visite*, a fast thirty seconds.

Leaving Paris

By the time you're ready to wrench yourself away from Paris, you should be able to do this part walking on your hands. But just in case:

In railway stations: Departure times, train numbers, destinations and track numbers (*voies*) are marked in huge letters, on an immense blue board in mid-station. Trains leave very strictly on time, and with almost no warning whistles or horns. If anyone is coming to see you off they will need a platform ticket, although as there are few officials actually at the gate this can sometimes be dispensed with.

Airport buses: Air France takes you to Charles de Gaulle from Porte Maillot (16e *arrondissement*) and the Étoile (avenue Carnot, 16e *arrondissement*). They claim half an hour travelling time; knowing traffic, you should double that. Buses leave every 15 minutes between 5:50 a.m. and 11:00 p.m. Fare 36F. (Unless you are actually staying near Porte Maillot or the Étoile, the Roissy-Rail service from Gare du Nord is faster, easier, and cheaper.)

The Air France bus to Orly leaves the Aerogare des Invalides (rue de Constantine, just north of the Invalides Métro, 7e *arrondissement*), and also from the Gare Montparnasse (15e *arrondissement*), every 12 minutes, and takes at least half an hour – allow plenty of leeway for traffic. Buses run between 5:50 a.m. and 11:00 p.m., and the cost is 60F.

Trains: *Roissy-Rail*: Gare du Nord to Charles de Gaulle. Tickets from automatic dispensers in the hall leading to the train, marked Roissy-Rail, or from a ticket window – but be wary of this last, as the booking clerk also issues the *Carte Orange* and *Coupon Jaune*, student passes, etc., and you can get blocked for ever while he does the paperwork. If you are well organised and don't lose things easily, get your return ticket to Charles de Gaulle when you arrive from the airport and are not pressed for time, and put it with your airline ticket. Trains run every 15 minutes from 5:30 a.m. to 11:30 p.m., 27F.

Orly-Rail runs between the Gare d'Austerlitz and Orly every 15 minutes, and takes about 35 minutes to reach Orly Sud and Ouest. Departures from 5:50 a.m. to 10:50 p.m., cost 17F30.

Service buses to airports: DON'T, unless you're a masochist with plenty of time to waste, take the bus to Charles de Gaulle, even if you have the *Paris Visite* and the ride is free – the nervous strain is just too much. However, the new fast direct service to Orly, from Denfert-Rochereau in the 14e *arrondissement*, is great – about 30 minutes' travelling time to Orly-Ouest, 35 minutes to Orly-Sud. Every 15 minutes, 6:05 a.m. to 11:00 p.m., 35F.

Buses and Métros to railway termini: Consult your maps. If you're on a direct route, with no changes, there should be no problems. But if you must change anywhere on the Métro, forget it: negotiating stairs and intersections with luggage is out of the question. Take a taxi. In hot weather, and in rush hours, Paris buses are intolerably hot; the windows are made to keep out draughts, not to let in fresh air. Doors are closed when the bus is in motion – and sweaty human bodies can be really unpleasant.

Aux alentours
(Getting around)

You'll probably spend much of your time in Paris getting from place to place, or just wandering around with eyes open. Nowhere in the world will you have such beauty to absorb as you go, but getting muddled can take the shine off anything, even Paris. Make the most of your wandering by arming yourself with a really first-class 'atlas' of Paris.

The best we know is a thick little book called *Plan de Paris*, published by Éditions A. Leconte and available in bookshops and *papeteries*. The hardcover edition is dark red, and costs 65F, which seems like a lot, but it's packed cover to cover with everything you need to know. There are cheaper, paperback editions of the *Plan*, but with hard use they tend to lose the cover, the maps drop out, and you end up frustrated. Other atlas-type books exist, some with larger and more legible maps, but none we have found includes so much and such accurate information.

The *Plan* of M. Leconte lists all streets, alleys, *quais* and squares alphabetically, with their beginning and ending points, *arrondissements*, nearest Métro stops, and a keyed map reference which takes you to the individual, coloured *arrondissement* map.

Each *arrondissement*, from 1 to 20, has its own page. Métro lines and stops are printed in red. The maps themselves are laid out with alpha-numerical grids. Some plans (not, to be sure, the estimable M. Leconte's) are smallish and blurry, and therefore useless no matter how cheap. A good copy is child's play to use, and a treasure to keep long after your visit to Paris. Don't lend it to anyone.

The suburbs (*banlieues*) are also mapped in this book with the same format of street listings, map reference, etc., but probably won't be of much interest to you at this point.

A highly useful section lists addresses and map references for anything you want to know, and quite a lot you might never need: embassies, theatres, hospitals, schools, churches, monuments, police stations, city halls, race tracks, museums, post offices, state ministries, stadiums, tennis courts, swimming pools, shops, radio and TV stations, principal cinemas, cabarets, concert halls.

All the Paris bus routes are listed in numerical order, and what is even more important, shown in chart form, each with its starting and ending point and the principal stops in between. For that alone, the Paris Office de Tourisme should give M. Leconte a gold medal, as it is the only thing lacking in their own otherwise excellent bus folder.

If you are in Paris for more than a day or two, and intend to move more than a quarter mile from your hotel in any direction, the *Plan* is indispensable. The good news is that you can get a copy before you leave London, from the French Bookshop, 28 Bute Street, SW7. Cost £4.20 for the paperback edition. Tel: 071-584 2840.

Less detailed but very useful maps of Paris, with pictured locations of principal tourist attractions – museums, monuments, and so forth – are available free from the Bureau de Tourisme. And the big department stores (Printemps, Galeries Lafayette, among others) have prepared very much the same sort of thing, showing of course where *they* are located.

Guide Paris Autobus: if you plan to use buses often, on this visit to Paris and in future, invest in this sturdy pocket-size treasure published by Ponchet Plan Net. It gives you an alphabetical list of streets; which buses go there; the nearest Métro stop; maps of each *arrondissement*, with bus routes in colour, and keys to street names; Métro and RER maps, information on tickets - all in four languages! It's 60F from bookshops, and can save you endless hours of walking and searching.

Most Paris streets are one-way, so a bus going east, for example, may run along one street and its westbound route on another, possibly ten minutes' walk away. It's all laid out for you on the clear and simple bus route charts at the end of the 'Guide Paris Autobus'.

The Streets of Paris

The *arrondissement* system

In the mid-nineteenth century, Paris was thoroughly overhauled by Napoleon III's urban planner, Baron Haussmann. Slums were cleared (fortunately, he didn't get around to the Marais), sewers and aqueducts installed where the Romans had left off, and a web of wide thoroughfares, the Grands Boulevards, was laid. The city was thereupon divided into twenty *arrondissements* (there had previously been twelve, based on the old traditional *quartiers*, some dating back two thousand years). Numbers 1 to 7 cover the three historic parts of Paris: the *cité* (official and religious, located on the central islands), the *ville* (the Right Bank, commercial and industrial), and the *université* (Left Bank, commercial and scholastic). To a great extent these medieval distinctions hold true today.

The *arrondissements* spiral clockwise from the centre of Paris (1er, part of the Ile de la Cité and the area around the Louvre). The numbers which you will see on street signs and in newspapers and magazines (and in this book) are expressed thus: 1er, which means *Premier*; 2e, which stands for *Deuxième*, and so forth. Each *arrondissement* has quite distinct identifying features or landmarks which can serve to give you your bearings. The Eleventh (you might as well get used to seeing it written as 11e) is roughly the area which stretches outwards from the Bastille; the 8e is Gare St Lazare and the Madeleine; the 7e is the Invalides and the Tour Eiffel. Street signs in Paris are large, legible, and almost always include the *arrondissement* number (thus: avenue de l'Opéra, 1er).

With map, *arrondissement*, landmarks, street signs, and clearly written house or shop numbers, you shouldn't ever get *totally* lost, but it can happen, and for some reason even people with a good sense of direction find it hard to work out which way is north in Paris.

When you do feel really lost, the simplest thing to do is seek out the nearest Métro station: ask anyone, with the simple formula, 'Pardon, monsieur (or madame) – le Métro?'

Le Métro

It's impossible to lose your way in the Métro. You can't walk ten paces without a clear, explicit sign informing you of your destination. How to use all this information:

1 In the *Plan de Paris*, look up the name of the street you want to go to, and you will find the nearest Métro stop.

2 Find the station on the Métro map in the front of the *Plan*, or in one of the small free maps dealt out by the municipal transport system at every chance. Or look on the big map outside the entrance to the nearest Métro station, or near the ticket office, or on the platform from which the trains run.

3 Trace your route. Each Métro line is known by its beginning and ending points. Between any two stations in the system, you will be coming from and going towards one of the terminals of the line. For example, line 12 runs from Mairie d'Issy to Porte de la Chapelle. If you were at Gare St-Lazare and wanted to go to Pigalle, you would take a train in the direction of Porte de la Chapelle. From St-Lazare to Sèvres-Babylone, your direction is Mairie d'Issy. You then follow the appropriate signs to the platform where your train comes in. On Métro maps, each line is numbered and colour coded. The terminals are marked in good big capital letters on the map, at the outskirts of the city.

4 If you need to change trains to get to the stop you want, it's equally easy. Paris Métro lines are linked together in a remarkable system of *correspondences* (intersections) of two, three, sometimes five or six lines. You may have to walk underground for what seems like miles before you find your train, and it's hard on the feet. But keep calm, and you will never be lost. The signs simply don't allow that to happen.

Each Métro has a first-class carriage in the middle of the train, but even if you have a second-class ticket, you can travel first-class after 5:00 p.m.

The Métro runs every day, but with reduced services on Sundays, holidays, and after about 8:00 p.m., when intervals between trains become longer. Most trains begin running at 5:30 a.m., and stop at 1:15 a.m. – but if you have to change trains you can easily find yourself stranded at the connecting station after 12:45 a.m.

L'autobus

Trickier, and takes longer to get you from A to B, but infinitely more fun than the Métro. Like the train system, each bus is marked large and clear with its point of origin and destination. The buses are designated primarily by number. On the sides of the bus, the major stops are displayed so that when it moves past you, you can read the route in a flash. An overall bus map, available at Métro stations, bus termini, and the Office de Tourisme at 127 Champs-Élysées, gives a fairly clear, colour-coded overview of the routes. But it's intricate, and you could miss your bus while you're trying to work it out. Best of all is the chart-form bus information in the *Plan de Paris*, and the pricey but useful *Guide – Paris Autobus* (page 38).

Le Guide Paris-Bus, published by Prat/Europa with the RATP is out of print as we go to press, but may have come back by the time you read this – and it's a treasure, for about 35F. It shows you every bus route, the street address opposite each bus stop, and best of all, what other buses connect at every bus stop on every route. Using it, you can quickly learn which combination of buses will serve you best and save a lot of walking. In addition, the index tells you which bus or buses take you to every point of interest in the city.

Bus stops are recognisable by yellow kerbside shelters, with a red disc on a standard above them. This displays the number(s) of the bus or buses that stop here. Inside the shelter is a clear chart of the bus route, all its stops, a helpful marker that shows exactly where you are on the route, and the nearest place where you can buy tickets. On the bus you will only be able to buy tickets singly and expensively.

Inside the bus – just in case you've missed the other information – there are two or three route maps, either overhead or on the sides above the windows at eye level for those standing. This makes it easy to keep track of where you are, what the next stop will be, and even if the worst comes to the worst and you are really mixed up, which direction you are going in. The bus stops have their names clearly and legibly displayed so you know where you are at all times.

Times: In general, buses leave their starting points at 7:00 a.m., and run to about 8:30 or 9:00 p.m. Others have a night service (these all begin at the place du Châtelet, avenue Victoria, 3e). Sundays and holidays: buses 20, 21, 26, 27, 31, 38, 43, 44, 46, 52, 62, 80, 91, 92, 95, 96, and the Petit Ceinture bus which runs around the outskirts of Paris.

All Paris buses run on the request-stop system. If you are at a stop marked for only one bus, the driver will stop (if he sees you) but it may be safer to wave your arm or an umbrella. If more than one bus serves your stop, you *must* signal the one you want.

The same system applies when you want to get off. No automatic stops. You must push a small, well-concealed button on one of the upright stanchions near entrance and exit doors. This activates a sign in the front of the bus: *Arrêt demandé*. This system lets Paris buses move fairly fast, considering the narrow, often crowded streets in which they run.

Noctambus

There are ten night-service buses which run from 1:30 a.m. to 5:30 a.m., all beginning at Châtelet and fanning outward to the outskirts of Paris:

A:	Châtelet to	Porte de Neuilly, via Étoile
B:		Mairie de Levallois, via Opéra
C:		Mairie de Clichy, via Pigalle
D:		Mairie de St-Ouen, via Gare du Nord
E:		Église de Pantin, via Gare de L'Est
F:		Mairie de Lilas, via Belleville
G:		Mairie de Montreuil, via Gambetta
H:		Château de Vincennes, via Nation
I:		Rungis, via Place d'Italie
J:		Porte de'Orleans, via Luxembourg

As the RATP says, 'Pas de voiture? Pas de taxi? Pas de vélo? Pas de panique.' – Just signal the bus. Night buses will stop anywhere you hail them, not just at bus stops. They run only one an hour. With *'Formule 1'*, *Carte Orange*, *Coupon Jaune*, or *Paris Visite*, you travel free; otherwise it's three or four tickets, depending on distance.

Métro and bus travel

Paris transport is heavily subsidised, a great break for the travelling poor as well as for hard-working Parisians. Tickets can be used on Métro and buses interchangeably, which saves a lot of time and trouble. Prices have risen only fractionally since the last edition of this book, and although in 1990 they may go up slightly from those listed here, the increases will in all probability be gentle. Beginning with the least expensive – and why we prefer these – here we go.

Carte Orange: this is a catch-all heading for cards that give you all-inclusive travel by the week or by the month (you can even get a yearly ticket). The *Carte* itself is a bright orange card in a plastic case which has a pocket for your weekly or monthly *coupon*. It's free. Take a passport-size photograph to any Métro station. You then buy a *coupon jaune* (valid from Monday through Sunday) or a *coupon orange* (good for one calendar month). The *coupon jaune* is on sale from the Sunday before it becomes valid through Wednesday of the following week. The *coupon orange* goes on sale on the 20th of the previous month.

In our experience, these coupons are the greatest travel buy ever invented. If you're in Paris even for four or five days, the *Coupon Jaune* will give you your money's worth in hassle-free travel.

If you're a really dedicated money-saver, arrive in Paris on a Monday morning, pick up your *coupon jaune* and be on your way. Use it 17 times and you're travelling free the rest of the week.

On the Métro, push your ticket through the turnstile and immediately slip it back into the plastic pocket of your *Carte*. On the bus, flash your *Carte* at the driver. On no account feed the ticket into the ticket-punch machine. This will invalidate it. There are no refunds for idiocy.

What you get for your money: unlimited travel on Métro, buses, certain segments of the high-speed RER, and the Montmartre funicular.

Coupon jaune   2nd class 49F
                 1st class 72F
Coupon orange 2nd class 173F
                 1st class 260F

Formule 1: This one-day pass gives you unlimited travel as above, second class only. You get an identity card (no photograph needed) which you can keep for ever. Buy a ticket (*coupon*) for each day you need it. 21F.

If for some mysterious reason your ticket won't open the gate, go back to the ticket window and show it to them; they'll press a magic button and buzz you through. This is no great help if you've used one of those entrances without ticket booths (marked 'reservé aux passagers munis de billets'), because then you'll have to trudge along to a manned entrance.

Tickets and *carnets*: You can buy them singly (extravagantly) at Métro station or on the bus, or in *carnets* of 10 from Métros or in many tobacconists' shops. On the Métro, push the ticket through the turnstile but don't discard it until you leave the train – there are occasional spot-checks of travellers, and the *controlleurs* can be fierce, even taking you and your passport to the nearest police station to be fined. On the bus, tell the driver where you are going and he'll tell you whether to punch one or two tickets. Suburban buses – those with numbers higher than 100 – will cost two to six tickets. Bus drivers do not sell *carnets*, only single tickets. And you can be *controléed* on the bus too, so keep your ticket handy.

Single tickets 2nd class 5F
           1st class (Métro only) 7F20
Carnet of ten 2nd class 31F20
           1st class (Métro only) 47F

You can buy *Carnets*, *Coupon Jaune* and *Coupon Orange* with your VISA (*Carte Bleu*) card, from automatic ticket machines at main Métro stations, using your PIN number.

Paris Visite replaces *Le Billet de Tourisme* and *Paris/Sesame* cards. It gives you unlimited travel on Métro, bus, RER, the Sacré-Coeur funicular, and is valid for three or five days, on two 'zoned' schedules. Travel on the Métro is first class.

The more expensive includes travel to and from Charles de Gaulle/Roissy, and Orly airports, and to and from Versailles and other suburban points of interest on the SNCF (railways). The cheaper tichet sets you free in the three inner zones of Paris.

	3 days	5 days
Inner zones	70F	110F
Outer zones	130F	160F

You can buy *Paris Visite* cards at the SNCF station at the airports, and at main Métro stations, railway stations, the RATP office at 52 quai des Grands Augustins, 6e, and from the French Railways Office at 179 Piccadilly, London W1 (Mondays through Fridays).

Now that you know how to get around – where to?

You might just want to set off at random – head in any direction on foot; hop on the first bus that comes along; take the Métro to the end of the line and try to find your way back as a pedestrian – no matter what, something will come of it.

Or perhaps you could use some pointers on the *quartiers* before you set out – a few landmarks – some guaranteed bus routes. Possibly some areas to avoid, as well.

Major monuments (the Tour Eiffel, the Arc de Triomphe, the Louvre, and such) you should be able to find with one hand tied behind your back. If you're really in doubt, ask a tourist. What follows is a sampler: general reflections on a few *quartiers* (central and out of the way) and some routes you might like to try, on foot and otherwise. It's anything but exhaustive. You'll discover far more than we have space for on your own.

Paris by bus

Commercial sightseeing buses in Paris cost an arm and a leg, as the saying goes. Why pay 110F for a trip when the glorious RATP (the municipal transport system) offers you an incomparable set of bus trips for practically nothing? If you are armed, as you should be, with the indispensable *Carte Orange* or *Carte Orange* (see page 42), or the very useful *Paris Visite* (page 42), your sightseeing is on the house, so to speak. The RATP has laid out, in a well-designed folder called 'Billet de Tourisme', available at all major Métro stations, a list of seventeen 'sightseeing' bus routes that can show you the most beautiful, historic, curious, and provocative parts of Paris. These seventeen could take up your entire time in the city, of course, so we've narrowed down the choices to a magic seven – some of which will show you parts of Paris most tourists haven't even heard about.

If you have time for only one leisurely, luxurious bus ride, choose No. 24.

Bus 24

From Gare St-Lazare, it takes you round the place de la Madeleine (luxurious shops) into the place de la Concorde, then sweeps along the quai des Tuileries beside the Seine, past the Louvre. As you go, you have a most enticing view of the silvery buildings lining the opposite side of the river (the Left Bank – Rive Gauche). Glancing to your left, you can see the exquisite church St-Germain-l'Auxerrois, where all the kings of France worshipped privately. At the pont des Arts, look across the river at the Hôtel des Monnaies (the Mint) and the Institut de France which houses the 'Immortals' of the Académie Française. Crossing the river on the pont Neuf to the Ile de la Cité, the bus passes the Palais de Justice before continuing over the Petit Pont to the Rive Gauche. From the boulevard St-Germain, the route follows the quai St-Bernard, skirting the edge of the four-centuries-old Jardin des Plantes. If you stay on the bus all the way to its destination at Alfort, you will catch sight of the monumental new Palais Omnisport built on the site of the razed wine warehouses along the quai de Bercy – passing a real working-class area on the way. On the return journey, the bus goes along the left bank of the Seine, with a good look at Notre-Dame; then past the Mint and along the quai Voltaire (where Ingres, Delacroix, and Wagner lived at various times), before recrossing the river by the pont Royal and returning to St-Lazare by way of the place de la Concorde and the magnificent rue Royale. Monday to Saturday, 7:00 a.m. to 8:30 p.m.

Bus 29

Also from Gare St-Lazare, the 29 takes you around the Opéra, down the rue du 4 Septembre, passing the Bourse (the stock market headquarters), and the place des Victoires with its statue of Louis XIV on horseback. You suddenly come to the great ultra-modern dazzler, Beaubourg (Centre Georges Pompidou), towering over the small crooked streets of the Marais, almost the oldest part of Paris. The bus goes past the elegant place des Vosges, built for the king in 1612, then into the wide boulevard leading to the place de la Bastille. The Bastille prison itself is gone; but the immense circle is very impressive. If you like, get off here and catch the No. 87 bus for another fabulous sightseeing trip to the Champ-de-Mars (for the Tour Eiffel and Napoleon's tomb), or stay with the No. 29 and go on, past the Cimetière de Picpus where many of the victims of *la guillotine* lie buried. Many of the 29s have an open platform at the back, great for sightseeing. Mondays to Saturdays, 7:00 a.m. to 8:30 p.m.

Bus 32

It begins at the Gare de l'Est, but you may want to catch it at one of its more interesting stopping places, such as place de la Trinité, going in the direction of Porte de Passy. The route takes you through the 'Quartier d'Europe', so called because almost every street is named after a capital city: Amsterdam, Budapest, London,

Stockholm. Past the Gare St-Lazare, you are in the faded elegance of the boulevard Haussmann, named after the man who reshaped the city in the 1860s. Along the rue de la Boëtie, look for the wildly expensive and beautiful boutiques and galleries. Then up the Champs-Élysées, and to the Trocadéro, the palace built for the Paris World's Fair in 1937 and now the home of three museums. You may want to stop off here and see the Museum of Mankind – fascinating. The bus goes on to the smart, but not entrancing, Passy neighbourhood with its mansions and streets overhung with huge old trees. On the return trip, the route is slightly different, and you'll pass along the avenue Matignon and through Faubourg St-Honoré, wall-to-wall with the great couture houses. The bus will give you an overview, but this is really for people who like to walk. File it for future window-shopping. No. 32 runs Mondays to Saturdays, first bus from Gare de l'Est at 7:00 a.m., last one at 8:30 p.m.

Bus 52

Begins at the Opéra, takes you around the lovely shopping area of the boulevard des Capucines, past the Musée Cognacq-Jay (again, file for future reference), and through the place de la Madeleine with its magnetic food shops: Fauchon, Hédiard and Michel Guérard. Around the place de la Concorde (a circus of killer traffic has taken the place of the guillotine that stood here for years), and a wonderful view up the vista of the Champs-Élysées. The big avenue de Friedland takes you to the Étoile/place Charles de Gaulle, where there is always a silent crowd at the Eternal Flame that burns over the tomb of France's Unknown Soldier. Beyond that, you are in the streets of the 16e *arrondissement*, a smart, conservative residential area. The avenue Mozart on the return journey is charming; the local café is called The Magic Flute. This is a pleasant place to step off the bus and have coffee, and walk around a neighbourhood that is real Paris, far off the tourist beat. The bus continues to the place de la Porte d'Auteuil and takes you to pont de St-Cloud, a fairly sterile area, so you might want to end your trip at the place de la Porte d'Auteuil and either walk west into the Bois de Boulogne, or head back into central Paris on the Métro. No. 52 runs seven days a week, including holidays, first bus at 7:00 a.m. weekdays and 8:00 a.m. Sundays, last bus about 10:15 p.m.

Bus 63

Begins at the Gare de Lyon, takes you along the quai St-Bérnard, and almost at once you are in the *Quartier Latin*, the home of Paris students from the time of the monks in the Middle Ages to the motorbikes and demonstrations of the 1960s. It traverses the rue des Écoles, crosses the boulevard St-Michel, and passes the church of St-Sulpice before threading its way through the stately streets of the 7e. The 63 touches the fringe of the boulevard St-Germain, then takes you along the quai d'Orsay (political and diplomatic Paris). If you stay with it to the end of the route at Porte de la Muette, you see 'untourist' Paris – but it's more interesting to get off at the Trocadéro stop for an unparalleled view of the city from high on the hill. Take the bus back in the direction of the Gare de Lyon, and this time step off at St-Germain-des-Prés: yes, it's a cliché, but not to be missed because of its bookshops, its galleries, its cafés. There are still those who swear that a costly coffee at the Deux Magots is worth the price, just to see and be seen by *le tout Paris*. And it costs nothing to browse in the side streets, to see Picasso drawings or primitive paintings. Bus 63 runs seven days a week, from 7:00 a.m. to midnight (leaving times from the Gare de Lyon).

Bus 72

Runs from the pont de St-Cloud to the Hôtel-de-Ville, and back again, and on the way gives you sight of both modern and historic Paris. In between you will see some of the glitter and splendour, and some of the less savoury and picturesque parts too. To get the most from this 'tour', catch the bus at the Hôtel-de-Ville end: from here you have a view of the pont Neuf (begun in 1578, so only relatively new), the great sweep of the Louvre, the Cours de la Reine and the Horses of Marly rearing over Paris on their pedestals. It passes the Jeu de Paume, the real tennis courts, which housed the staggering collection of Impressionist paintings until their removal to the new Musée d'Orsay. It continues along the Seine, along the boulevards named after the City of New York and after President Kennedy. And it runs along the avenue de Versailles, most interesting for its buildings such as No. 142 by the architect Hector Guimard, in art nouveau style. Beyond this point, the ride isn't particularly exciting, except as all Paris's 'real' neighbourhoods are; you may want to get off in the avenue de Versailles, wander a bit and absorb its feeling, then return by No. 22 to the Opéra. Mondays to Saturdays, first bus from pont St-Cloud at 7:00 a.m., last one at 8:50 p.m. On Sundays, there is a partial service, from pont de St-Cloud to Concorde only.

Bus 83

Begins at place d'Italie, in the 13e arrondissement, a seldom-visited but quite interesting part of Paris (some very good hotels and restaurants there, see pages 89 and 145 for more about them). Running down the avenue des Gobelins, it traverses the boulevard du Port-Royal. On Saturdays, there's a street market worth stopping for in this street, near the rue St-Jacques. Here it skirts the 5e *arrondissement*, the Latin Quarter. The rue d'Assas on this route is absolutely littered with good little bistros and cafés. The bus passes the Jardin du Luxembourg, where you might want to stop to inhale some fresh air and watch the Paris kids at play; then it runs along the river by the quai d'Orsay, past Invalides. Along the way, you glimpse the Tour Eiffel, and the dome of the Invalides with Napoleon's tomb. The bus crosses on to the right bank into fashionable haute-couture Paris, around the Rond-Point des Champs-Élysées and the Métro station of St-Phillipe-du-Roule. The bus goes as far as Levallois, but you have really had the most interesting part of its route by now, unless you want to see working-class Paris as it really lives. If you prefer, finish your trip at the Rond-Point, and sit for a while on a bench in the pretty little park while all Paris goes by, or walk up the Champs-Élysées towards the Étoile. This is a wonderful bus ride to take late in the afternoon (but be prepared for crowds during rush hour), as you may be lucky enough to see the lights along the Seine and the Champs-Élysées coming on as dusk approaches. Mondays to Saturdays, first bus from place d'Italie at 7:00 a.m., last one at 8:30 p.m.

Montmartrobus

A minibus service for the inhabitants of the steep streets that snake around the Hill of the Martyrs, new, enchanting, hardly publicised, and as yet sussed out by only a handful of tourists. For one ticket, or free with *Carte Orange*, *Coupon Jaune*, *'Formule 1'* or *Paris Visite*, you get a breathless, bumpy, roller coaster ride from Pigalle to the end of the line at Métro Jules Joffrin. On the way you are treated to the Moulin de Galette, the place des Tertres, the lovely place des Abbesses, the pure-Utrillo rue Tholoze, the centuries-old Montmartre vineyards, and more views up and down each winding street than you can take in. If the scenery goes by too fast, you can hop off, take pictures or merely wander and gasp, and catch the next bus in fifteen minutes or so. The return trip takes a slightly different route, if anything even more *pittoresque et historique*. The drivers are nerveless and daunted by nothing: not even a beer *camion* stuck in a hairpin turn will blow their cool. The marvellous thing about Montmartre is that the moment you're out of the sleaze of Pigalle, the landscape reverts to quotidian serenity: an area in which real people live and work as they have for centuries. If you jump off the bus at the northern end (Mairie du XVIII) you can pick up a snack lunch in one of the unbelievable places in the rue Poteau, and sit in the exquisite square de Clignancourt among flowers, trees, and children. If you have any luck at all you'll get there when the band is playing in the toy-town bandstand. The Montmartrobus runs every ten minutes northbound from Pigalle from 7:30 a.m. to 8:00 p.m., returning from the Mairie du XVIII with the last southbound bus leaving at 7:50 p.m. promptly.

RATP tours

In addition to these free or almost free bus routes through Paris, the RATP has some extraordinary tours of its own from the place de la Madeleine (8e) to – among other places – the châteaux of Chambord, Chenonceaux, Poitiers, to Bayeux for the Tapestry, to Colombey-des-Deux-Églises to see de Gaulle's house, to Beaune for the wine country, to Cabourg for Proustiana, to Mont-St-Michel, to Domrémy for the route of Jeanne d'Arc – and even a day trip to Luxembourg if that's a thrill for you.

For information: Services Touristiques de la RATP, place de la Madeleine, near the flower market. Pick up the yellow folder called 'Excursions (plus de 100 circuits)' from major Métro stations and all railway stations. Prices are low, compared to commercial bus tours, but you will need at least a minimal command of French to make sure you understand their instructions about leaving times and boarding places. They also have guided tour buses to Versailles, Malmaison, Paris by night, and so on, but only in French.

Footwork

The Batignolles

Just north of the Gare St-Lazare, 8e, in the web of streets named after European capitals, begins a pleasantly varied, fairly gentle cluster of neighbourhoods. Heading north up the rue de Rome, you begin to run into music stores: lutenist, guitar makers, violin shops, sellers of sheet music. This is the *quartier* of the Paris Conservatoire. The bar-tabacs, cafés and restaurants cater to music students; the prices are accordingly low and the whole neighbourhood is a find for the pauper astray in Paris. And it leads you, very quickly, into an oasis of calm. Take a left on the boulevard des Batignolles, past the Théâtre Hébertot, and you are in the beginning of the rue de Lévis – a street market, jammed on Saturday mornings, which most tourists miss because they've never heard of it. This leads to an airy little square, and you are in the rue Legendre, heading towards Montmartre. In three blocks, you've arrived at the Église Ste-Marie. Behind it is the square des Batignolles – placid, delightful, a good place to sit for a while. It's a small park rather than a 'square', and contains a series of artificial duck-ponds, a carousel, and raked gravel paths. If you're still feeling energetic, continue eastward and gradually uphill into Montmartre. The Batignolles is a backwater of calm in Paris – quiet, unimposing houses, a petit-bourgeois population. At one edge is the place de Clichy, the epitome of sleaze; at the other, the tracks that lead back to the Gare St-Lazare. In between, absolute peace.

The rue Mouffetard and the Fifth

Since medieval days, the precincts of the 5e *arrondissement* have been the student quarter of Paris. The rue Mouffetard itself has somewhat more diverse origins. It began as a Roman road from Lyons, developed into a rich residential area in the twelfth to fourteenth centuries, then fell into the hands of skinners, tanners and dyers (the Gobelins factory nearby is the only remnant of this period). The resulting stench gave the street its name: *mouffette* is French for skunk.

The Mouffetard today consists of a street market at its southern end, and a string of small shops and restaurants running north:

boulangeries,   triperies,   boucheries   chevalines   (for   horsemeat),
fromageries.   The restaurants run mostly to Greek, Arab, and
Vietnamese/Chinese food. Everything here is startlingly good
value: it's impossible to pinpoint a restaurant that offers a better
meal than its neighbour, for about 55F–70F, usually with reasonably drinkable wine and service thrown in.

At its north end, the rue Mouffetard becomes the rue Descartes.
At No. 39, the poet Verlàine lived and died – it has always been a
quartier for the artist, the writer, the poet, the student, the poor
scholar, and although it has been thoroughly discovered by generations of tourists, the Mouffetard and its neighbouring streets
remain triumphantly what they are.

The surrounding streets include the rue Geoffroy-St-Hilaire with
the only fully-fledged mosque in Paris; the Arènes de Lutèce
(remains of a Roman arena), the place Monge (outdoor market), the
Panthéon, and the Bibliothèque Ste-Geneviève, probably the first
use of structural steel supports and lots of glass, worth having a look
at. The 5e is loaded with schools, technical colleges, branches of the
sprawling University of Paris, and at odd times of the day bands of
students flood the streets. It's wonderful walking country. The most
you'll spend, perhaps, will be the price of a good, cheap lunch or a
sandwich eaten sitting on a college wall, or, extravagantly, a coffee,
sitting at a café table resting your feet and watching the world of
student Paris wander by.

Rue St-Dominique and the Seventh

The 7e is rich but sterile. You'll see that the hotels and restaurants
we have picked in this area are rather few and far between. Lots of
trees, wide streets, and most of the *arrondissement* seems to be made
up of the Tour Eiffel and its gravelly park, and the Invalides –
haunted grandeur, with Napoleon's tomb as the major *frisson*. In
general, we find the neighbourhood parched and almost devoid of
interest, certainly very low on anything that counts for strolling,
listening and enjoying the free delights of Paris.

But turn the corner off the boring boulevard de la Tour
Mauborg into the rue St-Dominique, and it's like opening the top of
a magic trunk. Bustle, laughter, shops, sales, ebullient cross-bred
dogs instead of blanketed Yorkshire terriers, girls in tight skirts and
men in faded jeans, a most typical and joyous neighbourhood
restaurant or two (see page 131), even a few noteworthy hotels (page

76). The little side streets that dangle from St-Dominique are equally beautiful, and it's almost impossible to believe that a hundred yards away are the flat-faced, dull apartment buildings and pompous antique shops. Spend a day in this neighbourhood: you'll spend almost no money unless you decide to splurge on a down-filled ski jacket for a big 110F, or a slightly used Christian Dior scarf from a street barrow.

Another startling street that redeems the whole 7e from its sterility is the little rue Cler, a pedestrian precinct that is like a microcosm of a French provincial town set down whole in one of the richer areas of Paris. The shopping is entrancing, and there is an hotel (see page 76) which has a faithful year-after-year clientele, French, English, American, Japanese. Perhaps there are other rue Clers and rue St-Dominiques which we haven't found; if so, we apologise to the 7e and some day will perhaps take time to discover its 'villages'.

The astonishing Eighth

One of the least homogeneous *arrondissements* of Paris that we've encountered is the 8e, which ranges from the quiet music-student life beyond Gare St-Lazare, to the bustling commercial area around Au Printemps department store, the boulevard Haussmann, and the rue Caumartin; and takes in the supreme elegance of the rue Royale and the place de la Madeleine. Imagine a neighbourhood that encompasses both a public bath-house where a hot shower costs 5F, and the super-luxury atmosphere of Fauchon, the most expensive food shop in the world! Hermès, with its silk scarves and perfectly made saddle-stitched handbags – £400 is nothing here – is in the rue Boissy d'Anglas. So is Lanvin, which seems to exhale Arpège from its windows.

Look into the lovely Jeu de Paume on the edge of the place de la Concorde to see if there's an exhibition there. If you think of having a meal within a thousand yards of its doors, be prepared to blow the week's budget – Maxim's is a few steps away. Yet in the same street that houses the creations of the couturiers is a pleasant little café which feeds the mannequins and the *vendeuses* (not the customers, of course) for about 60F a lunch. The Hôtel Crillon is only a few feet away from the American Embassy, and it costs nothing to smell the expensive hyacinths in its window boxes, or to sit for a few minutes in the downy chairs in the lobby (looking as though you are waiting for a rich friend). Yet in the immediate neighbourhood, just off the place de la Madeleine, is a very good, moderately-priced hotel, such remarkable value that it is only sheer generosity that makes us put it in this book, instead of keeping the name for a few favoured friends.

The bit of the 8e that surrounds the Gare St-Lazare is too little known to those who merely take trains or buses from the station. Real people live here, work here, send their children to school, look for jobs, buy flowers and pastries, newspapers, electric toasters, shoes, get their hair done and their cars repaired. Walk along the rue Rocher, or the rue de Vienne, have a very good meal at a price that would not even buy you a pub lunch in London, go into a sheet music shop in the rue de Rome and you might find a flat, a cello, a baby-sitter, a ride to Marseilles, a tandem bicycle or a chance to play chamber music. Walk ten minutes towards the river, and (if it pleases you) go in and try on a Dior mink jacket, or decide whether you really like the new Hermès scent or not.

The 8e is not as beautiful or as historic as the Marais, not as bubbling as the student quarter, the 5e, not as snobbish as St-Germain-des-Prés, not as pretentious as Passy and the 16e – it's dead at night except for the rich sweeping out of Maxim's – but for daytime walking its mix of characteristics make it very special indeed.

The other Paris

Jewish, Tunisian, Algerian. If you have a fancy for seeing what foreign parts of Paris are like, take the Métro to Pyrénées or Belleville, in the 19e/20e, on a Saturday night after sundown, or from about 9 o'clock on Sunday morning. Walk the length of rue Belleville, and here you will find that the old traditional Jewish working-class quarter is gradually meeting and mingling with the new wave of Arab Paris, without political thought or collision. Belleville dies at sundown on Friday, comes alive again on Saturday nights and Sundays. Whatever the weather, all Belleville is out on the street, talking, eating, embracing, arguing, smoking, shopping. Here you gradually begin to realise that almost every face you see is male. Arab women, if they have been brought to Paris, keep steadfastly to their houses and families. The Arab man in Paris lives to work, and works very often in the low-end job no one else wants to do. On weekends, they are all out drinking coffee in crowded cafés and socialising on street corners. The women, if any, are buying fruit, vegetables, dripping-sweet pastries, fresh-killed chickens.

Here in the rue Belleville and the rue Ramponeau, you have the feeling of being surrounded by a world infinitely more exotic than anywhere else in Paris. Half a dozen varieties of Arabic, plus Yiddish or a strange French that is heavily injected with words from both languages, are all around you.

It is true that the civilisation of North Africa has affected Parisian life in all its aspects. Hardly a quarter of Paris (except perhaps the stuffy 7e and the formal 15e and 16e *arrondissements*) is without its restaurant serving couscous, mloukhia, merguez, bric à l'oeuf, sugary Oriental pastries. But none is like Belleville.

In the last few years, the racial mix of Belleville has been further enriched by a new wave of Chinese residents, restaurants, shops, and mini-supermarkets. The Belleville area, historically, is the preserve of not very well-to-do Jews, many who survived concentration camps, many strictly orthodox. Then came the influx of Arabs, and with them many North African Jews; from Algeria, Tunisia, Libya, Morocco. It is intensely alive, with a cosmopolitan mixture of cinemas, posters, newsstands, food stalls – and if you want to get your hair cut on a Sunday, make for Belleville.

If you are there on a Sunday morning, and of an adventurous turn of mind, go into one of the numerous places that sell take-away food. A 'sandwich tunisien' is a North African/French sandwich: a crusty loaf split open and crammed with tuna, black olives, tomatoes, lettuce, hot green peppers, capers, bathed in an orange sauce that could start a fire. Drink only beer or mineral water, not wine (too sweet and too expensive). Finish with ruinously sweet Arab pastries and you will have had a very adequate meal which will have cost you about 18F all told.

Tourists are not exactly fawned upon in Belleville, any more than in Brixton, but nor is the casual stranger sent packing. We suggest you keep a low profile: flashy clothes and expensive cameras will do nothing for your image; at best you'll feel uncomfortable and out of place. But if you can manage not to look or behave like a gawker, there's no reason to avoid the area.

If you decide that you want to see this *quartier*, so rich in life and colour, don't wait, as its crumbling buildings are coming down fast before the push of modernisation. Already the bulldozers have done for the worst slums, and modern proletariat housing is going up. The boutiques will be the next to move in. One wonders where the Arab men – lounging, smoking, spitting, kissing – will go when the last 'hotel' is levelled.

Street scenes

Much of the beauty of Paris, ranging from the small and exquisite to surprising grotesques, is alive and thrilling to the eye and the – possibly furtive – touch of the fingers. Not just the endless turning vistas of streets, trees, mansions and monuments, but the decoration in the form of carvings, capitals and statues which reveal themselves often in unnoticed places, and always free.

Paris churches are part of this 'living museum', and although there is never an admission charge, it's a civilised gesture to leave a few francs in the unobtrusive offering boxes near the doors.

In the oldest surviving church of Paris, St-Julien-le-Pauvre (in the street that bears his name), look for a marvellous group of flying harpies among its twelfth-century stone capitals. Otherwise it's a dull little place crowded with columns, which comes to life only when its occupants, an Eastern Catholic sect called the Melchites, sing on Sunday morning.

The oldest bell in Paris is in the tower of the Church of St-Merri, 78 rue St-Martin, 4e – it was cast in 1331. The bell-tower porch of the church of St-Germain-des-Prés was begun in 1040, and two of the windows in the church itself date from the middle of the eleventh century; while just outside in the little garden is an astonishing head of a woman by Picasso.

The last period of Gothic architecture, known as the Flamboyant, blazed out as though in reaction to the stark horror of the fifteenth centry (plague, civil war and occupation by the English were all visited on Paris in a space of about thirty years). Perhaps the most fascinating survivor is in the vaulted interior of the church of St-Séverin, at 1 rue des Prêtres-St-Séverin, 5e: an extraordinary spiralling central column seems to move and vibrate as it flings upwards and outwards a series of interlocked ribs.

This might be an appropriate place to mention that Paris churches *are* churches, and are primarily for worshippers. It would be wisest and nicest not to talk loudly, walk heavily, or jostle the chairs and benches: and so for the groups of tourists who chatter and flash their way around Notre-Dame, we would cheerfully see them suspended by their cameras from the mouths of gargoyles.

It is almost impossible to write dispassionately about the Sainte-Chapelle, the most queenly example of Gothic architecture of Paris, built to hold relics of the Passion and consecrated in 1248. It is no longer a church, but an historical monument, and in changing identities it has been very nearly vandalised. Its lower chapel now sells guidebooks and cassettes, its frescoed walls are scratched with graffiti, and one of the unforgettable sights of recent years was a tourist who had taken off her shoes and was peacefully eating a sandwich under the great Rose Window.

For uncompromising medieval grimness, have a look at the tower of Jean the Fearless, built about 1374, and tacked on to the Hôtel de Bourgogne, at 20 rue Étienne-Marcel, 2e. At the other extreme is the Hôtel de Sens, aristocratic and elegant, standing at the corner of the rue de l'Hôtel-de-ville and rue Figuier, 4e. Its conical tower and superb doorway are among the gems of the Marais. All through this district are scattered beautiful examples of noble buildings of the sixteenth and seventeenth centuries, which survived wars, plagues, riots and revolutions but nearly succumbed in the heedless twentieth century. Mercifully, they have been saved, restored, cleaned. See the Hôtel de Lamoignon at 24 rue des Francs-Bourgeois, 3e, dating from 1580, and another beauty, the doorway with pepperpot turrets of the Hôtel de Clisson, even earlier, and now tucked into the National Archives at 58 rue des Archives, 3e.

Centuries later, Paris produced a most tremendous variety of 'pompous' architecture – a riot of academic taste, from about 1850 to 1900, so bad as to be utterly endearing. A classic is the Hôtel de Ville, 4e. Don't miss the main staircase, whose decorations mix up cowboys, Indians, and French merchants who are wearing solar topis in what seems to be Ceylon or Equatorial Africa.

The Universal Exposition of 1900 produced art nouveau and 'Le Style 1900', which has been loved, hated, collected and argued about ever since its birth. Many of Hector Guimard's sinuous, serpent-green Métro entrances still survive, and are now especially prized since the Museum of Modern Art in New York bought a discarded one and re-erected it in its garden.

At 10 rue Pavée, 4e, there's a synagogue designed by Guimard in 1913. A less famous architect, Jules Lavirotte, did a block of flats at 19 avenue Rapp, 7e, that has *everything*: peacocks, butterflies, enamel, entwined flowers, and – peering out of the maze of design – a bust of Ophelia with streaming hair that turns into tendrils of vines. At 33 rue du Champ-de-Mars, not far away, art nouveau lilies crawl all over the front.

At the corner of the rue Victor Massé and rue Frochot, 9e, where whores patrol the street from about 4 o'clock in the afternoon, there's a most delightful piece of art deco stained glass set into the walls. And don't fail to see a perfect Paris townscape: the avenue

Frochot, a locked private road with sedate houses, small front gardens, and an academy of painting, a prim little island in the midst of squalid Pigalle.

A series of Utrillo paintings unfolds as you walk into the rue Germain-Pilon, 18e, just off the place de Clichy. At No. 13 is a delightful courtyard and house, and nearby is the Grand Boulangerie Viennoise with beautiful painted glass art deco panels bordering its doors. Oddly enough, many Paris bakeries of the early 1900s have these little works of art.

At the top of the street you emerge into the rue des Abbesses — another Utrillo — and nearby is the tranquil place des Abbesses, with a famous and perfectly preserved Guimard Métro entrance.

Paris abounds in statues and carvings on its buildings, balustrades and pedestals — it's impossible to describe or even to list the main ones, and anyway they've been photographed and written about almost to the point of boredom. Our personal picks: the brackets that support the flying buttresses of the church of St-Germain-l'Auxerrois in the place du Louvre, 1er — a delightful nightmare of hippopotamuses, monkeys, madmen, and a rat busily destroying the globe of the world; the heart-stopping 'St Francis in Ecstasy' of the sixteenth-century master Germain Pilon, in the church of St-Jean–St-François, at 6-bis, rue Charlot, 3e; the rearing Horses of Marly at the bottom of the Champs-Élysées; and the Seated Lion, by the 19th-century sculptor Barye, on the quay side of the Tuileries.

Scheduling

Prime time for Paris-watching varies for various events.

Early morning (really early) from about 7:00 a.m., is the time to see what Parisians are really made of. For the most part, they actively enjoy work. Sidewalks are sluiced and swept, shopfronts washed down (with soap and polishing cloths), market stalls are arranged like jewellery shops. The cafés are full of banter.

From noon on, life becomes more leisurely. Lunch may be drawn out over a couple of hours; by 4:00 p.m. the population strolls rather than bustles. At dusk, the fountains and monuments are illuminated: at least once, try to be standing in the place de la Concorde, ideally inhaling the scent of money from the Hôtel Crillon, at the magical moment when the lights in the square, along the river, and all up the Champs-Élysées, go on.

Au lit *(Sleeping cheap)*

The hotels that follow have been personally and recently vetted by our experienced Paris people. We emphasise *recently*, because it has been our experience that hotels can change, renovate, redecorate, re-price, even disappear, with extraordinary speed in Paris. Because of the uncertainties of the French economy in 1989/90 – despite our diligence – we're certain that many hotel prices will shoot up after this book has gone to press. So be warned, and try not to be affronted.

Many of our choices are those officially classed as 1-star in the *Guide des Hôtels* produced by the Office de Tourisme in Paris. They collect their information from three professional bodies (the Syndicat Général de l'Industrie Hôtelière, the Chambre Syndicale des Hôteliers, Caffetiers, Restaurateurs de Paris, and the Syndicat National des Chaines d'Hôtels et de Restaurants). With all that expertise, you aren't taking much of a chance. This professionalism means that hotels have been inspected for adherence to certain standards, their prices have been registered, their amenities and number of rooms verified.

On the whole, the *Guide des Hôtels* is accurate, but between the time the data comes in and publication date, many things – including prices – can alter, especially if the hotel has upgraded its services or accommodation.

Every hotel we have included here is clean, well run, and well above what we would consider minimum standard of comfort. A certain number we have found are actually classed as 2-star, but with prices that bring them within our budget. Most of them are, as you would expect, walk-ups, but a surprising number even of 1-star hotels have lifts, which makes life easier with luggage, for older people, and for those with small children. About 98 per cent of them have a telephone in each room, and a switchboard service night and day. In most cases, someone on the hotel staff speaks

English, and where no English is spoken we have noted the fact. You will then have to get by with smiles, good will, and a little French remembered from school.

The price of every room in any hotel vetted by the tourist office must be displayed at the registration desk and again in the room. Many hotels, in the last year or two, have taken to displaying their range of prices, coordinated with the accommodation offered, on a printed notice on an outside door or window, so you know even before entering what you are getting into.

These days, few hotels include *petit déjeuner* (the Continental breakfast of croissants, bread, jam, coffee, tea or chocolate) in their prices. If it *is* included, and you don't want to eat it or pay for it without eating it, say so politely but firmly *when you register*, and ask how much the room *alone* costs. Breakfast in an hotel can range from a fairly moderate 15F to a shocking 20-25F. Even at its cheapest it will be double the price of coffee and croissants taken standing at the zinc counter of the nearest bar-tabac or brasserie – and there you have the fun of tuning in on the conversation of Parisians going to work.

The 1-star classification of hotels is rather a loose mesh, taking in anything from a radiantly clean, newly-painted hotel ten minutes from Beaubourg – efficient but not the friendliest in the world – to a strange little hostelry where the hot water runs out early, the towels are child-size, the proprietor never visible – but where you can have charcuterie lunches in your room, hang dripping laundry from the radiators, without anyone taking the least bit of notice. A sweet, rather shabby, warmly friendly place right off the glossiest part of the rue St-Honoré is 1-star, and so is a much statelier, frighteningly clean, chillingly unfriendly hotel in the now fashionable Marais.

A very few of the hotels we have found have no stars at all, although they are comfortable and spotless – many of them hope to be reclassified for the next *Guide des Hôtels*, but the inspectors haven't got around to them yet.

On the whole, we have found that even in times of inflation you can get a single room with a *cabinet de toilette* (that is, basin, bidet, and constant supply of really hot water) in a pleasant hotel for as little as 90F. A double room with a big bed is even more of a bargain, as it costs as little as 155F even in a very remarkable hotel in the Marais. If you want a shower, expect to pay from 130F for a single, and up to 235F for a double room with a large bed. Twin beds, and a bath instead of a shower, can push prices up towards

250-275F, but in terms of other capital city prices, they are still cheap. Usually, the price of a room with shower or bath and WC is the same for one or two persons; cheaper rooms, with running water or *cabinet de toilette* alone, may charge less for a single occupant. Some rooms have a big bed, plus a narrow single, meant for a family but perfectly OK for three travelling paupers.

Rooms that have no lavatory are always within ten feet or so of such a facility, and every hotel we have listed is careful to keep a shower or a bath on almost every floor, for which you can expect to pay about 10 to 15F for each use. You'd be surprised at how clean you can keep without a daily bath, in a room with that luxurious and versatile necessity, the bidet.

On the whole, expect to pay the highest rates for location: near the Opéra, around the Louvre, almost anywhere in the 1er, 6e, 7e, 8e, or 16e. St-Germain-des-Prés, which was for decades the refuge of the poor traveller, is now one of the costliest areas of Paris. A few old faithful hotels in the much loved Latin Quarter, 5e, try to keep their prices down, but they seem to be closing for good or else renovating and upgrading. The Grand Hôtel des Balcons, near the universities, was home from home for generations of American, English and German students. It has finally tottered under the weight of breadcrumbs, empty wine bottles and dripping laundry, and has been renovated to emerge blazing with three stars.

If you are willing to spend an extra ten minutes on the Métro, away from the tourist heart of Paris (with your *Paris Visite* or *Carte Orange*), you can save up to 25F per day for hotel rooms. Some of the hotels we have found are in what may seem unlikely neighbourhoods often brushed off by travel writers as 'uninteresting, working class, too far from the action' – beyond the Bastille, around the place de la République, up near the place d'Italie, in quiet Passy, and so forth. Actually, every one of these *quartiers* has an indigenous life of its own, well worth getting to know. Far more truly Parisian than the more obvious areas known as 'historiques et pittoresque', where they've seen tourists floating around for generations, and where they sometimes couldn't care less if they never see *you* again. In more out-of-the-way places, you have only to take breakfast two days running at the counter of a bar-tabac, and on the third day it will be 'Bonjour, Monsieur – comme d'habitude?' – the usual? The news-stand lady will be ready to hand you *Le Figaro* without being asked.

Some hotels which have been mentioned repeatedly in guide books begin to lean back and take it easy. One of our researchers spent a night recently in a well-known, well recommended 1-star place in the Quartier d'Europe, the quiet and pleasant area beyond the Gare St-Lazare. There, the shower head had fallen off the wall, the windows didn't quite close, and the blankets were like Kleenex. Since the clients didn't actually storm out, the management didn't see much reason to make improvements. As it is being renovated, we have dropped it – sad, as the management is kind, the location superb; we'll wait for new prices to restore it one day.

In contrast, one of our Paris-wise friends recommended a hotel in a quiet courtyard in the 18e *arrondissement* (Montmartre, but far from the brassy connotations of that word), with pretty coloured glass windows in the attractive rooms – where you could sleep for 75F; and a double with shower and WC is only 240F (about £23 at the time of writing).

Most hotels listed here have shaver points with 220-volt current, so you can use your electric razor, blow-dryer, mini-boiler for a cup of tea, and so on. For Americans used to 110 volts, all appliances must be dual voltage, or you should carry a converter (see Electricity, page 231). Almost every hotel has reading lights above or near the bed, which is a must for those who can't close their eyes without a book in hand, or if you want to have a lie-in with the newspaper.

If you use the telephone from your hotel, expect it to cost more than a phone box would, but you do have the convenience of having someone else deal with getting the number for you. If the concierge has done anything extra for you – getting a taxi, theatre tickets, or whatnot – it's polite to leave about 15F in an envelope at the end of your stay. If the *femme de ménage*, who cleans the rooms and brings fresh linen daily, does anything like washing or ironing for you (not something our readers will want, probably), leave her some money when you go. How much depends on what you feel the service saved you.

If you can dust off your school French and smile a lot, you will find that in almost every case the atmosphere in these hotels will be astonishingly warm, personal and friendly. A few phrases of hotel French are on pages 63–4, and more general conversation about *la politesse*, which oils the wheels of Paris, on page 249.

Eating and laundry in your room

Many Paris hotels have had their hospitality really abused by travellers brought to France by budget airfares and charters, in the last fifteen or twenty years. So they are, many of them, now posting polite notices in their lobbies or in their rooms: Please, no eating and no washing. We can well understand this, having seen such places as the Grand Hôtel des Balcons as it was before renovation: an absolute mess. We can only advise that if you *do* want to picnic, for breakfast or lunch (and it's a great temptation, with the most succulent pâtés and jewel-like patisseries sold almost under your nose), do it with neatness and discretion. Tidy up after yourself. Don't carry an obvious, warmly smelling roast chicken in a plastic bag right past the desk. Put down newspapers on the floor, pick up your crumbs, don't stain the table with wine-glasses, don't get grease stains and lipstick on the towels. We have picnicked with impunity, and perfect neatness, in hotels in Paris from the elegant Montalembert to our current favourite small hotel a few streets from the place de la Concorde without anyone ever saying boo.

When it comes to laundry, it's obvious that it isn't the washing, it's the *dripping* that drives Paris hoteliers up the wall. Hangers with wet shirts, draped over radiators, can make a soggy mess of a carpet. In one hotel, since completely renovated, students draped wet tights, bras, jeans and jerseys on the curtain rails until even the walls ran with damp.

If you must wash your smalls in a hotel basin or bidet, and why not, have the courtesy to blot them reasonably dry in a towel, and hang them over the basin or a tiled floor so that no drips will damage the carpet or curtains. And be discreet enough to whip them into the cupboard before the chambermaid comes to clean. She's not a management spy, but part of her job is to let the front desk know what condition the hotel is in every day.

Indispensable for staying in inexpensive hotels: a few extra light-weight plastic-coated hangers, four clip-type clothes pegs which can serve to hang up socks or tights, or to pull together curtains over an open window. An over-sized safety-pin comes in handy, too, for all sorts of things.

Hôtel French

The notice-board dealing with prices of rooms is often couched in an esoteric shorthand, but once you've cracked the code it's quite easy.

Chambre avec e.c. – room with hot and cold running water, basin, no bidet

Chambre avec cabinet de toilette − *room with basin and bidet in their own compartment*
Chambre avec douche − room with basin, bidet and shower
Chambre avec bain − basin, bidet and bath (often with a hand shower)
Chambre avec douche/bain et WC − basin, bidet, shower or bath, and lavatory
Petit déjeuner - Continental breakfast (see page 60)
En sus means 'extra charge', e.g. *petit déjeuner en sus, 10F.*

Baths, showers

As noted, if you are staying in a room without these amenities, you can command one by ringing down to the office. The charge will appear on your bill at the end of your stay. Really skinflint travelling couples can manage to work in two showers for the price of one if they are quick and wily, but don't say you read it here.

Part of a poor traveller's experience in Paris can be the public baths. Don't shudder and turn the page. They are clean, supervised by the city, offering showers with plenty of really hot water in private cubicles, and catering to the nearly 700,000 Parisians who have no baths in their homes. They are open Thursdays, Fridays, Saturdays and Sunday mornings, and a fairly fastidious friend agreed to try one recently. Great value, is the report, clean as can be. For 5F you get a shower stall and a dressing cubicle with mirror, tiled floor, hooks and shelf, endless hot water for twenty minutes which is plenty of time to get really clean and to wash your hair. Everything is mopped up between clients. It's a good alternative to spending 15-20F for a shower in your hotel. See pages 225–6 for addresses and more information.

Finding an hotel on your own

If all the hotels listed here are full, wander around the neighbourhood you like best, after stashing your luggage at the station. Even have a look at hotels that have no stars at all. They are often clean, respectable, cheap, run by a couple who may not speak much English but want you to be satisfied. If you are staying more than three days, you could try asking if they have a weekly or monthly rate. They save on laundry, you save on hotel costs.

Note: The hotel day begins and ends at noon, sharp, and if you overstay you will be charged for an extra day. Most of the hotels in this book are very good about letting travellers leave a small amount of luggage, coats, and so on (at their own risk, of course) in lobby or office until time for the train or plane. Some, however, have been so thoroughly imposed upon by those who dump rucksacks, skis, carrier bags and raincoats for days on end, that they are no longer so willing. Others may have little space and really don't want their lobbies cluttered up with the increasingly hideous magenta and bright orange nylon luggage that travelling paupers lug around – don't be offended if they politely refuse to keep them for you. Take the stuff to the nearest *consigne* at a railway station, making careful note of their opening and closing times.

Never book without looking

Go hotel shopping in the middle of the day, or not later than teatime, not at night or when you're dropping with fatigue. If they won't let you look at the room, say a polite 'merci' and be on your way.

For some cheap alternatives to hotels

See Other options, pages 94–98

Recommended Hôtels

1er arrondissement

Hôtel Lion d'Or 1-star

5 rue de la Sourdière, 1er
Tel: 42 60 79 04
Métro: Tuileries

Room with *cabinet de toilette*	1 person	140F
	2 persons	170

with shower	1 person	160
	2 persons	210
with bath	1 person	190
	2 persons	240
Petit déjeuner		15
Shower		15

This small hotel on a quiet street is a long-established favourite of 'Paupers' Paris' readers. It is in the process of being redecorated and generally polished-up. The location is superb, close to the Louvre, the Palais Royal, the Tuileries, the Seine, and a fair number of good restaurants. And they accept VISA and American Express cards. The *patron*, M. Damane, speaks excellent English.

Hôtel du Palais 1-star NN

2 Quai de la Megisserie, 1er
Tel: 42 36 98 25
Métro: Pont Neuf, Châtelet

Room with *eau courante*	1 or 2 persons	120F
with *cabinet de toilette*	1 person	126
	2 persons	150
with shower	1 person	166
	2 persons	184
Petit déjeuner		17
Shower		15

Really basic accommodation, this, but the welcome is warm and the rooms clean – and just at its feet is the delightful plant and flower market along the Seine. Rooms facing the Quai have a view of the river but, be warned, will get the noise of traffic continuously – ask for one at the back of the hotel. 'NN' means redecorating is either in progress or imminent, but on our visit nothing was happening. The *patron* is M. Saidi, and his English becomes more fluent as you talk to him. No credit cards, but Eurocheques with a Eurocard are accepted.

Hôtel Richelieu-Nazarin 1-star

51 rue de Richelieu, 1er
Tel: 42 97 46 20
Métro: Palais-Royal, Pyramides

Room with *cabinet de toilette*	1 or 2 persons	160F
with shower	1 or 2 persons	220
with bath and WC	1 or 2 persons	260
Petit déjeuner		22
Shower		10

A minute hotel – only fourteen rooms, and these usually snapped up by regulars – and to be booked well in advance. It's clean and tidy, recently re-done, panelled in wood, decorated with posters (the earth seen from the moon), and very pleasantly staffed. Somewhat noisy on the street side, but location is all: you can hardly stay in a more central spot – a stone's throw from the gardens of the Palais Royal. No lift, and very little English spoken, but the *patron*, M. Daniel, makes up for it with smiles and good will. No credit cards, no Eurocheques.

3e arrondissement

Hôtel Chancelier Boucherat 1-star

110 rue de Turenne, 3e
Tel: 42 72 86 83
Métro: Filles-de-Calvaire

Room with *eau courante*	1 person	147F
	2 persons	167
with *cabinet de toilette*	1 person	164
	2 persons	184
with shower or bath	1 person	200
	2 persons	221
with bath and WC	1 person	240
	2 persons	260
Petit déjeuner		20
Shower		12

This pleasant, quiet hotel is steadily improving: tatty carpets replaced, and a washer and dryer installed. The prices given are not those of the cheapest rooms – so you might be lucky and pay less. And if you arrive between November and May, ask for the winter prices - they are cheaper. The breakfast room is cheerful and full of plants and sunshine; the rooms and bathrooms immaculate; the street noiseless at night. Nearby: the Musée Picasso. Carte Bleu/VISA and Eurocheques accepted. *Patronne*: Mme Martin

4e arrondissement

Grand Hôtel Jeanne d'Arc 2-star

3 rue Jarente, 4e
Tel: 48 87 62 11
Métro: St-Paul

Room with bath and WC	1 person	240
	2 persons	280
Petit déjeuner		22

Now resplendent in its two-star status, this charming little hotel is very clean, perfectly neat, and decorated in white-lace bourgeois style. The rooms are well-arranged, the bathrooms large, and the street is a peaceful one, leading toward the rue de Turenne. A *little* English is spoken. M. Aymard, the *patron*, sounds just like Yves Montand. Traveller's cheques, and Carte Bleu/VISA and Eurocheques accepted.

Grand Hôtel Malher 1-star

5 rue Malher, 4e
Tel: 42 72 60 92
Métro: St-Paul

Room with *eau courante*	1 person	120F
with *cabinet de toilette*	1 or 2 persons	150
	3 persons	200
with shower or bath	1 or 2 persons	200

with bath and WC	1 or 2 persons	275
	3 persons	320
Petit déjeuner		20
Shower		15

Just across the street from the Hôtel Sévigné, this is rather a mystery hotel. Spotless, good carpeting and wallpaper, old-fashioned wardrobes and bedframes, marble-floored lobby, perfect location in the Marais, great restaurants all around. A little English is spoken by the receptionists, although the *patronne*, Mme Fossiez, whom we haven't met, is said to speak it well. On the busy rue Mahler, rooms can be noisy, but the rest of the hotel is almost eerily quiet. No credit cards, but travellers' cheques and Eurocheques with Eurocards are accepted - and the Mahler has a FAX machine!

Hôtel Castex 1 or 2 stars

5 rue Castex, 4e
Tel: 42 72 31 52
Métro: Bastille, Sully-Morland

Room with *cabinet de toilette*	1 person	100F
	2 persons	130
with shower or bath	1 person	160
	2 persons	235
with bath and WC	2 (double bed)	275
	2 (twin beds)	260
Petit déjeuner		20
Shower		20

This little family hotel was just finishing a complete overhaul when we last called, and they didn't know how many stars they would be awarded when the work was finished. They did have the new room prices – and it's a very good buy. The location is superb, surrounded as it is by restaurants of remarkable quality. The rooms in the Castex are shining clean, and most have telephones. The *patrons*, M. and Mme. Bouchan, are sociable and pleasant; and their enthusiastic son Blaise speaks English and is a gymnast. The rue Castex isn't one of the really picturesque streets of the Marais, but only two minutes away, across the rue St-Antoine, is the place des Vosges, and the haunting beauty of the Hôtel de Sully, the Hôtel Lamoignon, and the Carnavalet Museum. Carte Bleu/VISA and traveller's cheques in francs accepted, and Eurocheques with a 30F bank surcharge.

Hôtel de Nice 1-star

42 bis, rue de Rivoli, 4e
Tel: 42 78 55 29
Métro: Hôtel-de-Ville, St-Paul

Room	with *eau courante*	1 or 2 persons	130F
	with *cabinet de toilette*	1 or 2 persons	150
	with *salle de bains*	1 or 2 persons	200
	with bath and WC	1 or 2 persons	260
Petit déjeuner			20
Shower			16

This is a treasure: sparkling clean, well painted and wallpapered, and run by eager, helpful (and English-speaking) people. However, traffic on the rue de Rivoli is continuous, night and early morning, and you are advised to take earplugs. The site is superb, only minutes from Beaubourg and on the edge of the Marais. Very popular, so book at least two weeks in advance for peak periods; reservations should be accompanied by a deposit for the first night's lodging – traveller's cheques in francs only, or in Eurocheques. No lift. Mastercard and Carte Bleu/VISA accepted, and Eurocheques. *Patrons*: M. and Mme Vaudoux.

Hôtel Pratic

9 rue d'Ormesson, 4e,
Tel: 48 87 80 47
Métro: St-Paul

Room	with *eau courante*	1 or 2 persons	90F
	with *cabinet de toilette*	1 or 2 persons	100
	with shower	1 or 2 persons	120
	with shower and WC	1 or 2 persons	180
	with bath and WC	1 or 2 persons	180
Petit déjeuner			15
Shower			15

Clean, and with evidence of extensive renovation: hall and staircase, breakfast room, showers and bathrooms, and almost all the rooms have been re-done. The Pratic closes at midnight, and getting back to your room in the small hours is something of a task; the staff are a trifle cool, though always correct. But the prices are *rock bottom*. No credit cards, but traveller's cheques and Eurocheques accepted. *Gerant*: M. Zaidi.

Hôtel Sévigné 2-star

2 rue Malher, 4e
Tel: 42 72 76 17
Métro: St-Paul

Room with shower or bath	1 person	226F
	2 persons	242
with shower	3 persons	320
with bath and WC	1 person	226
	2 persons (double bed)	262
	2 persons (twin beds)	277
	3 persons	400
Petit déjeuner		included

Formerly known as the Grand Hôtel du Sud et du Pole du Nord – madness to change such a sonorous name! The easy-going atmosphere is gone, but it's still well-run, and extremely clean and tidy. The lobby now has a shiny, mirror-faceted column in it, which is pretty weird. Unusually for a hotel so well renovated, they will accept three people to a room, which brings down the prices. Every room has a bath or shower; there's a minute, padded lift which starts half a flight above the lobby. The receptionists usually speak good English. Drawback: hard by the rue Rivoli, hence noisy. No credit cards, but traveller's cheques and Eurocheques with Eurocards. *Patron*: M. Claude Rantier.

Hôtel Stella 1-star

14 rue Neuve-St-Pierre, 4e
Tel: 42 72 23 66
Métro: St-Paul

Room with *eau courante*	1 person	160F
	2 persons	180
with shower or bath	1 person	190
	2 persons	210
with shower and WC	2 persons	270
with bath and WC	2 persons	290
Petit déjeuner		20
Shower		20

This seems to be one of several Stellas in Paris: either a chain or a coincidence. A simple, clean and sober hotel, undistinguished but cheap (for the location) and decent, on a quiet street just south of the rue St-Antoine. It has been renovated: new beds, new carpets, and it has a lift. Traveller's cheques accepted, and Eurocheques (with a 10% surcharge). The *Patron*, M. Chartier, speaks good English.

5e arrondissement

Grand Hôtel d'Harcourt 2-star NN

3 boulevard St-Michel, 5e
Tel: 43 26 52 35
Métro: St-Michel

Room with *cabinet de toilette*	1 person	170F
	2 persons	210
with shower	1 person	200
	2 persons	270
with bath and WC	1 person	270
	2 persons	310
Petit déjeuner		25

A re-done two-star *with a lift* in an area where prices are usually over the top. It faces the St-Michel fountain, and is a short walk from

Notre-Dame, the Cluny Museum, Luxembourg Gardens, and the liveliness of the streets around St-Michel and St-Germain. Rooms are freshly painted and papered, there's a spacious breakfast room, and even in summer a bed is sometimes available on very short notice. The street can be noisy, early and late into the night. VISA, Mastercard, Eurocheques and traveller's cheques (in francs) accepted. The *patron*, M. Abed, speaks good English, and the reception is genuinely friendly.

Hôtel des Grandes Écoles 2-star

75 rue du Cardinal Lemoine, 5e
Tel: 43 26 79 23
Métro: Cardinal Lemoine

Room with *eau courante*	1 person	170F
	2 persons	210
with *cabinet de toilette*	1 person	210
	2 persons	230
with shower or bath and WC		300-330
twin beds or a double		350
Petit déjeuner		25
Shower		free

This is an unbelievably pretty hotel. To reach it, you walk through a rustic-looking courtyard off the rue Cardinal Lemoine; turn the corner, and you face a miniature country mansion set in its own gardens. The rooms are delightful, each decorated differently – and the elegance and charm of the furniture and decorations are worthy of at least two more stars. There's a lift, but steps to the entrance would make it difficult for wheelchairs. Telephone reservations (and we suggest you book well ahead of time) are taken between 2 p.m. and 6 p.m. *Patronne*: Mme LeFloch.

6e arrondissement

Hôtel Alsace Lorraine 1-star

14 rue des Canettes, 6e
Tel: 43 25 10 14
Métro: Mabillon

Room with *cabinet de toilette*	1 person	140F
	2 persons	200
with shower or bath	1 person	210
	2 persons	230
with bath and WC	1 or 2 persons	260
Petit déjeuner		20
Shower		20

We're told that a former *gérante* of this hotel was Mme Proust, and it has been an off-and-on haven for artists and writers. The building is a *monument historique*, hence neither modern nor aseptic – but if you wanted a germ-free environment you'd be in Switzerland. The hotel is a dream. Some of the walls have visible beams; showers and bathrooms are absolutely huge; the furniture is in the old 'rustique' style, the decor tasteful; the street is quiet and the yard dead still. From the façade windows you can see one of the St-Sulpice towers . . . it's Paris as one imagines it (and the clientele is made up entirely of nostalgic Americans). VISA, Diners Club, American Express, Eurocard, and traveller's cheques in francs accepted. *Patrons*: M. and Mme Kenniche.

Hôtel Nesle

7 rue de Nesle, 6e
Tel: 43 54 62 41
Métro: Odéon

Room with *eau courante*	1 person	90F
	2 persons (includes showers and breakfast)	180
with bath and WC	1 person	210
Petit déjeuner		20
Shower		20

The Hôtel Nesle is a riot. Full of students and back-packers, it has the atmosphere of the hippie days of the sixties. It may seem chaotic, but the *patronne*, Reneé, runs the place with a benign autocracy that doesn't interfere with her sense of fun. Each room is decorated in a different style – one is 'Grandma's room', complete with lace, old furniture, sepia photographs; another has medieval murals. There's a Turkish bath, the 'Hammam', with deep blue tiling and lion's head basin. Breakfast is served on brass trays to the sound of Arab music – and staff and guests join forces to keep the place cheerful. When we were there, one American motorcyclist was helping to plant shrubs in the back garden while another guest acted as landscaper. Drawbacks? Some of the rooms are small, and the partitions thin, so it might be noisy. There's a washer and dryer, but cash (and in advance) is the only acceptable currency.

Regent's Hôtel 2-star

44 rue Madame, 6e
Tel: 45 48 02 81
Métro: St-Sulpice

Room with shower	1 person	240F
	2 persons	300
with bath and WC	1 person	300
	2 persons	350
Petit déjeuner		27

Almost too expensive – but those who can afford it will love it. The little garden is beautiful, full of flowers, and breakfast is served there in good weather. The hotel itself is quiet, clean, neat, respectable, and with an aura of space and ease. And, as a 2-star hotel, it has a lift. Carte Bleu/VISA, Eurocheques, and traveller's cheques accepted. *Patron*: M. Crétey.

7e arrondissement

Hôtel du Champ de Mars 2-star NN

7 rue du Champ-de-Mars, 7e
Tel: 45 51 52 30
Métro: École-Militaire

Room with shower and WC	1 or 2 persons	270F
with bath and WC	1 or 2 persons	300
	(with twin beds)	330
Petit déjeuner		25

A 2-star hotel with more spacious rooms than some others in the neighbourhood. While not cheap, it does offer good value for two people travelling together, not so economical for a solo voyager. It's clean, comfortable, and with a friendly atmosphere, highly recommended by people who stay there year after year. However, breakfast in one of the nearby *tabacs* or bars is a far better bet than paying 25F here. The street by day is a microcosm of 'neighbourhood' Paris, with children, dogs, sparkling shops. At night it is very quiet. A little English is spoken, but smiles and goodwill on both sides fill the gaps. Carte Bleu/VISA and traveller's cheques accepted. *Patron*: M. Guillochon.

Grand Hôtel Leveque 1-star NN

29 rue Cler, 7e
Tel: 47 05 49 15
Métro: École Militaire

Room with *eau courante*	1 or 2 persons	160F
	3 persons	225
with shower	1 or 2 persons	240
with shower and WC	1 or 2 persons	260
Petit déjeuner		15
Shower		no charge

Most of the 7e *arrondissement* is so correct, so sterile, that it's a happy shock when you turn a corner and stumble into anything as full of life as the rue Cler. It's a pedestrian street bubbling day long with shops and stalls, and at night as quiet as a country lane. The Hôtel

Leveque has smallish, cosy, nice rooms, which have all been recently renewed. Some of the 240F rooms have room for three persons. Rates are remarkably low, and people seem to stay forever. Carte Bleu and traveller's cheques accepted.

Hôtel Malar 1-star

29 rue Malar, 7e
Tel: 45 51 38 46
Métro: Latour-Maubourg

Room with shower	1 person	180F
	2 persons	200
with shower and WC	1 person	240
	2 persons	260
with bath and WC,	1 person	260
twin beds	2 persons	300
Petit déjeuner		22

This isn't exactly an undiscovered hotel, as people keep rushing up to us and divulging its existence. But it is very good value still, well-kept, friendly and with a feeling of warmth and welcome. It's not very far from the amusing rue St-Dominique, one of the streets that makes the 7e worth staying in. Prices (except for the rather expensive breakfast) are still low enough to come as a surprise in this pricey neighbourhood. All rooms have shower or bath, and many have WCs. It's run by the same manager as the 3-star Jardin d'Eiffel around the corner, and if there's a problem with languages, he'll send a three-star member of staff around to help.

Hôtel Prince 2-star NN

66 avenue Bosquet, 7e
Tel: 47 05 40 90
Métro: École-Militaire

Room with shower or bath	1 person	230F
and WC	2 persons	260-280
	3 persons	300
Petit déjeuner		23

A spectacular bargain – only 29 rooms, each with bath or shower and its own WC, on a broad boulevard which is typically *haut-bourgeois* Parisian. The neighbourhood has a life of its own which makes it considerably more interesting than most of the rest of the bland, rich 7e. The rooms facing onto the avenue Bosquet are double-glazed, so it's reasonably quiet. The Prince has a lift, and facilities for those in wheelchairs. It gets booked up in summer and autumn, mostly with businessmen and families, so write or phone several weeks in advance. English is spoken and American Express, Carte Bleu/VISA and Eurocheques accepted. The *patron*, M. Roussel, is very cheerful, and likes to joke.

Hôtel du Résidence du Champ de Mars 2-star

19 rue de Champ-de-Mars, 7e
Tel: 47 05 25 45
Métro: École-Militaire

Room with *cabinet de toilette*	1 or 2 persons	165F
with shower	1 or 2 persons	165
with shower and WC	1 or 2 persons	269
with bath and WC	1 or 2 persons	289
Petit déjeuner		21

A two-star hotel with a lift, just off the smart, tree-lined avenue Bosquet, at prices that are hardly more than some one-star establishments. The rooms are adequately furnished, varying in size, and well arranged for comfort: quiet ones face the yard, less quiet on the street side. The street is one of the few lively 'shopping' ones in the staid 7e. For a picnic lunch, explore the delights of Marc Tattevin at No. 15, whose prepared foods are seductive; and 'Fromage in Piú' nearby makes cheese-lovers faint with pleasure. Carte Bleu/VISA and Mastercard, and Eurocheques (in francs) accepted. *Patron*: M. Guyot.

Le Royal Phare 2-star

40 avenue de la Motte-Picquet, 7e
Tel: 47 05 57 30
Métro: École-Militaire

Room with shower and WC	1 person	220F
	2 persons	240
with bath and WC	1 or 2 persons	280
Petit déjeuner		22

M. Le Rousic, the *patron*, speaks little English but understands it well and is extremely helpful. He is gradually re-doing the hotel with new showers, carpets, wallpaper, bedspreads, and it all shows his considerable personal involvement. A happy atmosphere and very good value. Close to excellent shopping (a good Prisunic and Fran-Prix), and close to the charm of the rue Cler for shopping, strolling, gazing. The avenue de la Motte-Picquet traffic begins early, about 7:00 a.m., if that matters to you, but it's quiet at night. Reading lights and a lift. American Express, Carte Bleu/VISA, Eurocheques and traveller's cheques accepted.

8e arrondissement

Hôtel de Marigny 2-star

11 rue de l'Arcade, 8e
Tel: 42 66 42 71
Métro: St-Lazare

Room with *cabinet de toilette*	1 person	165F
with shower or bath		
and WC	1 or 2 persons	340
Petit déjeuner		24

A truly remarkable bargain, if you can manage to get one of the six 165F rooms in this charming two-star establishment. It's about a hundred yards from the Madeleine and five minutes walk to the Gare St-Lazare and the place de la Concorde. The Marigny actually provides pillows in addition to the usual Paris hotel bolster, and is one of the few that provides an individual piece of soap for the traveller. Sparkling clean and prettily furnished, too. But watch out for the self-service lift as the doors can give you a rap on the elbow if not firmly controlled. Reading lights. Carte Bleu/VISA, traveller's cheques and Eurocheques accepted. *Patron*: M. Maugars.

9e arrondissement

Hôtel de Berne 1-star NN

30 rue de Châteaudun, 9e
Tel: 48 74 37 66
Métro: Le Peletier

Room with *cabinet de toilette*	1 person	140F
	2 persons	160
with shower	1 person	170
	2 persons	190
with shower and WC	1 person	190
	2 persons	210
Petit déjeuner		15
Shower		15

A re-done hotel (apart from the staircase and corridors), pleasant and easy on the eye. Its distinguishing feature is an accommodating attitude, a willingness to cater to individual needs. An English breakfast, for example – eggs, ham, cheese, croissants, unlimited coffee – can be had; groups are welcome; inquire ahead for details. Drawback: noisy on both sides of the building. No credit cards or Eurocheques accepted. *Patron*: M. Neubert. (Note: there's another Hôtel de Berne in the 8e arrondissement – with three stars and prices to match. This is not it.)

Hôtel Confort 2-star, NN

5 rue de Trévise, 9e
Tel: 42 46 12 06
Métro: Rue Montmartre

Room with *eau courante*	1 person	150F
with shower	1 person	215
	2 persons	240
with bath and WC	1 person	260
	2 persons	280
Petit déjeuner		22
Shower		15

This is a pleasant hotel with not much to distinguish it from hundreds of others, except that it is two-star with the NN classification, which means they have done a lot of painting and sprucing up. It has a lift, and facilities for people in wheelchairs, and you can bring your dog with you. And there's a TV in every room. It's cheap, considering all these amenities, and is run by agreeable and helpful people, who speak English. Reading lights. VISA, Eurocheques and traveller's cheques accepted. *Patronne*: Mme Francis.

Hôtel de Lille no stars

2 rue Montholon, 9e
Tel: 47 70 38 76
Métro: Cadet

Room with *eau courante*	1 person	80F
with *cabinet de toilette*	1 person	120
with 2 beds		150
with shower	1 or 2 persons	150
with shower and WC	1 or 2 persons	180
Petit déjeuner		15
Shower		15

Although the entrance looks a bit dark, persevere. The rooms have been smartened up and are very clean and tidy. And it's still absurdly cheap. No lift, and no English spoken. Traveller's cheques accepted, but no credit cards. *Patron*: M. Amir.

Hôtel Montyon 2-star

15 rue de Montyon, 9e
Tel: 47 70 92 70
Métro: Rue Montmartre

Room with *eau courante*	1 person	125F
	2 persons	180
with shower	1 person	200
	2 persons	220
with bath and WC	1 person	235
	2 persons	260

Petit déjeuner	25
Shower	15

This attractive hotel is moderately priced, has a lift, a pleasant small reception-breakfast room with a TV, and a bar in the lobby which sounds rather awful but in fact is quite a good idea if you feel like having a quiet drink before dinner. Reading lights. Carte Bleu/ VISA, traveller's cheques and Eurocheques accepted. *Patronne*: Mme Annick Plusquellec.

10e arrondissement

Hôtel Bonne Nouvelle

125 boulevard Magenta, 10e
Tel: 48 74 99 90
Métro: Gare du Nord

Room with shower	1 person	120F
	2 persons, double bed	150
	twin beds	200
Petit déjeuner		17

A very Parisian hotel, this, somewhat old-fashioned but remarkably well located and certainly *bon marché* . . . good value. All rooms have showers, although none has a private loo. Some English is spoken, there's a lot of good will and willingness to be helpful, even school-level French will get you a long way here. No credit cards, but Eurocheques are accepted. *Direction*: Cransac.

Hôtel du Centre 1-star NN

4 rue Sibour, 10e
Tel: 46 07 20 74
Métro: Gare de l'Est

Room with *eau courante*	1 person	137F
	2 persons	154
with *cabinet de toilette* and WC	1 person	147

with shower or bath	1 person	187
and WC	2 persons	204
and with two beds,		30% supplement
Petit déjeuner		included
Shower		17

In this rather unpromising neighbourhood – notable mostly for its bargain shoe and handbag shops – we fell into the doorway of the Centre Est out of a cloudburst and turned up a little gem of a hotel. Five minutes from the Gare de l'Est, which is a centre of bus and Métro lines that will take you anywhere, the Centre Est has a lift, facilities for wheelchairs, even accepts dogs. The rooms are big, the bathrooms spotless, the patron speaks a bit of English, it has reading lights. Recent renovations include more rooms with showers and WCs, though the carpets and wallpaper are not the newest. Many of the rooms have huge mirrors, wooden wardrobes and tables, and some have a view of the Église St-Laurent. No credit cards, but traveller's cheques in francs and Eurocheques accepted. *Patron*: M. Glas.

Hôtel Jarry 2-star

4 rue Jarry, 10e
Tel: 47 70 70 38
Métro: Château d'Eau

Room with *cabinet de toilette*	1 person	95F
	2 persons	130
with shower	1 or 2 persons	150-185
with shower and WC	1 or 2 persons	150-185
Petit déjeuner		15
Shower		No charge

In the not very interesting 10e *arrondissement*, this hotel is a pleasant surprise: very clean, sober, nicely re-done with considerable taste, and the concierge speaks good English. Conveniently located for the Gare de l'Est, and there are some goodish restaurants and brasseries in the neighbourhood. No lift, and no credit cards or traveller's cheques accepted. *Patron*: M. Mahfouf.

Hôtel du Jura 1-star

6 rue Jarry, 10e
Tel: 47 70 06 66
Métro: Château d'Eau

Room with *cabinet de toilette*	1 person	110F
	2 persons	145
with shower	1 or 2 persons	170
Petit déjeuner		included
Shower		15

A more modest place, but comfortable, neat and respectable, and a remarkable bargain with well-arranged rooms and breakfast included. It can be a bit noisy and is beginning to need redecoration and repairs, but they're on the way, we're told. And while the 10e isn't one of the 'historic' areas of Paris, it has its own neighbourhood character, and some very good shopping. Those who run the hotel are kind, helpful, and willing to speak English of a sort and to help you with your French. No credit cards or traveller's cheques.

Little Hôtel 2-star NN

3 rue Pierre Chausson, 10e
Tel: 42 08 21 57
Métro: Jacques-Bonsergent (and close to République)

Room with shower	1 person	90F
with bath	1 person	260
	2 persons	280
with bath and WC	1 person	280
	2 persons	310
Petit déjeuner		20

A clean and pleasant place, which has been renovated in stages – hall, reception area and breakfast rooms first, and most recently the bedrooms. The furniture is not the newest, but the rooms have a home-like feeling, and the *patron*, M. El Baz, is a sociable man who likes to take personal care of his customers. Carte Bleu/VISA, Eurocheques and traveller's cheques accepted.

Hôtel de la Nouvelle France 1-star

23 rue des Messageries, 10e
Tel: 48 24 70 74 and 48 24 66 29
Métro: Poissonnière

Room with *eau courante*	1 person	90F
with *cabinet de toilette*	1 person	140
	2 persons	170
with shower or bath	1 person	230
and WC	2 persons	260
Petit déjeuner		included
Shower		free

A complete delight, and very good value for the price. It's been renovated, and now looks very cheerful and clean. The rooms are large, fresh and quiet, even on the street side; and the prices are still low. The reception was friendly and helpful and spoke a bit of English. *Patron*: M. Boissier.

11e arrondissement

Auberge de Jeunesse Jules Ferry

8 boulevard Jules-Ferry, 11e
Tel: 43 57 55 60
Métro: République, Parmentier

For more notes on Youth Hostels, see page 96. The Jules Ferry is an excellent example.

Dormitory room (sleeping 2, 3, 4 or 6)	68F per person
Shower and breakfast	included
Drap de couchage jettable	13F
(but it's obviously better to bring your own sleeping bag)	
Youth hostel card	90

    If you're not a Youth Hostel member, you pay 15F a day extra as a Guest, but after 6 days (90F) you become a member.

The Jules Ferry Hostel is an old building, with some renovated rooms (all have basins and running water), not very fresh paint, but a pleasant atmosphere and a feeling of safety. The *patron*, M. Fischer, is cooperative and kind, no matter how busy he is – and he speaks English. A Youth Hostel card is obligatory, but you can join by paying a Guest fee (see above). In summer it's advisable to reserve two weeks to a month in advance, *by mail*, and reservations for more than one night must be accompanied by a cheque in francs and an international postal reply coupon. You can check in any time between 8:00 a.m. and 9:00 p.m. and the building is open from 6:00 a.m. to 2:00 a.m. (rooms accessible round the clock).

Hôtel Notre-Dame 2-star

51 rue de Malte, 11e
Tel: 47 00 78 76
Métro: République

Room *cabinet de toilette*	1 person	145F
with shower	1 person	175
with bath	2 persons	230
with shower and WC	2 persons	280
with bath and WC	2 persons	280
	3 persons	315
Petit déjeuner		25
Shower		13

This is a gem. The reception area has been beautifully re-done, and the breakfast room is full of fine posters and fresh roses. The atmosphere is peaceful (though the rue de Malte is far from quiet in daylight) and the *patronnes*, Mme Damitio and Mlle Coudy are very pleasant. The Notre-Dame is closed in August, and you're advised to book well in advance from late spring through early autumn. Carte Bleu/VISA and traveller's cheques accepted. And it has a lift.

Hôtel Plessis 2-star NN

25 rue du Grand-Prieuré, 11e
Tel: 47 00 13 38
Métro: Oberkampf or République

Room with *cabinet de toilette*	1 or 2 persons	165F

with shower and WC	1 or 2 persons	235
and with television	1 or 2 persons	250
with 2 beds, for 2 people		280
with bath and WC and television	1 or 2 persons	270
	Extra bed	75
Petit déjeuner		25

Renovations were taking place when we last called, and the hotel has gained an extra star. It's very well run by an enterprising couple, M. and Mme Montrazat, who speak English and know a great deal about this quite interesting neighbourhood. It now has double windows and new doors – quite efficient against the noise. Closed from mid-July to mid-August. All credit cards accepted, and traveller's cheques and Eurocheques.

Hôtel Printania

16 boulevard du Temple, 11e
Tel: 47 00 33 46
Métro: Filles du Calvaire, République, Oberkampf

Room with *cabinet de toilette*	1 person	140F
	twin beds	195
with shower and WC	1 or 2 persons	225-240
with bath and WC	1 person	280
	twin beds	350
Petit déjeuner		22
Shower		18

The Printania has been revamped, gradually, in fresh, pleasant colours, even to the corridors and stairs, and the extra touches are refreshing: plants and a pair of light brown doves in the hallway, for example – and two dogs and a cat. It's clean and tidy, and the *patronne*, Mme Cochennec, is warm and friendly (and speaks no English). The rooms facing the boulevard are double-glazed, but even so it can be a touch noisy on that side. There's a lift. Carte Bleu/VISA accepted, and Eurocheques with a 35F surcharge.

Hôtel Rethia 1-star

3 rue Général-Blaise, 11e
Tel: 47 00 47 18
Métro: St-Ambroise

Room with *eau courante*	1 person	90-100F
with *cabinet de toilette*	2 persons	135
with bath and WC	1 or 2 persons	175-220
Petit déjeuner		included
Shower		10

In the past few years, rooms have been decorated but prices have climbed hardly at all. Although it is in a rather out-of-the-way neighbourhood, this would be our choice for a long inexpensive stay: for writing; for exploring Paris; for discovering a quiet and peaceful bourgeois *quartier* where one soon puts down roots. A pretty square opposite is bubbling with children after school. No credit cards, but traveller's cheques in francs accepted. *Patron*: M. Aguer.

Hôtel Sans-Souci 1-star NN

113 boulevard Ménilmontant, 11e
Tel: 43 57 00 58
Métro: Ménilmontant, St-Maur

Room with *eau courante*	1 person	80F
	2 persons	120
with shower or bath	1 person	160
Shower		15

Basic, but clean and respectable. Most of the rooms are off the boulevard, hence quiet, and the hotel is two steps from the Père-Lachaise, if the *tombeaux* of the rich and famous are what bring you to Paris. A pleasant atmosphere and excellent value. The 1-star NN rating means that renovations and upgrading are in the offing. Eurocheques accepted, but no credit cards. *Patron*: M. El Djama.

12e arrondissement

Hôtel de Marseille

21 rue d'Austerlitz, 12e
Tel: 43 43 54 22
Métro: Gare de Lyon

Room with *cabinet de toilette*	1 or 2 persons	130F
with shower	1 or 2 persons	190
Petit déjeuner		18
Shower		15

In a short street lined with hotels, only about 200 metres from the Gare de Lyon, the Marseille is a pleasant find. The rooms are clean and tidy, and although not much English is spoken there is an air of welcome and good will. No rooms have private loos but the communal ones are well-kept. *Patron*: M. Soumar. No credit cards or traveller's cheques.

13e arrondissement

Hôtel Pacific 1-star

8 rue Philippe-de-Champagne, 13e
Tel: 43 31 17 06
Métro: Place d'Italie

Room with *cabinet de toilette*	1 or 2 persons	150F
	3 persons	180
with shower or bath	1 or 2 persons	180
	3 persons	210
with bath and WC	1 or 2 persons	200
Petit déjeuner		20
Shower		15

A fairly large hotel, with a lift, unusual in a one-star establishment. It's rather old-fashioned, and agreeable in every way though reception was polite rather than friendly. The rooms are comfortable, the baths small but with very good tiles and plumbing, and *shower curtains* – not a usual thing in moderate-priced Paris hotels. It's a few minutes from the place d'Italie (good shopping and a big branch of Au Printemps), and just off the avenue des Gobelins which is rich in small good restaurants. But it is right next to the gendarmerie, so it might be a bit noisy if *les flics* get busy. No credit cards or traveller's cheques. *Patronne*: Mme de Roode.

Hôtel Rubens 1-star

35 rue de Banquier, 13e
Tel: 43 31 73 30
Métro: Campo-Formio

Room with *cabinet de toilette*	1 or 2 persons	100F
with shower	1 person	115
	2 persons	140
with bath and WC	1 person	140
	2 persons	175
Petit déjeuner		17
Shower		12

A lovely hotel in an interesting 'bourgeois' neighbourhood, high up, good transport (the No. 83 bus from the place d'Italie is one of the great ones). This is another one-star hotel with a lift. The street is very quiet with no through traffic, but it's close to a variety of good restaurants (Lebanese, Vietnamese, Italian), and is just off the avenue des Gobelins which has a great *traiteur* (takeaway for hot and cold delicacies). The rooms are delightful, the baths unusually large. Reading lights. No credit cards or traveller's cheques. *Patron*: M. Quintino Caputo.

14e arrondissement

Hôtel des Bains 1-star

33 rue Delambre, 14e
Tel: 43 20 85 27
Métro: Edgar-Quinet

The Hôtel des Bains was in the throes of being renovated, preparing to be upgraded to two stars in December 1989, so we don't know the latest prices. As of this writing, a room with a shower and WC for 1 or 2 people costs 200–250F, but it will go up. If you want to be within walking distance of the Tour de Montparnasse (a towering purgatory if there ever was one), and near the immense and formidable Gare Montparnasse with its spiderweb of Métro lines, this may be for you. The rue Delambre is a happy hunting ground for bargain clothes and food. And the Hôtel des Bains would be a pleasant place from which to explore the less touristic parts of Montparnasse itself. *Patron*: M. André Regis.

Hôtel du Parc 1-star

8 rue Jolivet, 14e
Tel: 43 20 95 54
Métro: Edgar Quinet, Montparnasse-Bienvenue

Room with *cabinet de toilette*	1 or 2 persons	160F
with shower and WC	1 or 2 persons	220
with bath and WC	1 or 2 persons	220
Petit déjeuner		15

The view from the Hôtel du Parc is of a little triangular square off the boulevard Edgar Quinet – or, from the rear, over the roof-tops. And the windows are double-glazed, so in any event it's quiet. The building is old, but much improved by the *patrons*, M. and Mme. Jacob, and the rooms are freshly decorated, clean and cheerful. There are plans to install a lift, and when that happens, the prices will go up too. The neighbourhood is interesting, with two Japanese sushi restaurants in the nearby rue Gâité, and a big branch of Galeries Lafayette around the corner on the rue du Départ. No credit cards or Eurocheques.

Hôtel de la Loire 2-star NN

39 bis, rue du Moulin-Vert, 14e
Tel: 45 40 66 88
Métro: Alésia, Plaisance

Room with *cabinet de toilette*	1 or 2 persons	150F
with shower or bath	1 or 2 persons	200

with bath and WC	1 person	250
	2 persons	300
	3 persons	350
	4 persons	430
Petit déjeuner		23
Shower		15

This is a quiet hotel, on a quiet street, and the atmosphere is more that of a country town than an international metropolis. It has a range of small but efficient rooms, set out along one side of a pretty little garden; and upstairs, it has some huge rooms – certainly big enough for a family. Mme Noël, the *patronne*, is generous and welcoming. Carte Bleu/VISA accepted, but no Eurocheques.

16e arrondissement

Hôtel du Ranelagh

1-star
56, rue de l'Assomption
Tel: 42 88 31 63
Métro: Ranelagh

Room with *eau courante*	1 person	85-92F
with *cabinet de toilette*	1 person	95
	2 persons	110-130
with shower	1 person	170-200
	2 persons	180-210
with bath and WC	1 person	220
	2 persons	230
Petit déjeuner .		19
Shower		12

Pleasant, undistinguished *hôtel familial* which has barely raised its prices for two or three years. The rooms are exceedingly comfortable and clean. The Ranelagh is very near the delightful avenue Mozart, with good cafés and shops – much quieter than the more obviously touristy parts of Paris. Closed the last two weeks in July. English understood, but not spoken unless the *patron*'s daughter is available – then it's spoken fluently. No credit cards or traveller's cheques. *Patrons*: M. and Mme Cheve.

Hôtel Stella 1-star

133 avenue Victor-Hugo, 16e
Tel: 45 53 55 94
Métro: Victor-Hugo

Room with *cabinet de toilette*	1 person	110F
	2 persons	120
with shower	1 person	140
	2 persons	160
with bath and WC	1 person	191
	2 persons	211
Petit déjeuner		16
Shower		16

Rooms are very pleasant with handsome modern cane beds, good bedspreads, and beautiful little gilded bamboo chairs (like ballroom chairs); the bathrooms with WC are small but comfortable and the showers have curtains. The bath-towels are large enough to be comfortable. In the summer it gets very booked up and one should reserve a month or so ahead; off season, at times when Paris is not crowded with visitors for fairs or special events, it is sometimes possible to get a room at a day's notice, but hardly ever possible to walk in and get one for that night. 'English is no problem,' said the man at the desk, in French – you decide for yourself when you go in. Considering its amenities, it's one of our best choices. No credit cards or traveller's cheques. *Patron*: M. Abderahman

18e arrondissement

Hôtel André Gill

4 rue André Gill, 18e
Tel: 42 62 48 48
Métro: Pigalle

Room with *eau courante*	1 person	75F
with *cabinet de toilette*	1 or 2 persons	150
with shower	1 or 2 persons	187
with shower and WC	1 or 2 persons	210
with bath and WC	1 or 2 persons	240

	3 persons	312
Petit déjeuner		19F50
Bath		25

An oasis of peace and calm, on the Montmartrobus route (see page 49) and very close to Pigalle, yet a world away in feeling, the André Gill is in a pretty courtyard with trees. Completely renovated. The rooms are pleasant and some have attractive coloured glass windows. All credit cards accepted. *Patron*: M. Brahim Lounis.

Hôtel du Bouquet de Montmartre 2-star NN

1 rue Durantin, 18e
Tel: 46 06 87 54
Métro: Abbesses

Room with *cabinet de toilette*	1 or 2 persons	130F
with shower	1 or 2 persons	190-227
with bath and WC	1 or 2 persons	235
Petit déjeuner		18
Shower		12

The rue Durantin leads directly into the green and tranquil place des Abbesses, where one of the rare canopied art deco Métro stations of Hector Guimard survives. It's hard to believe that a quiet little hotel can be only three minutes' walk from Pigalle with all that it implies. The outside of the hotel is not prepossessing, but it's friendly, quiet and clean inside. Use this as a base to explore, on foot or with the miraculous Montmartrobus, the hidden streets of the Butte Montmartre (staying well away from the place du Tertre). Dogs and cats are permitted if you give advance notice. English is spoken; no credit cards. *Patronne*: Mme Gibergues.

Other options

Bed and Breakfast: B & B on the English plan is slowly catching on. 'Café Couette' is an organisation which operates all over France and has recently started up in Paris. Write to, or visit, them at 8 rue d'Isly, 75008 Paris. An English-speaking representative is usually in their office which is at the back of a courtyard and hard to find, but persevere. Single rooms with bed and breakfast are about 90F, doubles from 120F. In England, write or telephone Bed & Breakfast (France), P.O. Box 66, 94 Bell Street, Henley-on-Thames, RG9 1XS. Tel: 0491-578 803.

Rooms to let: check the notice-boards at the American Church, 65 quai d'Orsay, 7e (*Métro*: Alma Marceau, Invalides) which is a mine of room and flat offers, usually for two weeks or a month in the holiday seasons. Take a notebook, go early, provide yourself with a Télécarte or a pocketful of one-franc pieces, and start phoning. (See pages 253–4 for peaceful, unvandalised phone locations.) St Michael's Church of England, 5 rue d'Aguesseau, 8e (*Métro*: Madeleine) has a similar service, very helpful staff and delightfully friendly atmosphere.

Student Housing: students are well catered for in Paris. Take your International Student Identity Card, or if you don't have one, a current photograph and proof of your full-time student status with 30F, to CIEE, 49 rue Pierre-Charron, 8e (*Métro*: Alma-Marceau).

The Cité Universitaire, in the quiet southern part of Paris, often has rooms to let during university holidays. Contact them at 18 boulevard Jourdan, 14e (*Métro*: Cité-Universitaire), where you may find someone who speaks English.

A very useful organisation for the young is UCRIF (Union des Centres de Rencontres International de France), which has 11,000 beds on offer all over the country. Find them at:

> Office de Tourisme
> 127 avenue des Champs-Élysees
> Tel: 47 23 61 72

> Gare du Nord
> Tel: 48 74 68 69

> Siège Social UCRIF
> 21 rue Béranger, 3e

They have ten hotels in Paris ranging from one with 230 beds and a top price of 230F per person for bed and breakfast, to a much smaller one which is about 70F a night.

Also first class at finding accommodation for young people:

Accueils des Jeunes en France:
139 boulevard St-Michel, 5e
Métro (RER): Port Royal
Tel: 43 54 95 86
Open from March to October, Monday through Friday,
9:30 a.m. to 6:30 p.m.

and near the Bastille at:
151 avenue Ledru-Rollin, 11e
Tel: 43 79 53 86

and at the Gare du Nord, near the Halle des Arrivés:
Tel: 42 85 86 19
Open from 8:00 a.m. to 10:00 p.m.

and near the Pompidou Centre at:
119 rue St-Martin, 4e
Métro: Rambuteau or Hôtel-de-Ville
Tel: 42 77 87 88
Open from 9:30 a.m. to 6:30 p.m.

and at:
16 rue du Pont Louis-Philippe, 4e
Métro: Pont-Marie, St-Paul, Hôtel-de-Ville
Open June to September, Monday through Friday, 9:30
a.m. to 6:30 p.m.

There are four beautiful and historic converted houses in the Marais, 4e, given over to housing students. Check at the Maubuisson Hôtel des Jeunes, 12 rue des Barres, 4e. (*Métro*: Hôtel-de-Ville, Pont-Marie.)

Youth Hostels: *the Ligue Francaise des Auberges de Jeunesse (LFAJ)*, 38 boulevard Raspail, 7e (*Métro*: Sèvres-Babylone) is *the* address to use if you have a YHA card, no matter what age you are. Paris hostels are not comfortable, not very well located, and certainly offer little privacy, but at these prices who can complain? A three-day stay is generally the limit, but that's probably all you would want. For a more detailed look at one of the better hostels, see page 85, Auberge de Jeunesse Jules Ferry.

Your own college or university may be able to add to this very brief listing of student-type places to stay. For longer stays, look for notices of short rentals of flats or studios, which may be posted in the entrance halls or around the restaurants and cafeterias in the various university buildings scattered around Paris. A friend of ours, on sabbatical from Cambridge, found himself a free room for a year in exchange for teaching the flat's owner some English. Check these:

CROUS, 39 avenue George Bernanos, 5e (*Métro*: Port-Royal)

Assas, 92 rue d'Assas, 6e (*Métro*: St-Placide)

Cité Universitaire, 19 boulevard Jourdan, 14e (*Métro*: Cité-Universitaire)

CIDJ, 101 quai Branly, 7e (*Métro*: Bir-Hakeim)

Renting a flat in Paris, for a family or group planning to stay a long time, can work out cheaply: two agencies which handle furnished, well-equipped flats or studios, for a minimum of two months, are Paris Promo SARL, 18 rue du Cardinal Lemoine, 5e, and Inter-Urbis, 1 rue Mollien, 8e. Both charge tenants a fee but are said to be efficient. Find out everything that can be a problem: lease, electricity, gas, service charge, inventories, and if possible, take along a French-speaking person to deal with this.

Exchanging: perfect for paupers. A French person or family occupies whatever you have to offer, from a bed-sit to a house, and *you* go to their room/studio/flat. An experienced 'exchanger' has these tips to offer:

1 If you can, make your arrangements through an exchange agency which lays down certain well-established rules. Or check the Announcements column in *The Times*, London.

2 Be specific about what you are offering – number of bedrooms, baths, equipment, use of telephone, daily help, linen, washing machine, car, motorbike, exact dates when you plan to leave and return.

3 Be sure you understand what you are getting: same as above, but with such important extras as how many flights of stairs, lift, concierge, etc.

4 Pets and plants can be catered for in exchanges, but specify *that* early on; some exchangers may be allergic or not willing to tie themselves down.

Everyone we know who has done exchanges has been satisfied and plans to do it again. Most have had happy surprises: one family thought it was getting a four-room house and found they had four *bedrooms*: another was invited to spend the weekend in a Normandy cottage during their Paris stay; a third has established a long family friendship which includes the free use of a Paris flat over Christmas week. *Not* so great: the exchanger who arrived late at night and found the cupboard bare, not so much as a teaspoon of instant coffee or a slice of bread for breakfast, in an intimidatingly clean kitchen!

Recommended: Intervac, 6 Siddals Lane, Allestree, Derby, DE3 2DY. Also: Worldwide Home Exchange Club, 139a Sloane St, London SW1.

La nourriture *(Eating well)*

What to expect

For anyone coming from a country where even 'alternative' magazines don't shrink from saying that a lunch costs 'only £12.50' and recommending wines at £6 a bottle; where only Indian, Chinese or Greek food is inexpensive; Paris seems like the bargain paradise of the world. True, prices have gone up sharply in the past few years since most price controls have come off. But you can still eat well as the Parisians do, in interesting surroundings, for roughly half what a comparable meal would cost you in London or Manchester or Edinburgh.

The great Paris restaurants, admittedly, can cost you a month's salary at one sitting, but that's not what this book is about. Everywhere in Paris there's an immense range of affordable and very good food. There's no equivalent whatever in English cuisine at any price that can compare with Paris food today. To eat well in England in the 1990s comes far too high for the likes of travelling paupers.

Our basic requirement in setting out this list is what is called *le menu*, or sometimes *le menu touristique*. It is price-fixed, posted in the window (even some of the three-star restaurants will publicly display their menu, but these will be from 400F up). Some offer a three-course menu, with a quarter-litre of wine, beer or mineral water and service (at 15 per cent) included. Others will include service, or will say 'prix net' which means the same thing, but will not include drink. In most cases wine will be modestly priced at from 6 to 9F for a quarter-litre, two good glasses.

Some restaurants we have chosen do not offer three courses, but have opted for a two-course *formule* – starter and main course. A few have no set menu, but their à la carte choices seem so good, and the total is not staggering, so they are included here.

Now for the good news: almost every one of the restaurants here will feed you well, with a glass or two of drink, for not more than 80F – as this is written, you'll get 10F50 for your pound, so a meal to enjoy will be about £7.50. A few go as high as 90F, all inclusive, but they have been chosen as special occasion meals despite their extravagant prices. Only one is 104F – roughly £10 all-in.

We have to warn you here about the restaurants which offer all inclusive three-course meals for about 43-45F: our experience this year is that quality has been sacrificed for the sake of the low price. This is fuel food only, with steaks that need a hacksaw, scrawny pieces of chicken, or small anonymous fish with the ubiquitous *pommes chips*. You might be better advised to have a snack lunch – pizza, omelette, or some of the walking-around sandwiches of the 6e *arrondissement* mentioned on page 38 – and splash out on a real meal in the evening. This will give you good food, eaten at leisure in a pretty place, and a feeling of what Paris is all about.

Some of our much-loved restaurants, however, have managed to produce, year after year, food of quality at really low prices – read on. Many can only offer a special menu at lunch. Others will give you just *passable* food, but will make up for it in fun, atmosphere, and convivial surroundings – and have been described very frankly in these pages. Make your own choices.

Follow the lead of many Parisians: if wine, beer or mineral water is not included in the menu price, feel free to skip it. Contrary to what you have heard, not all Parisians drink wine with every meal. Ask for *Une carafe d'eau, s'il vous plâit*, and you'll get a jug of clean, safe, cold drinking water just as agreeable as some of the bottled waters which can cost up to 14F a bottle.

We have grouped these restaurants by *arrondissements* (see page 38 to find out how these work), so that if you find your first choice is packed, another won't be far away. Almost all of them offer remarkably good food and a certain pleasantness of atmosphere. Many of these places hardly ever see a tourist, because they are good bourgeois eating-places patronised by serious eaters, and no one eats more seriously than the French. Each year, more and more accept credit cards, but see page 245. In the main they are clean, simple, usually with a spotless paper tablecloth put down over a longer-lasting cotton one; paper napkins – but sometimes linen ones – endless baskets of fresh, good French bread, and undistinguished but palatable wine, beer, or mineral water.

Sanitation (*le lavabo*) varies from spotless to mildly squalid, and a few places still have *toilettes à la Turque* reminiscent of the Dark

Ages. Not once in our experience has the bill been padded in any way. Coffee is never included in the fixed price menu, and ordering it in a restaurant can bump up the price by as much as 9F. You'll sleep better without it anyway.

Many Paris restaurants close on Sundays, and some are open only for lunch or only for dinner. Most close on public holidays, some close Christmas Eve and New Year's Eve. Many which open on Sunday are closed one other day during the week, and very many still, despite the tourist demand for food, do the traditional thing of closing for the entire month of August, when all Paris moves to the beach. But even that is not immutable!

Paris restaurants are changing their hours of opening, weekly and annual closing times with the speed of light to adjust to the changing patterns of tourism and variations in economic circumstances. Many that formerly closed in August are now taking off earlier or later in the year – some not at all, others disappearing for six weeks in slack times. The information herein was accurate in July 1989, but don't be too disappointed if things have changed when you arrive.

Have the occasional snack lunch or dinner in your room (or outdoors), which can save you 18 to 20F on a restaurant meal (see page 62, about hotel eating). Or go to one of the very good value 'Selfs' (page 153), where three courses with your choice of drink can be as little as 40 to 50F.

Café eating – those alluring little corner spots with outdoor tables and awnings – can tear a carefully-calculated budget wide open. But if you're exhausted in mid-morning or late afternoon, sit down and be prepared to spend 10F for a cup of coffee, or 12F for a *citron pressé* (real lemonade), and calculate that the chance to rest your weary feet and sit as long as you like is worth the money.

For breakfast, if you choose not to eat at your hotel (often over-priced and not nearly as enjoyable as mingling with the French on their way to work), take your coffee and croissants at *le zinc* (the counter), not sitting down at *la terrasse* (a table) which ups the bill by about fifty per cent. And never order tea in Paris! You get a cup, a teabag, and a jug of water that's hottish but never boiling, and you'll pay about 8F. Brandy would be cheaper.

All Paris tap water – in hotels, flats and restaurants – is safe to drink. But if you worry about what a change of water can do to your digestive system, it's good to know that you can buy a huge (1½ litre) plastic bottle of Vittel, or private-label *still* mineral water, at supermarkets for about 2 to 3F. *Eau gazeuse* – Perrier and the like –

obviously are available only in glass bottles, but cheap over the counter, and you'll get back 1F when you return the bottle to the shops.

Restaurant manners

Restaurants – except for Les Selfs (pages 153) – are run by a *patron* or *patronne*, with waiters and waitresses. All very human, all very connected to their clients. We're not talking here about McDonalds or the like. Contrary to myth, those who work in restaurants are not to be addressed as *Garçon!* If you want fast, friendly service, and advice if you need it, it pays to be polite. As you enter the restaurant it doesn't hurt to say *Bonjour*, or *Bonsoir, Monsieur*; as you leave, *Au revoir, m'sieur/m'dame*. In between, you should fill out your sentences with *s'il vous plâit*, and *merci bien*, and such. In very small family-run restaurants, it's usually polite to include the entire clientele as well as the management in your goodbyes: *Au revoir, messieurs-dames*.

French restaurants – especially the ones you'll find listed here – don't give you a lot of elbow room, and curiously enough you find that you don't need it. You may find yourself just barely able to squeeze into your seat, or seated opposite a stranger instead of with a table to yourself and seated very snugly at that. Yet, such is the general air of *politesse* and enjoyment that such tight spacing doesn't seem like an encroachment.

You'll find it easy to adapt to. Your neighbours are absorbed in their food, or each other, and there is no lack of privacy. A *bonsoir* or *bon appetit, Madame* will not be taken amiss if you happen to catch someone's eye. If no one wants to get into conversation, it will be obvious; if everybody does, this soon becomes known. In any event, there is no stuffiness or awkwardness about your proximity. Best of all, women who eat alone in restaurants need not worry about being put at the worst table, near a draughty door, or in a forgotten corner. They are never ignored, and are always treated with respect, and even a little encouragement.

Recommended restaurants

1er arrondissement

Auberge du Palais Royal

10 rue Jean-Jacques-Rousseau, 1e
Métro: Louvre

With a menu at 65F, it's more expensive than many others, but well worth it. The walls are decorated with theatre posters, the room is candlelit and full of flowers, the *patron* is friendly and welcoming, the service unobtrusive. Recently: a choice of *saucissons à l'ail* or cucumbers in cream, or fromage frais with garlic and herbs, then escalope of turkey with tagliatelli or delicious *andouilles* with sautéed potatoes. Fruit or crème caramel are always on the menu, and sometimes unbelievable pastry, *faite à la maison*. Drink is extra: 12 F for a quarter of wine or a bottle of beer. Open noon to 2:00 p.m., 7:00 to 10:00 p.m., closed Sunday evenings. No annual closing.

Chez Fernand

81 rue Rambuteau, 1e
Métro: Les Halles

Not easy to find, a restaurant of this quality so near Beaubourg and Les Halles! The menu is 56F for two courses: and our report from Paris friends is 'very good food, very French cuisine. The duck baked with cider was excellent, and who could be unhappy with a *chèvre* salad to start?' Other choices would be onion soup (getting rarer in Paris), grilled *entrecôte* with herbs, or an *entrecôte marchand de vin*. This is all very filling, but if you want to add a dessert it will cost about 12 to 15F for the usual *tartes* and crème caramel. Service is included, beer is 12F and wine is 15F for a quarter. Chez Fernand is open noon to 2:30 p.m., 7:30 to 9:30 p.m. Closed Sundays and two weeks in August.

L'Incroyable

26 rue de Richelieu, 1er
Métro: Palais-Royal
Tel: 42 96 24 64

This is on everyone's discovery list, but success hasn't gone to its head: the perfection of French bourgeois cooking and ambience. Very crowded at lunchtime on weekdays; Saturday is a better bet. The 45F menu, with drink and service included, may offer *rillette* or *terrine*, then grilled pork chops, *tripe à la mode de Caen*, or steak with steamed potatoes and petit pois, with a fruit compote to follow.*Tarte maison* is 6F extra: local *habitués* love it for its thin, crisp pastry, while our scout would have preferred a little more heft. Open from 11:45 a.m. to 2:15 p.m., and from 6:30 to 10:30 p.m., Tuesdays through Fridays, open for lunch only on Mondays and Saturdays, and closed on Sundays. No annual closing.

La Fauvette

46 rue St-Honoré, 1er
Métro: Louvre, Les Halles

When the market of Les Halles packed up, it left behind a semi-wholesale area of butchers and *charcutiers* and a few of the very characteristic small 'market' restaurants. Fortunately, the crowds of tourists, attracted by the gloss of the new Halles, haven't noticed this one. A recent visitor enjoyed its friendly ambience and what she called the ' simple, delicious and *filling*' food. A meal is 48F for a selection of the usual starters, wonderful roast beef or chicken, *tartes* or cheese. Service is included, and inexpensive drink – 5F50 for drinkable wine – is extra. Open for lunch only, 11:00 a.m. to 3:00 p.m., and it's best to go early because it fills up by 12:30. Closed Saturdays, Sundays and during August.

Le Galtouse

Corner of rue de la Grande Truanderie and rue Pierre Lescot, 1er
Métro: Les Halles, Etienne-Marcel, Châtelet

Somehow this one has slipped past the guidebooks. The two-course *formule* at 65F, service included, is one of the best meals you can find in the pricey environs of Les Halles. The restaurant is so attractive that you'd expect it to be really costly: mirrors, flowers, candles, globe lighting indoors, well decorated café tables outside. Recently: a big salad with melted goat's cheese on grilled bread and walnuts and shallots, followed by a really good veal escalope with two vegetables. Service is excellent, and you're advised to go not later than 8:15 for dinner, as by 9:00 it's fairly crowded. Wine is not cheap – a 33 cl *pichet* (2 glasses plus) is 16F – but even so you'd only spend about 82F for a first-class meal. Open noon to 2:30 p.m. and 7:00 to 11:00 p.m., seven days a week. Another Galtouse is in the rue St-Denis opposite the Fontaine des Innocents, noisier and somewhat rushed in feeling, but with the same good food and service.

Pasadena

rue du 29 Juillet between rue de Rivoli and rue St-Honoré, 1er
Métro: Tuileries

Such a perfect restaurant that our friends ate there three nights running. Madame, who runs the house, can be temperamental, and must be approached with smiles; she gets distinctly chilly if grilled about the food. Her husband does the cooking, and it couldn't be better. The menu is 80F including service but not drink – and unlike many Parisian restaurants the temperature didn't go down when we asked for a *carafe d'eau* and a Perrier only. Highly recommended are the fish soup with *rouille* and *croûtons*, the *escalope de veau* or *boeuf bourguignon*, and grilled salmon. On a summer evening there were fresh strawberries with heavy cream, and 'a chocolate mousse cake unlike any other ever eaten'. Open 12:30 to 2:30 p.m. and 7:00 to 10:00 p.m., closed Sundays, holidays and August.

Au Petit Ramoneur

74 rue St-Denis, 1er
Métro: Châtelet, Les Halles

Very near the Forum des Halles, and about five minutes from Beaubourg (where no one should eat), this is a most delightful and popular place in an (almost) pedestrian shopping centre. It's jam-med at lunchtime, while other inexpensive places are three-quarters empty: a great place to talk to people as you are practically eating from each other's plates. The menu is 50F *tout compris*, and they do a nice thing: a bottle of red wine is put on the table and you help yourself. Food is hearty, bourgeois, big helpings of everything. Nineteen first courses, including lentils vinaigrette and *pâté de foie* with green peppercorns; ten main courses such as tripe in Calvados; and cheese, fruit, or ice-cream. Lunch from 11:30 a.m. to 2:30 p.m., dinner from 6:30 to 9:30 p.m., open on holidays but closed Sundays and from August 20 to September 7.

Le Relais du Sud-Ouest

154 rue St-Honoré, 1er
Métro: Louvre, Palais-Royal

An astonishing place so close to the Louvre, and selfishly, we're glad that it hasn't been mobbed by tourists. Stone walls, old photos, *faux-bois* painted wall panels, and briskly efficient service that still manages to be friendly. Who could ask for anything more? The menu changes every day, but the last time one of our extended family was there, the first courses were a seafood cocktail, *salade Niçoise*, avocado, salad with frizzy lettuce and walnuts, and *pâté*: then roast guinea-hen, duck with prunes, or an entrecôte steak, with raspberry *tarte* or a creamy custard or cheese to finish. To drink, rosé or red wine, or mineral water. All for 60F including service and drink. The Relais is open for lunch from 11:30 to 2:30, but it is very busy from 12:15 to 1:15 p.m. For dinner, 7:00 to 11:00 p.m. Dinner is 80F, all-in. Closed Sundays, open 'most' holidays, usually closed for one week in August but not always.

Le Stado

150 rue St-Honoré, 1e
Métro: Louvre, Palais-Royal

The patron of Le Stado is a former rugby player, and the stone walls are hung with mementoes of his career and many of the teams of the Tarbes (south-west) region. The cooking is extremely good, hearty Pyréneés food, and the service is warm and welcoming. Starters are the usual *cruditeés*, *charcuterie* and *pâté*, with a fine garlicky *rillette du pays* or a salad with nuts; typical main courses are beef brochette, rumpsteak, *lapin chasseur*, steak tartare or veal kidneys, with cheese, fruit *tartes*, or a coffee dessert called Moka St Michel. Service and wine included, the whole feast comes to just 60F at lunch, 80F at night. Le Stado is open seven days a week, noon to 2:30 p.m., 7:00 to 11:00 p.m. Open in August, but closed on major holidays, 14 July, Christmas, New Year's.

Le Ver Luisant

26 rue du Mont-Thabor, 1er
Métro: Tuileries

In this very elegant and expensive street, close to the Jeu de Paume and to the Meurice and other classy hotels, is an astounding restaurant, narrow, full of mirrors and very crowded even at 12:30 on a Saturday. The clientele is bright and attractive; be prepared to be elbow-to-elbow. Choose from *crudités*, *oeuf mayo* or various *terrines*, then steak with *frites* or omelette, or such interesting specials as salt cod with potatoes. Sorbets, *tartes*, and a superb chocolate mousse. Very good food, good value, and brisk efficient service, which is included in the 51F menu; beer and wine are extra at 10F. Open 7:00 a.m. to 7:30 p.m., closed Saturdays, Sundays, and August.

Au Vieil Écu

166 rue St-Honoré, 1er
Métro: Louvre
Tel: 42 60 20 14

A pleasant place if you can stand piped music (mercifully soft) and rather vulgar décor. The food is tasty and well presented, but definitely not for the starving as portions are small. On the 55F menu (service and wine, beer or mineral water included) you can choose from salad with smoked salmon, or soup, then roast beef or grilled haddock filet, followed by a *tartine* (diminutive) of strawberries, or sorbet. Open for lunch, noon to 3:00 p.m., dinner from 7:00 to 11:00 p.m., closed Sundays and holidays, with no annual closing.

2e arrondissement

Country Life

6 rue Daunou, 2e
Métro: Opéra

Imagine a restaurant only steps away from the Opéra where you can eat as much as you like – and healthy food at that – for 52F? That's Country Life-Paris, and the only catch is that they're open only for lunch and are closed on weekends. Go through the health-food shop, collect a ticket, serve yourself and pay after you've eaten lunch upstairs in a green, airy loft room. The menu offers a huge salad bar, good soups which are different every day, and a range of hot dishes such as *gratin dauphinois*, *tarragon courgettes*, and various grain concoctions; for meat-eaters, there's usually beef stew. Desserts (nut tart, fruit salad and the like) are 12F, no alcohol is served, but fruit juices are only 8F50 and coffee or herbal tea is 3F50. Open 11:30 a.m. to 2:30 p.m., closed Saturdays, Sundays and holidays, but no annual closing.

Le Drouot

103 rue de Richelieu, 2e
Métro: Richelieu-Drouot

The same management as Chartier (page 136), it's large, too well known, but excellent value. It's near the Opéra, hence useful for pre- and post-Printemps and Lafayette excursions. A three-course meal with wine recently was 49F, plus twelve per cent service – leek salad, *boeuf bourguignon* with steamed potatoes, and caramelised apple tart, with a quarter litre of slightly-better-than-ordinary wine. A cheese or ham omelette was only 8F50! Open 11:30 to 2:30 p.m., 6:30 to 11:00 p.m., seven days a week. No annual closing, but closed on major holidays.

La Maisonette

59 rue Montmartre, 2e
Métro: Sentier, Les Halles

A stone's throw from Les Halles, but a world away from its frantic tourists. The Maisonette is agreeably old-fashioned and informal – the waiters tend to *tutoyer* their customers. In warm weather the doors open wide to the outside, in winter it's cosy with ceramic tiled walls and floors. At lunch you could eat well for 52F including service: vegetable *pâté* or fresh asparagus vinaigrette, then stuffed pepper or really good steak or *quenelles de brochet* with saffron sauce, and the usual desserts. In the evening, expect to spend from 70F to about 90F, with good salads, seafood in pastry, chicken breast with hazelnuts, and other unusual choices. Wine is 7F50 for a quarter, and very drinkable. Open noon to 2:30 p.m., 7:30 to midnight, closed Sundays and the last week of August.

3e arrondissement

Le Helium

3 rue des Haudriettes, 3e
Métro: Rambuteau, Hôtel-de-Ville

The chef of the Helium seems to have been on a gourmet tour of the world, from which he has returned with a handful of exotic recipes. This very small place is a find. Tucked away in a minor street of the Marais, very plainly decorated, all the emphasis is on the food. Although there's no fixed-price menu, the à la carte prices are reasonable. You could spend as little as 70F for a superb three-course meal, including wine and service, with something like Mexican *tartelettes* to begin, then *Poulet à l'Antillaise* (rather special, according to Jonathan Gilbert) only 32F before 10:00 p.m., but mysteriously escalating to 40F after that time; then white chocolate cake, 20F, or profiteroles, 30F, or *fromage blanc* with nuts and honey, 15F. Wine is only 6F. Open noon to 3:00 p.m., 7:00 p.m. to after midnight. Closed Sundays, no annual closing.

L'Oreé du Marais

29 rue des Francs Bourgeois, 3e
Métro: St Paul
There are no great surprises at L'Oreé, but it's a useful little place in what is becoming an over-priced and over-crowded neighbourhood now that the world has discovered the ancient Marais. The menu at 59F gives you a salad with walnuts, steak, then cheese or conventional desserts such as pear tart, chocolate mousse, or apple tart. The more expensive meal at 69F offers artichoke vinaigrette, cucumbers in cream or a mixed salad – then kidneys in mustard sauce, usually steak with garlic butter, or a cold dish which might be chicken or rabbit with salad, and desserts as above. Service is included, wine is extra and not cheap – 13F to 15F for a quarter-litre, so you may want to ask for *un carafe d'eau*. L'Oreé is open every day of the year, noon to 2:30 p.m., 7:00 to 10:00 p.m.

4e arrondissement

Le Beautreillis

18 rue de Beautreillis, 4e
Métro: St-Paul, Bastille, Sully-Morland
Tel: 42 72 36 04

This intimate stone-walled place must be one of the best values in the Marais, a district no longer much frequented by paupers. A meal is 45F including service, and it's open for Sunday lunch which is a boon. The menu offers as a first course a choice of beautiful salads, one with chicken livers and the other with hot *chèvre* on toast, then various steaks, usually a chicken dish, or fish in a creamy sauce with matchstick potatoes. Desserts are conventional but good: the crème caramel is to be recommended, or you could have ice-cream or *fromage frais* with sugar. A quarter-litre of wine is 12F. Open noon to 2:30 p.m., 7:00 to 11:45 p.m., closed Sunday evenings and all day Monday, and for a week in August – dates not set. Open most holidays except Christmas and Easter.

La Canaille

4 rue Crillon, 4e
Métro: Sully-Morland

One of our student scouts of years past wrote 'Very cool – assez sympa, décontracté,' and now our reviewer Gloria finds it 'sort of campy'. Whether this is progress, or devolution, or creative linguistics, we don't know, but the food is imaginative and very good. The menu is 58F at lunch, 70F at dinner: *terrine* of *daurade* (a sea-bream), or a flan of courgettes with chervil, or pumpkin tart; then grilled steak *Bourdelaise*, or duck à l'orange, or a fillet of *rascasse* (scorpion fish) with lumpfish eggs; followed by Camembert or the usual desserts, including a crème caramel with almonds. A 52F lunch menu, with no choices, was an onion and potato tart, squid *Basquaise*, and a crisp biscuit topped with whipped cream and fresh strawberries. A quarter of wine is 9F extra, but service is included. Open 11:45 to 2:15 p.m., 7:30 p.m. to midnight. Closed for lunch on Saturdays and Sundays, and one weekend in August.

Le Chateabriand

6 rue de la Bastille, 4e
Métro: Bastille

Simple, relaxed and warm, with 1950s décor of a certain charm: wire chairs and coat racks, vivid pink paint on the woodwork. The menu at 55F, including wine and service, is simple but good: to begin with, homemade vegetable soup – not easily come by in Paris – or *crudités*, or radishes with butter (which only the French mind could conceive), mackerel fillets in white wine; then sautééd trout, salmon with chives in cream, with steamed potatoes, or leg of lamb, or *andouillette*. Desserts are, predictably, cheese or fruit, ice-cream, pears in wine. As the neighbourhood around the Bastille becomes the hottest in Paris, it's refreshing to find a place like this. Open noon to 2:30 p.m., 7:00 to 10:00p.m., closed Saturday lunch and all day Sunday. Annual closing is August 12 to 31.

La Crêpe Comix

6 rue Castex, 4e
Métro: Bastille

'Terrific crêperie,' report David Gaines and Susan Thompson, with comic-book posters all over the walls to keep you amused while you wait for your very good food. The dishes are named for French *bande dessineés* characters – Hercule, Romuauld, and so on. This last-named brought forth various superlatives – WOW!! GEE WHIZ!! MMMM! – consisting as it does of melting *chèvre*, nuts, and salad – for 34F; and a gluttonous dessert crêpe of chocolate ice-cream with chocolate sauce was 23F. These were the most costly choices on the menu; other main-dish crêpes are 19F, and sugar-dusted dessert crêpes are 11F and up. Service is included, cider is 10F for a quarter-litre and wine is only 8F. Lunch from noon to 2:00 p.m., dinner 7:30 to 10:30 p.m, closed Sundays, Mondays and holidays, and usually for three weeks in the summer.

Le Cristal

13 rue Beautrellis, 4e
Métro: St-Paul, Bastille, Sully-Morland

The Cristal goes from strength to strength. If you're feeling extravagant, splash out on its 76F menu, so good we can't resist listing everything. First courses: chicken liver salad, vegetable *pâté* with a creamy sauce, frog's legs flambeéd in whiskey of all things, salad with hot goat's cheese, avocado with crabmeat, marinated seafood salad. Main courses: skate in cream sauce with capers, duck, seafood brochette, pork *filet* in prune sauce, steak with bacon. To finish, a choice of various cheeses, apple tart, lemon pie, ice-cream or sorbet. The 58F menu is conventional but good. Service included in both menus, but drink is extra and not cheap: half a bottle of wine is 38 to 42F. The Cristal is very small, with only about eight tables, prettily decorated, in a quiet Marais street – and for the quality of food, very hard to match. Both menus are served at lunch and dinner, increasingly a rarity in this fashionable neighbourhood. Open noon to 2:30 p.m., 7:00 to 11:30 p.m., closed Saturday lunch and all day Sunday. Open on holidays, including Christmas and Easter, closed 'some time in September but not every year', if you can work that out.

Le Municipal

7 rue du Temple, 4e
Métro: Hôtel-de-Ville

The Municipal is caught in a time-warp from the 1950s, with formica-topped tables on wonderful period bases, lots of glittering neon and mirrored glass. At the long bar you can stand to eat sandwiches and drink beer. It's directly across from the big department store BHV, and a short walk from Beaubourg, yet a world away from the tourist trail. For 48F at lunch, the menu recently offered tasty although basic choices such as *crudités* or *fromage de tête* for starters, then grilled steak, roast chicken, pork chop, or ham all with crisp *frites*, or cold chicken with mayonnaise and potato salad. Desserts were apple sauce, fruit, yoghurt or cheese. This is one of the very few restaurants remaining in Paris which has *pensionnaires*, regular customers who pay by the week or the month and so save money. At night, à la carte prices are reasonable: a meal of garlic sausage with butter, lemon sole, and homemade chocolate mousse would add up to about 78F. Service is included, and a quarter-litre of wine is 7F. Meals are served without interruption from 11:00 a.m. through 7:30 p.m. (the doors close at that hour but service goes on), Mondays through Saturdays. Closed Sundays, holidays and August. Worth considering as a glimpse of a Paris that is rapidly vanishing.

Le Petit Gavroche

15 rue Ste-Croix de la Bretonnerie, 4e
Métro: Rambuteau, Hôtel-de-Ville
Tel: 48 87 74 26

An odd, scuzzy little restaurant, with zinc bars upstairs and down, peeling paint, toilets in the last stages of degeneracy, a revolting stuffed deer in one corner, too-loud radio, and one redeeming quality: good food. Lunch and dinner menus are 37F and 40F respectively. For dinner, cucumber in cream, or *pâté* Breton, pork chop or veal cutlet, and cheese, yoghurt or pastry to finish. Lunch, according to the owner, is better than dinner because 'someone's mother does the cooking', and what is served apparently depends on her whim. À la carte offerings: a salad of lettuce, tomatoes, blue cheese and walnuts in a delicious vinaigrette, 22F; or asparagus vinaigrette, 20F, or *terrine de saumon*, 32F. Duck breast in green peppercorn sauce, or duck leg à la orange, or salmon with mint, each 42-48F; and a delicious Floating Island for 14F, or *tarte maison* or crème caramel. A quarter of wine is 9F, and service, though very slow, is amiable and included. Friendly customers, no tourists. Open noon to 2:30 p.m., 7:00 p.m. to midnight, closed Saturday lunch and all day Sunday, and in August open for dinner only.

Les Piétons

8 rue des Lombards, 4e
Métro: Châtelet, Les Halles, Hôtel-de-Ville

The rue des Lombards, although it bridges the 1e and 4e *arrondissements* as it crosses the boulevard Sebastopol, is relatively quiet. This café is a useful place for a meal if you're bound for, or have just come from, Les Halles or Beaubourg and want to escape the worst of the crowds. The food is conventional brasserie fare: grated carrots or *pâté* or *oeuf en gelée* for starters, *filet* of cod or chicken or steak, and dessert or cheese to finish – we'd choose the gruyère or *chèvre* rather than the stereotyped crème caramel/mousse au chocolat/apple tart selection. It's inexpensive, three courses for 52F, service included, and wine from 6F to 17F for a quarter-litre. AND it's open the year round. Mondays through Saturdays, meals are served without a break from noon to 11:30 p.m.; summer Sundays the same hours; from 1 September to 30 June, Sunday hours are from noon to 8:00 p.m.

Le Pot

27 rue du Temple, 4e
Métro: Hôtel-de-Ville

We've included this because it's very French and the kind of place you'd pass by, in this busy street off the noisy rue de Rivoli near the BHV and the Samaritaine stores. It looks as though there's only one table available, but press on to the little back staircase, and upstairs you find what seems like a living room with long windows opening onto the street. There are wonderfully friendly people, a radio playing, and the food is conventional but good – all the dishes are about 35F, for a big mixed salad, or chicken with *frites*, or hamburger. Wine is 10F for a quarter litre. Making conversation, David Gaines and Susan Thompson somehow elicited this from the owner: 'If you can't pay now, that's all right, come back later!.' They hadn't intended to leave without settling the bill but were touched by his kindness. Open for lunch only, 11:00 a.m. to 2:00 p.m.; open on Sundays, no annual closing, but closed on Christmas and Easter.

Le Relais Saint Gervais

13 rue François Miron, 4e
Métro: Hôtel-de-Ville, St-Paul
Tel: 40 29 07 52

A treasure, according to one of our Paris student restaurant-sleuths. It's housed in one of the very few 14th-century buildings still standing in Paris, but that's not what impressed her most. The cooking is of a very high standard, and the service exceptionally friendly – so far, no Marais tourists have made their way here so go while it's still relatively undiscovered. (Not to be confused with the couscous restaurant, much simpler, with a similar name, very nearby.) The menu – salad or a wonderful *terrine* among the choices for first courses, then exquisitely cooked trout with almonds, or beef or a *plat du jour*, and cheese or chocolate mousse. It all sounds very conventional, but in fact it's done with finesse and there's obviously a talented pair of hands in the kitchen. All this for just 65F, including service – drink is extra. À la carte the prices whiz into a bracket that puts them out of a pauper's reach, so be wise and stay with the menu. At night the Relais becomes a piano bar! Open for lunch noon to 2:00 p.m., dinner 7:00 to 11:00 p.m., closed on Tuesdays, and no annual closing which makes it a find in August.

Le Temps de Cerises

31 rue de Cerisaie, 4e
Métro: Bastille or Sully-Morland

There's a poster of Jacques Brel on the wall of this friendly little corner restaurant in the Marais, and it's likely that he would have been at home here. You'll be caught up in the flow of talk from the workers in overalls and the young Parisians of the *quartier*, and Gérard, the *patron*, really does keep the lively spirit of the place going. The food, as Patrick from Brittany, who now lives in Paris, says, is honest and correct. But the quality is variable, and the best bet is to stick to simple dishes such as cold beef salad with ratatouille, or roast pork with *haricots verts*. The first courses are usually very good – smoked fish with potato salad, or charcuterie, or *crudités*, and excellent desserts, fruit compote, *gâteau fourré*, ice-cream. If *Far Breton*, a cake made with plums, is on the menu the day you're there, choose that. All this, and walls papered with photographs of the Marais as it once was, comes to just 46F, service included. A quarter-litre of house wine is 10F, but a better bet for two might be the Côtes-du-Rhone at 28F the half bottle. Open as a café from 7:30 a.m. to 8:00 p.m., but serving lunch only from 11:30 to 2:30 – go before 12:30 or after 1:30, otherwise there isn't a square metre of space. Closed Saturdays, Sundays, holidays and August.

Le Trumilou

84 quai de l'Hôtel-de-Ville, 4e
Métro: Hôtel-de-Ville
Tel: 42 77 63 98

This used to be the haunt of the neighbourhood's writers, painters, and craftsmen until it was taken up by (mostly French) guidebooks, but there seems to be no way it can be spoiled or changed. From the street it looks like a bar with an infestation of pinball machines, but wait until you get in: a big, brightly-lit room, lined with paintings, flowers everywhere, which even on a rainy Sunday evening tends to be crowded with those who know a good thing when they see one. The cost of meals has gone up only fractionally in two years. On the 54F menu, a good plate of *crudités* and roast chicken with tomatoes, then a choice of cheeses or seasonal fruit or crème caramel. The more lavish 70F menu had a *salade Niçoise* among its first course choices, and a very good *pintadeau* (guinea fowl), then *tartes* and ice-cream or cheese. Both menus include service but not drink. Beer at 7F is a great buy, but a quarter-litre of wine costs 12F. Trumilou is open Sundays and holidays, including Christmas, Easter, and New Year's Day; closed Mondays, and for a few days in August, unsettled at this writing.

Vancouver

64 rue de la Verrerie, 4e
Métro: Rambuteau, Hôtel-de-Ville

Surprisingly, the prices in this nice neighbourhood restaurant have not risen in two years. The *formule* at 53F still offers about a dozen choices of hors d'oeuvres ranging from half an avocado to leek tart, Baltic herring, quiche, rabbit *pâté*, then an utterly delicious turkey escalope with mushroom sauce or a very tender steak or *andouillette*, all served with thin crisp *frites*. If you're still hungry, be prepared to spend 25F for rather lush desserts, including profiteroles or chocolate cake. The 53F menu includes quite agreeable wine, and at the moment it's only being offered at lunch. But from October to the end of March there's a three-course menu for 59F, including service but not drink, which is a truly tempting reason for coming to Paris off-season. Service is polite, fast, and friendly. The two inside rooms are pleasant and serene, and the outside tables are in an agreeably *mouvementé* street. Open from noon to 2:30 p.m., and from 7:00 to 11:00 p.m. Closed Sundays and for three weeks in August, but open on all holidays except Christmas, so keep the Vancouver in mind if you're in Paris over New Year's Day when many restaurants are sleeping off the *Reveillon* of the night before.

5e arrondissement

Aux Savoyards

14 rue des Boulangers, 5e
Métro: Jussieu, Cardinal Lemoine
Tel: 46 33 53 78

Like most of the restaurants in these streets, Savoyards is jammed with students – and often staffed by them – which gives it a somewhat hectic atmosphere. Don't expect to linger, or have a quiet meal, or exchange confidential *mots*. The service is lightning fast – and well it might be as there is usually a line-up of hungry faces at the door. Since a meal, with service and perfectably passable wine, costs just 56F, it's no wonder. Servings are generous: a heaping plate of mushrooms in a spiced sauce, and *two* eggs with mayonnaise among other starters, then steak tartare or pork cutlets or two dishes of the day such as really good fish with butter and capers, or in a tomato sauce. There's a good selection of sorbets, cake, ice-cream or cheese. Open noon to 2:30, and 7:00 to 10:30 p.m., closed Saturday evenings, Sundays, holidays, and August.

Le Baptiste

11 rue des Boulangers, 5e
Métro: Jussieu
Tel: 43 25 57 24

A beautiful little room with provincial decoration on stone walls; copper jugs, plants and so forth. Lovely food. Menus are written on wooden paddles, and include, at 52F, a generous salad with blue cheese and walnuts, or chicken liver *terrine*, followed by *faux-filet au poivre* (tender thin-cut steak) or sautéed calves' liver (our esteemed spy Gloria Girton comments 'actually the liver of a female calf, as opposed to that of a male – only the French!'). Among the desserts are pears with hot chocolate sauce, and a perfect lemon *tarte*. Wine is extra and not cheap: 12F for a quarter of vin ordinaire. À la carte: a huge salad of warm goat's cheese on toast with lettuce and tomatoes for 32F (or a salad with chicken livers sautéed in raspberry vinegar for 25F) plus a dessert for 20 to 22F would make an ample meal, and you wouldn't miss a main course. The rue des Boulangers was laid out in 1350 and is practically paved with restaurants. Baptiste is open from noon to 2:00 p.m., then 7:00 to 10:30 p.m. for dinner. Closed for Saturday lunch and on Sundays; open only for dinner on holidays. The annual closing isn't settled as we write; best phone if you're in Paris in July or August.

Le Bouche Trou

20 rue des Boulangers, 5e
Métro: Jussieu

The Trou is truly in the heart of the student district, therefore always crowded, but nevertheless well away from the more touristy parts of the 5e. A genial atmosphere, where a good meal costs 52F, service included. You might start with charcuterie, then go on to a *plat du jour*, and finish with ice-cream, pastry, fruit, or cheese. A four-course menu at 72F is excellent value, with such first courses as a chicken liver omelette or a salad with quails' eggs and crisp bacon, and main courses including turkey breast with sorrel or trout with leeks, then salad or cheese, and a choice of desserts. Wine is only 7F for a quarter litre. The service is – to be realistic – very leisurely indeed. Open noon to 2:30 p.m., 7:00 to 11:00 p.m., closed for Saturday lunch and Sundays, and in August. Open most holidays except Christmas and Easter.

La Brouette

41 rue Descartes, 5e
Métro: Cardinal-Lemoine

La Brouette seems to have a slightly grasping hand out for tourists, but it's included here for its out-of-ordinary offerings. For 70F you can start with snails or leeks in vinaigrette; then frogs' legs, or mussels in garlic butter, or *colin meunière*, followed by an excellent *tarte*, or prunes in wine or profiteroles – and the price includes wine *and* coffee. Unbeatable for quantity and quality, but slow on service even when uncrowded. A fine place to spend a leisurely evening watching the street scene. Open 12:30 to 2:30 p.m., 7:00 to 10:00 p.m., closed Saturday and Sunday nights, open on holidays and in August.

Les Dégrés de Nôtre Dame

10 rue des Grands Dégrés, 5e
Métro: St-Michel, Maubert-Mutualité

The Dégrés announces on its card *Petite restauration à toute heure*, and since it serves food from 7:00 a.m. to 4:00 a.m., every day of the week, all year round, that's an understatement. And what food! They offer two menus, one at 65F including service. Onion soup, various hors d'oeuvres and salads to begin with, the brochette or rumpsteak with *frites* or a *plat du jour*, and a chocolate mousse that has been praised by three of our voracious Paris eaters – in addition, there's usually an apple tart, or ice-cream, or sorbet. For 75F, you might have a mixed green salad with delicious hot goat's cheese on toasted bread, steak *au poivre*, lamb brochette, fish, grilled chicken, ending with cheese or a choice of truly delicious desserts. Beer is 15F, wine by the big glass about 12F, half-litres of excellent white wine are 38F which would provide drink for three moderate bibbers. It's an attractive stone-walled room with flowers on the bar, with about seven tables plus some on the pavement when the windows are opened wide in good weather. The bread is a coarse, flavoursome country loaf served with a dish of butter and, says Patrick Boulard, that's enough to make the Dégrés a rare pleasure. Add the extraordinary hours, the fact that it's five minutes' walk from chaotic St Michel, and you can see why it's worth seeking out. Don't expect very fast service, but you'll enjoy sitting watching the strollers in the pretty little street outside.

La Fontaine Saint Victor

24 rue Victor, 5e
Métro: Maubert Mutualité
Tel: 40 46 12 04

This club-like restaurant is housed in the 'Maison de la Mutualité', a beautiful 1930s Art Deco building, just five minutes' walk from Notre Dame and completely unknown to tourists. Service is courteous, traditional, not very fast; the whole ambience is restful and restorative for the weary. There's one very inexpensive menu at 52F which offers two courses – typically, *crudités* and grilled steak. And a grander one at 84F with four courses: such as an exotic salad of stuffed grape leaves, chorizo sausages, and hearts of palm, then calves' liver with sautéed cauliflower, or steak tartare or chicken lavishly garnished with vegetables; cheese *and* such desserts as sorbet, pineapple *tarte* or ice-cream. Service is included, and wine in half-bottles is 21F, no quarter-litres available, so you may prefer to skip it. La Fontaine is open only for lunch, from noon to 2:30 p.m., which is a bit restrictive – but it *is* open for Sunday lunch which could be very useful. Open on most holidays except Christmas, closed in August.

Le Pavé aux Herbes

43 rue Mouffetard, 5e
Métro: Monge
Tel: 43 31 77 88

A restaurant in the Mouff' that attracts the French as well as tourists is a rarity; this might be the only one. A good mixture of French and Greek, it has a menu from Monday to Friday for 43F, including wine and service, with first courses that include avocado vinaigrette, stuffed grape leaves, lovely taramasalata, and *pâté* with green peppercorns. Then grilled brochette or squid or steak, finishing with Greek pastry or apple *tarte*. The best bargain is a plate of Greek appetisers with aubergine, taramasalata, grape leaves, mushrooms à la Grecque, tsatskiki, and such, for 39F. With a quarter-litre of red wine for 10F, you will have lunched well for 49F. A menu for 69F is available every day and includes snails in garlic butter and some good main courses and desserts. Service is included, drink extra. Open every day of the year, no annual closing, with lunch from noon to 2:00 p.m., dinner from 7:00 to 11:00 p.m. or possibly midnight.

Taverne Descartes

rue Descartes, 5e
Métro: Cardinal Lemoine, Place Monge
Tel: 43 25 67 77

An old faithful friend, where you can lunch on a two-course *formule* of hors d'oeuvres and a main dish and wine, *service compris*, for 37F to 48F, prices which have crept up only slightly since the last edition of this book. And for those prices, you can have mussels in garlic sauce or a good *terrine* or salad, then lamb or various steaks or *andouillette* sausages. More ambitiously, climb up to the 76F menu which gives you a dozen mussels, or six snails, or avocado with crab and several other starters, then grilled lamb with garlic butter, baked potato with cream, or fish in wine sauce, or an aubergine and lamb and tomato dish, then a choice of cheeses *plus* dessert – orange salad, *tarte tatin* (caramelised apple pie), sorbets and several more. Service is included on this menu, and another 12F will give you half a bottle of wine. The interior is imitation-old: dark wood, dim lights; and fast and friendly service of really generous proportions. No annual closing, and open every day except for Saturday lunch, from noon to 2:00 p.m., then 7:00 to 11:30 p.m. which on Saturday night stretches to midnight. The Taverne is open on most holidays, except Christmas and New Year's Day. You'll like the ambiance of the street which is full of shops, boutiques, strolling families, wandering musicians, late into the evening.

La Trattoria

5 rue d'Arras, 5e
Métro: Cardinal-Lemoine
Tel: 43 29 51 28

A fairly new Italian restaurant that offers surprising value in this interesting neighbourhood surrounding the University of Paris – and already discovered by the enterprising students. For just 60F including wine and service, they'll feed you lots of good food: salad or mortadella sausage or tomato salad to start with, then lasagne or tagliatelli or spaghetti Napoli, or veal escalope; cheese or home-made apple cake or fresh fruit salad, and a quarter-litre of wine or coffee as you choose. The small room is wood-panelled, with bright tablecloths and fresh flowers on each table, and a notably friendly welcome. There's piped music but don't flinch, it's soft Italian pop and doesn't interfere with your pleasure in the food. Open noon to 2:00 p.m., 7:00 to 10:00 p.m. from Monday through Friday; on Saturdays and Sundays it's closed for lunch but open in the evenings – good to remember on a weekend night. Open most holidays, but it might be wise to check by telephone about Christmas and New Year's Day. Open in August, 'possibly' closed in February but that isn't certain.

6e arrondissement

La Bolée

25 rue Servandoni, 6e
Métro: Odéon, Luxembourg

This pretty little street near St Sulpice is a short stroll from St Germain, and La Bolée is a wonderful escape from its never-ending crowds and noise. Créperies are a very good choice for vegetarians, and for times when you want a light but satisfying meal – possibly on a day when you've had a lavish lunch or are planning a *luxe* dinner. Adam, from Montreal, and an English friend, Melanie, liked the sarrasin (buckwheat) pancakes – with goat's cheese and walnuts for 25F, or with courgettes and egg, 20F, a green salad for 10F, and a really lush crêpe with chocolate, coconut and vanilla ice cream at 20F. The thing to drink is, of course, Breton cider (*une bolée*), a big glass for 8F. As a bonus, you can watch the friendly owner making crêpes with lightning speed and deftness. Open for lunch Mondays through Saturdays 11:00 a.m. to 2:30 p.m., for dinner from Monday to Friday 6:00 p.m. to 10:00 p.m. Closed Saturday nights and Sundays. No annual closing, and it's open all holidays including Christmas, Good Friday, Easter Monday.

Bistro de la Grille

14 rue Mabillon, 6e
Métro: Mabillon
Tel: 43 54 16 87

A charmer, this Bistro, which takes its name from the lovely old wrought-iron grillwork over the entrance. The dining-room is pure 19th century, with dark wood, Eugène Atget photographs of ancient store fronts, posters of long-forgotten movies on the walls. The food is very imaginative, and for 70F including service you can choose from such first courses as tomatoes with mozzarella, a warm salad of crisp bacon, omelette and lettuce, fish soup, or poached marrow on country bread; then a tartare of fresh fish with lime, Lyon sausage cooked in white wine, *carpaccio* (very thin raw sirloin of beef) with oregano and olive oil, *dorade* (red sea-bream) in a cream-and-shrimp sauce. Desserts are extra: 25F, for fresh pear with chocolate sauce, bitter chocolate cake, Floating Island, etc. – but after those first two courses you probably couldn't tackle them. One of our Paris friends suggests having a substantial starter for 30F, then going straight to the chocolate cake, a satisfying meal for a little more than £5. Wine is available only in half-bottles at 23F, so if you're alone this might be your day to skip the drink. Lunch from noon to 5:30 p.m., most unusual in a Paris restaurant – dinner 7:30 p.m. to midnight, and open every day of the year except for major holidays such as Christmas. As you would imagine, the Bistro is usually very busy with regulars from the neighbourhood eating and drinking at the bar, a lively crowd at night – reservations for dinner are a must, and better go early or late for lunch.

Les Byzantins

33 rue Dauphine, 6e
Métro: Odéon, St-Michel

The neighbourhood is packed with Greco-French restaurants, all with similar menus. Les Byzantins is 'banal but honest', with stuffed grape leaves, salad, taramasalata, and so forth as starters, then calamari or brochettes, and various predictable desserts, a filling meal for 65F including service. They're open every day of the year, which can be a help if you're frantic on 14 July or Christmas. The atmosphere is simple but pleasant, and the service wonderfully friendly. But beware the drink prices – half a bottle of wine is 35F and mineral water is 14F. Open noon to 2:00   p.m., 7:00 to 10:30 p.m.

Claude Valentino/Monteverdi

5-7 rue Guisarde, 6e
Métro: Mabillon
Tel: 43 29 53 04, 43 29 34 04

To find a really good meal for 70F in the pricey 6e *arrondissement* is a feat, and especially when it's two minutes from St Germain and just down the street from St Sulpice. This restaurant with the two names is Franco-Italian, two lovely rooms connected by an open archway – and gentle music played by a three-piece group in the Monteverdi side filters through. You may have to ask to see the 70F menu, but do so: you can have red peppers with hot anchovy sauce, or the house salad of avocado, mozzarella and red peppers among other starters, then steak tartare with parmesan and fennel, or lemon chicken, or *poulet suprême*, followed by lemon or orange *tartes*, and other desserts of the day. The tables are widely-spaced and there's a feeling of privacy. The service is so relaxed that you could easily spend an evening here. And although when Jeanne Corey and her husband dined there recently, the restaurant was full and would-be diners were turned away, they did not feel rushed or pressured. The menu includes service, and is served at lunch and until 9:00 p.m., after that it's pretty expensive à la carte. Drink is extra, but a half-bottle of wine for two at 26F still brings the total bill to only 83F each, about £8 – miraculous. While the servings aren't large, you'll find everything delicious and beautifully presented. Open noon to 2:00 p.m., 6:00 p.m. to after midnight, closed Sundays, open most holidays except Christmas Day; usually there's no annual closing, but you might check by telephone before going in August.

L'Ecaille de PCB

5 rue Mabillon, 6e
Métro: Mabillon

'This restaurant gets 8 out of a possible 10,' says Jonathan Gilbert, adding that its menu at 90F hits the top edge of a pauper's budget. But as he remarks, it's a spin-off of Les Charpentiers, one of the best known and priciest of St Germain restaurants, and he adds feelingly that here you get what you pay for. It specialises in fish which is always costly in Paris; each day there's a different and equally wonderful dish – *cotriade* (to call it a fish stew is inadequate), or ray with capers, or *brandade* (a velvety concoction of salt cod, cream and garlic), *aioli* (fish and vegetables with intensely rich garlicky mayonnaise-like sauce) – and so forth. You're given a choice of a few starters, and dessert (sorbet or crème caramel) or cheese, and a carafe of wine. And the surroundings are pleasant, a wood-panelled room, bilingual waiters, a helpful *patronne*. When you see the prices people are paying for the à la carte dishes, you realise that this menu is a bargain, even though it's the upper limit of your budget. Open noon to 3:00 p.m., 7:30 to 11:30 p.m., closed Saturday lunch and Sundays, and open in August and on most holidays except 14 July.

L'Enfance de Lard

21 rue Guisarde, 6e
Métro: Mabillon
Tel: 46 33 89 65

If you wait until one o'clock to go into L'Enfance, you're out of luck as it will be packed out. That's how good it is, and how unusual. The food is so imaginative that we can't resist listing one day's choices on the two-course *formule* for 70F: for starters, savoury profiteroles stuffed with escargots and dressed with garlic cream, or parma ham, minced goat's cheese with pepper, *confit* of chicken with fresh peaches, jellied rabbit, squid with fresh pineapple and lemon slices. The main courses were duck leg with orange sauce, steak tartare, fish *choucrôute* (fresh cod and smoked haddock with a creamy lemon sauce with sauerkraut), tuna steak with mustard sauce, and fish fillet on a bed of endives. Service is included and so is endless wine. Desserts are 30F to 34F and irresistible – we can only mention *chocolat delice* which is a cross between fudge and a rich almond brownie on a bed of coffee sauce. At night, the same menu is 89F for two courses, including service and wine. The rue Guisarde is a historic street, and the restaurant is warm and friendly, with beams and stone walls. Open 12:00 to 2:30 p.m., 7:00 to 11:00 p.m., closed Sundays; open most holidays except Christmas. No annual closing – what a blessing in August.

La Godasse

38 rue M.-le-Prince, 6e
Métro: Luxembourg, Odéon
Tel: 43 26 54 14

'A fashionable place in a fashionable area', one of our restaurant spies comments, with stone walls, wooden rafters, and a talkative, animated crowd of well-dressed people. 'This is for meat-eaters' was another remark, as the menu at 69F is almost entirely steak or pork. To begin with, thick slices of flavourful *pâté*, or Roquefort salad, spinach and poached egg, or a creamy well-seasoned goat's cheese salad. The desserts are very special - if the strawberry cake is listed, have it. The crème caramel is made with *real* caramel, and what a difference that makes. Don't be tempted by the à la carte menu unless you're feeling rich: it can add up to 130F or more in no time. Service is included but drink is additional and not cheap: beer is 15F, and half-bottles of wine are 35 to 50F. But a *pichet*, 33cl, is a reasonable 25F and can be shared by two. Open 11:00 a.m. to 2:30 p.m., and from 7:00 to 11:00 p.m. Closed Sundays, most holidays (but open on Easter), and the third and fourth weeks in August.

Jardin de Prunus

37 rue Mazarine, 6e
Métro: Odéon

This simple but elegant Chinese restaurant is excellent value – the menu is 48F80, *tout compris*, and the food is exceptionally good. A soup with poached egg and vegetables is delicious – or one could have bean-sprout salad or *pâté* imperial. Chicken with pineapple, or pork or beef with vegetables, or curried chicken are among the main courses, with the usual Chinese desserts: macaroon-like *gâteau chinois* or arbutus fruits in syrup. Open noon to 2:30 p.m., 7:00 to 10:30 p.m., closed Sundays, open on holidays and no annual closing.

La Macrobiotheque

17 rue de Savoie, 6e
Métro: St-Michel, Odéon
Tel: 43 25 04 96

Here's a rarity, recommended by a semi-vegetarian Paris friend – a no-meat restaurant that's pleasant and tranquil and only a few steps from the rush and scurry of St-Michel. And it's inexpensive, which is far from the case with most Paris vegetarian restaurants . . . lunch is only 40F, including service and fruit or vegetable juice, or tea! Our friend liked the vegetable *pâté* and the soup, the plate of rice and vegetables, and the simple but delicious desserts and fruit salads. At night, the price escalates to 68F, with a choice of soups or salads or eggs and the same excellent vegetable *pâté*, while main dishes include vegetable *tartes* which change every day, various *gratins*, and substantial dishes based on cracked wheat or rice or some other grain. It's all clean, fresh, and friendly, with a kind manager who speaks English. And you can put together a nice take-away lunch if you prefer and stroll down and eat it near the fountain in the place St-Michel. Open noon to 2:00 p.m., 7:00 to 10:00 p.m., closed Sundays, no annual closing.

Marco Polo

8 rue de Condé, 6e
Métro: Odéon
Tel: 43 26 79 63

Full of Italians, which means good food, Marco Polo will give you an excellent two-course meal for 70F but you must go there for lunch as in the evening everything's à la carte and not cheap. However, in this popular neighbourhood, food of this quality at this price is rare. And it's perfect for vegetarians, as both starters and main courses can be meatless if you choose. Begin with tomato and mozzarella salad, or *carpaccio* (raw beef sliced transparently thin), progress to a big plate of pasta, various meat dishes – Adam Steinhouse mentions the veal escalope in a black olive and tomato sauce, and his friend Melanie who doesn't eat meat had gnocchi gorgonzola. The *plat du jour* is always interesting. At night, you'll pay between 85F and 120F à la carte. All prices include service but not drink; a quarter-litre of wine is 15F. Open noon to 2:30 p.m., 7:00 to 11:30 p.m., closed Saturday lunch, Sundays, and from 15 to 30 August.

Osteria del Passe Partout

20 rue de l'Hirondelle, 6e
Métro: St-Michel

Tucked away on a little street, almost hidden from the crowds in the boulevard St-Michel, the Osteria is a real find in this usually vastly over-priced and over-crowded district. Remarkable food: ricotta and tomato salad, avocado with shrimp, orange-fennel-and-black-olive salad, or spinach salad with walnuts and gorgonzola to begin with; then the most delicious delicate taglionini (very thin pasta) with dried *cèpes* and fresh mushrooms in cream; and desserts like Tira Misu, pound cake drenched in Marsala-rich cream. These, and more, on the 70F menu which includes service but not drink. A bottle of Chianti is 64F and four can share it; otherwise drink beer at 12F as wine is available only in bottles and half-bottles. Open noon to 3:00 p.m., 7:30 to 11:00 p.m., closed Saturday lunch and Sundays, and all Saturday in August.

Orestias

4 rue Grégoire-de-Tours, 6e
Métro: Odéon

A wonderful little restaurant run by a troupe of manic Greeks who operate on the 'always room for one more' principle. The tables are long and open, offering minimum intimacy and maximum chance to get to know people. The food is Franco-Greek and there's lots of it (but go early as many of the best choices go fast). Unbelievably, the menu is only 40F, service included: things like vine leaves, green salad, or *pâté*, then brochette or roast chicken or lamb chops, and apple tart or yoghurt or fruit to end with. Wine is really inexpensive, 6F for a quarter-litre – as Jonathan Gilbert says, it's a lovely, entertaining little place you'll want to go back to more than once. Open noon to 2:30 p.m., 6:30 to 11:30 p.m. Closed on Sundays, but open holidays and August.

Le Polidor

41 rue M.-le-Prince, 6e
Métro: Odéon
Tel: 43 26 95 34

'Polidor is really Vieux Paris,' reports our able researcher, Gloria Girton. She adds that it is extremely popular and usually packed, so best to go early when daily specials are still available. A two-course menu is offered Mondays through Fridays at lunch only, with several starters including Andalusian rice, then main dishes such as ham with lentils, kidneys in Madeira sauce, and (recommended) *boudin* with creamy puréed potatoes. Desserts are priced from 12F to 14F, and a quarter-litre of wine is 7F, so a good lunch might add up to 69 or 71F. À la carte suggestions in the evenings: farm-raised chicken in Basque sauce for 46F, superb caramelised apple *tarte* with lots of *crème frâiche* for 22F, and wine at 7F – still a total of only 79F. Polidor was founded in 1845 and the dining-room looks untouched, with old floor tiles and drawers where the *habitués'* napkins were kept. The courtyard *cabinet à la Turque* also seems to belong to the period, be warned. Open 365 days, with lunch from noon to 2:30 p.m. and dinner from 7:00 p.m. to 1:00 a.m., except Sundays when it closes at 11:00 p.m.

Restaurant des Arts

73 rue de Seine, 6e
Métro: Odéon

Here's something rare in this very touristy area, a restaurant that seems to stay the same year after year and indeed generation after generation. It's always full of people chattering, waving forks in the air, eating heartily, and good news, most of them are French. It's good simple food, a three-course menu for 64F including service – recommended, the *salade composée* of rice, sweetcorn, tomatoes and lettuce as a first course, or *salade Niçoise*, then a choice of veal escalope, chicken in a creamy sauce, or an *entrecôte* steak; a big selection of *tartes* (the *tarte aux pommes* went down well with our restaurant spy). Skip the wine (8F50 for a quarter-litre), and be patient with the service – the mother and daughter waitresses are amiable and overworked during the busiest times. In hot weather, when it's very crowded, you can feel uncomfortably close to a lot of warm bodies. Open noon to 2:00 p.m., 7:00 to 9:00 p.m., and please note – closed *Friday nights*, Saturdays, Sundays, holidays and all of July.

Restaurant des Beaux Arts

11 rue Bonaparte, 6e
Métro: St-Germain-des-Prés
Tel: 43 26 92 64

Everyone knows this restaurant, and it has been in guidebooks for years, but nothing has changed its busy bustling character or the quality of the food. There's an amazing variety of choices – twelve different starters and as many main courses to pick from – all for 53F which includes service and wine. Four friends recently have all recommended, quite independently, the *boeuf bourguignon*, and another who doesn't eat meat opted for a vegetarian main dish. The high-speed shuttle service of the waitresses is something to see, and the wave of noise that hits you as you open the door can make you reel. In winter, there's usually a great *pot-au-feu* with marrow bones – choose that if it's on offer. There are perpetual queues, and you aren't encouraged to dally for long periods over choosing, so consult the menu posted outside and be ready to give your order quickly. Lunch from noon to about 2:00p.m., dinner from 7:00 to 10:45p.m., which is late for Paris, but don't be disappointed if the *boeuf* is gone by nine o'clock. Open every day of the year including holidays.

7e arrondissement

5 Au Ciel de Shanghai

33 avenue de Suffren, 7e
Métro: Bir-Hakeim

Enjoyable places around the Tour Eiffel are almost non-existent, so our friend Eric Bernard's report on this old favourite came as a relief. Expect to spend about 80F for a complete meal including wine and coffee, but you can eat for about 65F on the menu without a drink. Recommended: pork in a spiced sauce with mushrooms and 'brilliant' shrimp in a light crusty batter. Starters are conventional but our scout liked the light fresh soup. The Ciel is open seven days a week, and 'most' holidays, but not Christmas or Easter as far as we could find out, and open all of August. Noon to 2:30 p.m., 7:00 to 10:30 p.m. One of the friendliest Chinese restaurants we know.

Chez Germaine

30 rue Pierre Leroux, 7e
Métro: Vaneau

You *must* go early, otherwise prepare to queue for ten minutes to half an hour – it is that good, and that popular. It's a great place for people travelling alone, as the gregarious atmosphere will draw you into conversation that could last all evening if you weren't aware of hopeful eaters peering through the windows. It can even provide you with someone to show you around Paris, or a lifelong friend. Everyone Chez Germaine knows exactly what you've chosen for your meal, whisper it softly as you please, as it is then bellowed across the room to the kitchen. M. Babkine says *interdit de fumer*, and he means it, so this is a great place for non-smokers. The *menu conseillé* is 38F, but you can eat almost as inexpensively from the à la carte, as Adam Steinhouse and his Canadian friend Iris, remark . . . they had a very good meal with tomato salad, veal escalope sautéed in breadcrumbs, and a dessert, for the huge sum of 41F each. Prices include service, and wine is still very inexpensive, and perfectly drinkable, at 4F90 the quarter-litre. Prices are quoted in *francs anciens* which may give you a turn, thinking you're paying

380F for a meal, but makes you smile quietly as you realise that this idiosyncracy fits in with the very personal qualities of the owners. Open 11:30 a.m. to 2:30 p.m., 7:00 to 9:00 p.m., closed Saturday nights, Sundays and August.

Le Roupeyrac

62 rue de Bellechasse, 7e
Métro: Solférino-Bellechasse
Tel: 45 51 33 42

One of the few affordable places within walking distance of the Musée d'Orsay, the Roupeyrac changes little over the years. At lunch, it's crowded with people from nearby ministries, so go early. Saturday lunchtime is a wiser choice. The 58F menu gives you a limited number of first courses, then try brains in black butter which is one of our long-time favourites, or steak or pork chop; cheese or a perfect chocolate mousse, and plum cake, which Adam Steinhouse who dined there recently says is a treat. He comments that the food comes in big servings, and his steak, ordered *saignant* (very rare), was cooked exactly to that point. Tim Allan chose from the à la carte menu and put together a fine meal for 88F: mushrooms as a starter, then marinated salmon with spinach which was wonderful on a hot night, and *café liégeois* which he says was 'pure creamy extravagance' at 21F . . it's a very French confection of ice-cream, syrup and *crème frâiche*. Prices are 'net' which means *service compris*. Wine in a rather odd quantity – 22 cl – is 6 or 7F. The Roupeyrac is open noon to 2:45 p.m., 7:00 to 9:30 p.m., closed Saturday nights, Sundays, holidays, and all of August.

8e arrondissement

Étoile d'Asia

24 rue Jean-Mermoz, 8e
Métro: Franklin D. Roosevelt
Tel: 43 59 60 59

A pleasant, not-too-expensive, Chinese-Vietnamese restaurant in a ritzy neighbourhood; clientele mostly French. A few nice touches such as wood-panelled walls. First course: Chinese salad or two choices of soup; then something like chicken with almonds or curried pork, followed by fruit or almond cakes. À la carte it can run into real money, and drink is expensive and extra: wine is available only in half-bottles, the cheapest at 26F. However a carafe of fresh water is set on each table, the service is beautiful, the food perfectly cooked and very fresh, and the place feels twice as expensive as it is – which is 60F for the menu plus whatever tip you like to leave. Open noon to 2:30 p.m., 7:00 to 10:30 p.m., open on holidays but closed Sundays and probably in August.

Flora Danica

142 avenue des Champs-Élysées, 8e
Métro: George-V, Étoile
Tel: 43 59 20 41

Perfect Danish food served in a very attractive room set with classic Danish furniture and enhanced with paintings everywhere. It is open from noon to 11:00 p.m. without interruption, and from about 12:30 to 1:30 you'll have difficulty in finding a seat. Portions are generous and exquisite to look at as well as to taste. A plate of herring, liver *pâté*, hard-boiled egg with shrimp, sausage, cheese and miniature pork *frikadeller* with cucumber salad is 74F – the most expensive dish on the menu. Wonderful cold roast beef with potato salad is 50F, and there are various *smorgasbord*-type dishes to choose from which are all from 62F to 69F. Danish pastries are 15F, and beer which is perfect with this sort of cold meal is 16F. While not inexpensive, the Flora Danica is greatly to be recommended. It's open every day of the year except 1 May. Be sure you don't stray into its companion restaurant Copenhague, which is VERY expensive.

Galerie Point Show

66 Champs-Élysées, 8e
Métro: Franklin D. Roosevelt, St-Phillipe-du-Roule

Fast, frantic and a complete contrast to Le Moka just down the street – here's a Chinese snack bar inside this big gallery of shops.

Tim Allan, who works nearby, calls it the best place to have a quick and satisfying bite to eat on the Champs-Élysées. Try to get there well before 1:00 p.m. or go after 2:00 p.m., at the height of the lunch rush you'll be queueing for an appreciable time. While the food isn't typically French, the people who eat there are, knowing a good thing when they see or eat one. The menu changes slightly every day, but usually you'll find dishes like sautéed prawns with oriental vegetables, or various spring-roll-like delicacies, or stir-fried beef and rice – all about 30F. It's always delicious, and good fun as orders are shouted in shrill Chinese from the U-shaped bar to the chefs at the back. A far better choice than a chain-restaurant hamburger or a slice of pizza on a day when you are going to have a luxurious meal at night. Open from well before lunch to late into the night, 365 days a year.

Le Moka

25 rue d'Artois, 8e
Métro: George-V, St-Phillipe-du-Roule

Here's the perfect alternative to lunch in one of the expensive restaurants on or near the Champs-Élysées – inevitably, you'll be horror-struck by the prices and taken aback by the quality, or lack thereof, of the food in the touristy places. Le Moka is at the corner of the rue de Berri and the rue d'Artois, and is your chance to eat in a typical working-man's bar-restaurant. It's packed and noisy, full of building workers in paint-spattered dungarees, all eating and joking and shouting at each other. The menu changes every day, the food is well-cooked and garnished with excellent vegetables and sauces. There's no fixed-price menu, but the à la carte choices are reasonably priced and incredibly good value. You could have a salad or *terrine*, 15F, as a starter, then something like a steak *au poivre* for 40F, *escalope de veau* or tournedos for 50F – often there are less expensive dishes to choose from. Desserts are about 15F – service is included, and wine bottles on every table from which you help yourself. So for 65 to 75F, you'd lunch in a very French way, and be amused by the atmosphere. Open only from 11:30 a.m. to 3:00 p.m., closed Saturdays, Sundays and 'probably' two weeks in August.

Le Relais

44 rue de Londres, 8e
Métro: St-Lazare, Europe
Tel: 43 87 46 15

This cosy restaurant is far from the tourist round, and mainly popular with the smartly-dressed local people who live in this some-what bourgeois *quartier* tucked incongruously between the rather raunchy rue de Budapest and the scruffiness of Place de Clichy. Its menu at 75F, service included, seems to change every day which is, as Tim Allan and Adam Steinhouse remark, a good sign that the owners care about food. One night the main dish was an excellent veal escalope in a sauce of wine, cream and mushrooms – the next day the choices were rabbit and *gigot d'agneau* (leg of mutton). Try the herring to begin with, and one of the characteristic *tartes* as dessert – unless you'd rather choose from a selection of cheeses. Two people who have dined there recently have noted that the red wine – at 10F for a quarter-litre – was notably good. This is better than average food, at a slightly higher than average price, reflected in the ambience of the Relais. Open 12:00 to 2:30 for lunch, and dinner from 7:30 to 9:30 p.m., closed Saturdays, Sundays, holidays, and August.

Le Volnay

6 rue de Laborde, 8e
Métro: St-Lazare

From the side street, this looks like nothing more than a bar, but it's one of those deceptively simple, small and very French restaurants. The cooking is hearty and countrified, and the benevolent wait-resses treat you like family, all but reminding you that you haven't finished your vegetables. There's no menu, but even choosing the most expensive dishes you won't spend more than 82F, including half a bottle of passable wine. Try the chicken Marengo, and try to resist the ice-cream confections. Open 11:45 a.m. to 2:30 p.m., and 6:45 to 8:30 p.m. Closed Saturdays, Sundays, holidays, and July.

9e arrondissement

L'Auberge du Père Louis

7 rue de la Boule-Rouge, 9e
Tel: 45 42 52 59
Métro: Rue-Montmartre

A big place filled with lots of people getting together to have a good
time. Usually, we don't recommend restaurants that cater to groups
– but Père Louis has so much to offer that we must include it. If
you're alone or a twosome, make for the first floor and try for a
table near the window. The menu at 85F begins with a kir, goes on
to salad or cold ham for a start, then a main dish such as braised
beef, *blanquette de veau* (veal in a white sauce), or steak, and finishes
with good cheese or *tartes* or ice-cream, and coffee which is a most
unusual 'extra' to appear on a fixed-price menu in Paris. Wine is
included, as is service. The friendly waiters like to joke and to
practise their English, while you practise your French. If you can
collect half a dozen friends for dinner here, you might phone for
reservations as an informal group, in which case you could qualify
for menus which range from 50F for three courses up to 90F for a
sumptuous 5-course meal! Open noon to about 10:30 p.m., every
day of the year.

Chartier

7 rue de Faubourg Montmartre, 9e
Métro: Rue Montmartre

A cliché in restaurants, listed in all guidebooks, but the value is so
good it must be included. It's possible to eat a really superb meal for
61F, everything included: *terrine de lapin* (rabbit), *cassoulet parisienne*
or *escalope de veau forestière*, and *gâteau St-Sylvestre* or *mousse au
chocolat*, and a quarter of wine – just to give you the gist. Service is
quick, not too much Gallic charm, but the customers are always an
interesting mixture of students, tourists and impecunious Parisians.
Look for the *menu conseillé*, which is always good value, but note that
12 per cent service is added to its basic cost. The 1920s décor makes
Chartier worth a visit. Open 11:00 a.m. to 3:00 p.m., 6:00 to 9:30
p.m., seven days a week, no annual closing.

Chez Maurice

44 rue Notre-Dame de Lorette, 9e
Métro: St-Georges

There are those who love it, there are those who say it's full of
tourists; here we quote Tim Allan who lives in the neighbourhood
and says 'Highly recommended, worth a special trip.' The *menu
touristique* at 55F would seem to be a misnomer as when he was there
recently the restaurant appeared to be full of French people, from
'the two young lovers finding time to eat between seductive glances,
to the two stereotypical old French ladies nibbling in virtual silence
and keeping an eye on everyone'. To eat, there was a large inviting
plate of *crudités*, and a 'fantastic' cod fillet coated in herbs, with
boiled potatoes, not *frites*. The fruit salad was much like any other,
and chosen only because all the *patisserie* looked just too filling after
a hearty main course. There are other prix-fixe menus from 65F50
to 100F50, but the least expensive did him nicely. Open every day
of the year; lunch from noon to 2:00 p.m., dinner 7:00 to 10:30
p.m.

Chez Vincent

56 rue St-Georges, 9e
Métro: St-Georges

A cosy, friendly neighbourhood restaurant, generous with good
food: a big table of hors d'oeuvres one day recently included ratatouille, fresh mushrooms in cream sauce, shrimp, a selection of
charcuterie, tomatoes, olives, lentils and salads. Try duck breast
with green peppercorns, veal done in various ways, grilled shrimp,
pot-au-feu. Conventional desserts – *tartes*, crème caramel, chocolate
mousse. All for 73F, service included. Drink is extra and good, but
not cheap. A nice Valpolicella will set you back 14F for a quarter-
litre. Open 11:45 a.m. to 2:00 p.m., 6:45 to 10:00 p.m., closed
Saturday lunch, all day Sunday, and all of August.

Nine Rue Choron

9 rue Choron, 9e
Métro: Notre-Dame-de-Lorette

'I shall try not to be biased about this,' says Tim Allan who literally lives above the restaurant. It's for real paupers who want a decent filling meal which costs 30F. Not a misprint. Less than £3. And it's pretty good stuff. What's missing? Choice. For your first course, you choose whatever you like from a big tray loaded with *crudités*. Then you have a choice between two dishes, usually one meat or chicken, and one fish – on Thursdays, which is when we advise you to go, there's couscous with a tureen of vegetables in sauce, and meat. Usually there's fresh fruit salad as the only dessert, or cheese. Unusual in Paris, there's no service charge added, so leave about 5F; and wine, believe it or not, is only 5 to 7F for a quarter-litre. Your meal, therefore, will set you back about 40F. As you can imagine, Nine Rue Choron is almost always full, so go early. Lunch from 12:00 to 2:00 p.m., dinner 7:00 to 10:30 p.m., and it's open on Sundays! Open on holidays, but closed for the month of August.

Picpain

2 boulevard Haussman, 9e
Métro: Richelieu-Drout

Here's a breath of fresh air in the fast-food world! 'It should be a criminal offence to eat in the best-known hamburger-chain restaurants when there's something like the Picpain,' according to a Paris-based friend. Although the set-up is very much like any eat-and-run place, the ambience is quite different – cane chairs, prettier décor, and staff who actually smile. The Salade Picpain at 19F90 is very big, fresh, and filling. The burgers are 19F and taste pleasantly different, served as they are in crusty rolls rather than the usual cardboard. 'Try the Pic Crudité, 9F90, or the PicCroc (ham and cheese on great bread for 12F90', is another comment. Tim Allan says you go in for a snack lunch and come out feeling healthy, as the enormous orange juice for 9F90 probably gives you enough Vitamin C to see you through a week. Picpain is open every day of the year, from noon to midnight, and until 1:00 a.m. Fridays and Saturdays. Prices are 'net', that is, service is included.

Pupillin

19 rue Notre-Dame-de-Lorette, 9e
Métro: St-Georges

A stylish neighbourhood restaurant and much recommended for its bar salads, of which there are at least six, each enough for a full meal: avocado stuffed with fresh cheese, lemon, orange, ham, olives, and dill, for example; or a pasta salad with peas, hard-boiled egg, bananas, pineapple, tomatoes, ham, fresh cheese and seasonings, each 33 to 35F. The fare varies with available produce. The imaginative 69F menu features chicken liver or vegetable flans, courgette quiche or cold spinach soup for starters, and kidneys in Madeira sauce, squid *à la armoricaine* or *carpaccio* with salad to follow. Wine is available only in demis, at 32F50; beer is much cheaper. Desserts, says our delighted critic, are divine. Open 11:30 a.m. to 2:30 p.m. and 7:30 p.m. to 1:00 a.m., and closed only on Christmas Day.

Le Relais Savoyard

13 rue Rodier, 9e
Métro: Cadet, Notre-Dame-de-Lorette
Tel: 45 26 17 48

The same family has run the Relais Savoyard for the past quarter of a century, and it has its quota of regulars from the neighbourhood – visitors from the outer world, so to speak, are looked upon as rather an oddity. Service is efficient and polite but somewhat unsmiling. However, the food is good bourgeois cooking: among the hors d'oeuvres, warm sausage and potatoes, charcuterie, grapefruit, *crudités* – while a main course of whiting, crisply fried, got a verdict of delicious. Other choices could be, depending on the day, something like courgettes stuffed with a meat-and-rice pilaff, or cold ham and salad. Cheese, fruit, ice-cream or a dessert of the day are the last course. And the whole thing, including service and a quarter-litre of red wine, is just 62F. White wine will cost you slightly more. Open noon to 3:00 p.m., 7:30 to 10:00 p.m. or possibly a little earlier or later, depending on how busy they are. Closed Sundays, holidays, and August.

Taverne des Dauphins

8 rue de Châteaudun, 9e
Métro: Cadet
Tel: 48 78 66 99

A lively little restaurant where you can amuse yourself watching the other customers – many of them regulars – or find a seat by the window and look out on the busy street. The service is slow but pleasant. Lunch, including service and less-than-spectacular wine, is 43F, and consists of hors d'oeuvres, a *plat du jour*, and dessert: onion soup or cheese-filled crêpes, followed by roast pork or fish *à la Provençale* or *escalope de veau*, then sorbet or peach melba or pastry. Dinner menus, at 49F90, 58F or 73F, follow the same line, with more interesting alternatives: Parma ham or lobster bisque to start; grilled salmon with anchovy butter or steak with Béarnaise sauce, for example. A 75F 'Chilean' menu offers exotic-sounding soups and salads, *empanadas* and such, but our critic found them unexciting: back to basics, she recommends. Open noon to 3:00 p.m. and 6:30 to 11:00 p.m., closed Sundays and holidays, no annual closing.

Xavier Gourmet

21 rue Notre-Dame-de-Lorette, 9e
Métro: St-Georges

Serendipitously next door to Pupillin, another notable find, Xavier is a rather sophisticated blend of tea room and restaurant, always busy, always good. Examples: trout in aspic with smoked salmon sauce and a green salad, 35F. A crêpe stuffed with raw mountain ham, raclette cheese from the Savoie, with green salad and tomatoes, 30F. A sandwich, on wonderful chewy *Poilâne* bread, of tomatoes, mozzarella, fresh basil, and olive oil, served with a green salad, 30F. Best of all are the pastries, which our scout Gloria calls 'exquisite' and 'absolutely yummy'. A glass of good wine is 9F, service is included, and it's easily possible to walk out satiated for 55F. Open from 9:00 a.m. to 10:30 p.m., seven days a week, including holidays. No annual closing. They run a branch, as yet untested, at 89 boulevard de Courcelles, 8e.

11e arrondissement

Bois et Charbons

8 rue de la Main d'Or, 11e
Métro: Ledru-Rollin
Tel: 48 05 77 10

It takes persistence to find this small gem: but if you've been flea-marketing at the place d'Aligre, direct your steps toward the Faubourg St Antoine. Look for No. 133, and turn into the narrow unpromising alley of furniture-makers' shops called le passage de la Main d'Or. Just off that is the short street rue de la Main d'Or, and there you are. For 45F at lunch you'll have very good leeks vinai-grette (or *crudités*, or *oeuf dur*), then something like roast beef with ratatouille and rice (the menu changes daily), and chestnut cake or crème caramel. Bois et Charbons looks from the outside like a workman's café, but a number of well-dressed young business people from the neighbourhood have sussed it out. 'My kind of restaurant,' says Gloria Girton. On Thursdays and Fridays, between 1 September and 30 June, the restaurant is also open for dinner and becomes a Bistro Lyonnais with such specialities as *cerville de canut* – a delicious fresh cheese with fresh herbs – quenelles, Bresse chicken, Lyonnais charcuterie, and that great Lyons dish *tablier de sapeur* – literally 'fireman's apron', which is breaded, sautéed tripe served with homemade tartare sauce. Put this down in your notebook for a winter's night! Open noon to 2:00 p.m., closed Saturdays and Sundays, no annual closing.

Pho Dong Huong

14 rue Louis Bonnet, 11e
Métro: Belleville

This delicious little restaurant is always filled with happily-eating Asian patrons, not a tourist in sight, the place to go if you're meandering around Belleville in search of Vietnamese food. There is no fixed menu, but the large Tonkinese soup at 26F is a whole meal: flavoursome meat broth filled with rice noodles and beef, served with a side dish of lemon, fresh mint, lemon grass, hot peppers and a spicy satay sauce. Or choose chicken with lemon grass and rice, or cold noodles tossed with glazed roast pork, herbs and spices and *pâtés impériaux* (spring rolls), each 26F. Service included, drink extra: beer is 12F, tea 5F. Open from 11:30 a.m. to 10:30 p.m. without interruption; closed Tuesdays and July. Good for a fine Sunday lunch or dinner.

La Ravigotte

41 rue de Montreuil, 11e
Métro: Faidherbe-Chaligny
Tel: 43 72 96 22

This is one of our top-priced restaurants but very much recommended for serious eaters – plan to go there one evening when you've had a snack lunch and are feeling adventurous, and mildly rich. It's in an area with real character, and owned by the original proprietor's charming granddaughter, who will linger and chat with you and suggest the evening's best choices. The menu is 100F and worth every centime: first courses such as escargots, smoked trout with red berries, or *rillette* of salmon, then a masterly *cassoulet*, a choice of excellent steaks or *tête de veau*, ending with profiteroles, chocolate mousse or luscious *tartes*. The food is as good as it sounds, and the room is interesting with old black-and-white photos decorating the walls which show how the neighbourhood used to be. Service is included, but drink is extra – decide for yourself if you want to spend 18F for a quarter-litre of wine. If you specify *un carafe d'eau* it's perfectly all right, the friendly atmosphere doesn't go cold. Open for lunch Mondays to Saturdays, noon to 2:30 p.m., dinner served only Thursdays, Fridays and Saturdays, until 9:30 p.m. Closed Sundays, holidays and August.

Au Trou Normand

9 rue Jean-Pierre Timbaud, 11e
Métro: Oberkampf, or a brisk walk from République
Tel: 48 05 80 23

Not fancy, but attractive in its simplicity, and its à la carte prices are astonishingly low: a salad of potatoes in oil with smoked salmon was

9F10, calamari in tomato sauce with rice 25F30, chocolate mousse 7F, a quarter of Provençal vin rosé 9F: a whole meal, with a kir before dinner, only 58F90 including service. It's run by two nice women, and the service is leisurely but friendly. 'Peeping through the steamed-up windows one winter evening, I saw that all the clients were dancing,' says our diligent scout Annie Polatsek. Other items on the menu included various *pâtés* and *tabouleh* salad as starters, tournedos and lamb brochettes, all quite inexpensive. Open from noon to 2:30 p.m., 7:00 to 11:30 p.m. Closed Saturday evenings, Sundays, and holidays – and probably in August.

Le Val de Loire

149 rue Amelot, 11e
Métro: République

Don't be put off by the eccentric menus in English and German posted outside. Follow the French menus. One at 49F gives you very good vegetable soup or *pâté*, usually a choice of roast chicken or beef, and flaky fruit *tartes*. The 88F menu is tremendous: four courses which begin with a *terrine* of country *pâté* put on the table to serve yourself, then snails or frogs' legs or crab cocktail or ham, followed by steak *au poivre*, good fish, veal steak in a creamy mushroom sauce; then superb cakes, and a choice of cheeses. 'Very good food,' says a French friend who dined there recently, 'but almost too much of it.' The atmosphere is friendly, from the big dog stretched across the doorstep to the chatty and attentive waitresses who like to see you eat. Prices include service. Wine is extra but not expensive: a likeable half-bottle of red is only 12F. Open noon to 2:30 p.m., 6:45 to 9:45 p.m., closed Sundays and most holidays, and all of August.

12e arrondissement

Café Melrose's

76 bis avenue Ledru-Rollin, 12e
Métro: Ledru-Rollin
Tel: 46 28 10 82

Melrose's, which used to be one of the well-known gay restaurants, has changed hands, changed décor, and changed character in the past two years. It's worth walking the few streets from the place d'Aligre flea market to find it for lunch, which for 58F is rather sensational value (but you might be wise to telephone for a table) – seafood salads or smoked fish, cucumber with mint and other interesting things for a starter, then *moules marinière*, or steak, or squid with rice, and a choice of cheeses or sweets like lemon or strawberry *tarte*, sorbet, or plums in wine. At night, the price climbs steeply to 98F, but it's still a very good buy; Nicolas from Lille, Adam Steinhouse and Iris from Canada recommended the starter salad with nuts and plenty of Roquefort, *moules marinière* in a subtle and not overpowering sauce, and 'agreeable' herring, all as first courses, then a tender *bavette* (steak), or duck, or fish. The desserts were much as at lunchtime except for a memorable chocolate cake made with dark, bitter chocolate. Service is included, but not drink which can push your bill up sharply: the best bet was a half-bottle of Côtes-du-Rhône Vacqueyras at 32F, which gave each of three diners two small glasses. Open noon to 2:30 p.m. for lunch, 8:00 to 11:00 p.m. for dinner. Closes Sundays, open on holidays including Christmas and Easter Monday, closed 15 to 30 August.

Le Limonaire

88 rue de Charenton, 12e
Métro: Ledru-Rollin or Gare de Lyon

A tiny restaurant on a tree-studded corner, in turn-of-the-century style, decorated with musical instruments on the walls, plants, old photos, a piano in the corner and an old *orgue de barbarie*. The ceiling is pressed tin, the bar is beautiful, traditional zinc. There is no prix-fixe menu, but 85F will see you beautifully fed, and another 9 to 16F will go for excellent wine: Côtes du Rhône is featured, and our expert reviewer Gloria, who dotes on this restaurant, favours the fruity red Visan. Starters include a variety of *terrines*: tuna, or chicken livers with blueberries, or a Basque *terrine*, about 22F, or a warm goat cheese salad, 28F. A *plat du jour* at lunch was delicious country ham with melon and salad, 45F; for dinner, a *confit de canard* (duck), 58F. Desserts include walnut, hazelnut, or rich home-made chocolate cake with custard, 20F, or fresh fruit salad or ice-cream. Wednesday through Saturday evenings at 10:00 p.m., a player or singer comes through, passing the hat after performing: for this you'll need reservations. Open every day for lunch from noon to 2:30 p.m., dinner from 8:00 to 10:00 p.m. Closed in August.

13e arrondissement

Bangkok–Thailand

---

35 boulevard Auguste-Blanqui, 13e
Métro: Corvisart

Pure Thai restaurants, unalloyed with Vietnamese or Chinese cuisine, are rare in Paris, and the food is distinctively spiced and tantalising in flavour: cilantro (coriander) predominates. At lunch, for 46F including service and jasmine tea, you might have Thai soup or salad, then a choice of three dishes (always beef, pork, or chicken), ending with fresh fruit salad. If you eat à la carte, a meal can cost as little as 64F with service but not drink – or up to 100F for a banquet including half a bottle of wine at 25F. Subtle food and the most delightful service, according to our south-east-Asia buff. Open noon to 2:30 p.m., 7:00 to 10:45 p.m., closed Sundays and holidays. Annual closing not set as of this writing.

L'Espérance

---

9 rue de l'Espérance, 13e
Métro: Corvisart
Tel: 45 80 22 55

Don't be put off by the unprepossessing exterior of L'Espérance, or of the immediate surrounding neighbourhood. It's worth penetrating inside, and up the few steps to the restaurant itself where the atmosphere alters at once. The waiter makes you welcome, the other diners will smile at you and you can join in their conversation if you're so minded. And you won't believe the price: 38F50, including service and drink! You'll have a choice of starters such as leeks vinaigrette, herring or some other fishy dishes, then roast chicken, *limande* (flatfish), or a number of grilled meats, all with vegetables or spaghetti. For a supplement of 6F50, have the couscous. Desserts are fruit salad, fruit *tartes* or cheese including *chèvre* (goat's cheese). How do they do it? If you're looking for elegance, this is not the place for you. But it's a good place to have a satisfying meal before you go on to check out the music cafés and bars in the surrounding Butte aux Cailles. L'Espérance is open seven days a week, including holidays, Christmas and Easter, but closed (in 1989) from 1 to 20 September.

14e arrondissement

Crêperie de Saint-Malo

53 rue de Montparnasse, 14e
Métro: Montparnasse
Tel: 43 20 87 19

The rue de Montparnasse has always been rich in Breton restaurants, and this is one of the choicest. Despite its name, it's much more than a crêperie. Very 'sympa', and you can choose from three menus. Even the least expensive, the *Menu Forestière* at 56F50 gives you such choices as a salad of frizzy lettuce with chicken livers and bacon, then a Breton *galette* (a big flat pancake) wrapped round ham, cheese and egg or mushrooms, finishing with a crêpe with chocolate, honey or lemon. The Menu Marin at 58F50 offers a saucer of taramasalata, a smoked salmon or seafood *galette*, and sweet crêpes as above. For the top price of 68F50, luxuriate in *moules marinière* for a first course, or homemade fish soup, thick, delicious and partnered with a very good *rouille* – then grilled salmon with Béarnaise sauce, luscious grilled sardines in season or *dorade* (sea bream) – finishing with a sweet crêpe or crème caramel. Service is included in all prices, and Breton cider at 13F50 is a must. The Saint Malo is open 365 days of the year, from 11:30 a.m. to 3:00 p.m., and 6:00 p.m. to 2:00 a.m.

Mandarin des Vanves

10 boulevard Brune, 14e
Métro: Porte-de-Vanves

A dedicated flea-market shopper told us about the Mandarin, saying that it's the only place to go if you've been scuffling around the avenue Marc Sangnier on a Sunday (see p. 222). Go before 12:30

p.m., as this big, noisy, family place is packed after that. Menus are 45F and 65F including drink and service. The food is Vietnamese, Thai and Chinese, and comes in lavish helpings. On the more expensive menu, our friend ordered Nem (Vietnamese spring rolls with spicy sauce), and then had five main dishes to choose from, including red-cooked pork and chicken with mushrooms, accompanied by a heaped plate of rice with corn, beansprouts and strips of egg foo-yung. Desserts are fairly ordinary but after such a meal this hardly seems to matter. Open every day from 11:30 a.m. to about 10:00 p.m., but closed Sunday evenings. No annual closing. AMEX and VISA accepted.

Le Moule en Folie

5 rue du Maire, 14e
Métro: Edgar-Quinet

A seafood restaurant, all done up in blue for oceanic effect, a bit stilted and bourgeois and – like most Paris fish houses – not exactly cheap. But pleasant service and excellent food. *Soupe de poisson sauce rouille*, or *tomate aux fruits de mer* for starters; *truite meunière*, *sardines grillés*, or *moules marinière* to follow; and cheese, sorbets, ice-cream or *tarte au citron* to conclude. For lunch it's 69F, service included but not wine (18F for a half-litre of white, rosé or red). Open noon to 3:00 p.m., 7:00 to 11:00 p.m., and open every day of the year.

Au Vin des Rues

21 rue Boulard, 14e
Métro: Denfert-Rochereau
Tel: 43 22 19 78

This adorable little restaurant changes its menu daily, so we can only report on what Paris resident Gloria Girton greatly enjoyed on a hot summer's night. 'Wonderful mixed salad with crisp-fried duck skin and sautéed shallots' was 20F; and a plate of warm sausage with potatoes and salad 45F. If you are still able to eat another mouthful after all that, homemade sorbets and an extraordinary peach soup with mint, among other things, are 20F. Service is included, and an excellent Coteaux du Lyonnais red wine is only 9F for a quarter-litre. Without dessert, you'll be spending not more than 74F for a superb meal, in a very pretty room embellished with pictures, posters, maps and drawings. No tourists have yet found Au Vin, and we can't recommend it highly enough – it's hard by the lively and attractive rue Daguerre where a street market bubbles and sparkles. Lunch from 1:00 to 3:30 p.m.(!), dinner is served only on Wednesdays and Fridays from 9:00 to 11:00 p.m. On other evenings it's a wine bar presided over by the owner. Closed Sundays, Mondays, and August.

15e arrondissement

Bistro Bourdelle

12 rue Antoine Bourdelle, 15e
Métro: Montparnasse (use the Bienvenue exit)

A simple restaurant, with its own circle of *habitués*, oil-cloth covered tables, posters on the walls, a couple of tables outside in good weather, a cordial *patron*, and excellent, imaginative food. The two-course menu is 74F, and includes a number of salads to start (mushroom and cabbage, lentil salad, cucumbers in cream, salad with warm chicken livers, *fromage de tête*), followed by a *plat du jour* which varies daily, of *andouillette* in mustard sauce, *brochet quenelles* in Nantua sauce, steak in a choice of sauces, *boeuf bourguignon*. Desserts are extra at 26F, among them a favourite Floating Island, and chocolate mousse. A good house Côtes du Rhône from 12F to 15F. Lunch served from noon to 2:00 p.m., dinner from 8:00 to 10:00 p.m., closed Saturdays, Sundays, and an unspecified three weeks in August.

La Pomme de Reinette

48 rue Dutot, 15e
Métro: Volontaires

An old favourite, the Crêperie Dutot, has changed its name but is as attractive, friendly, and intimate as ever. While not the cheapest in Paris, it gives you blissful crêpes and the salads are large, varied, and beautifully presented. The 69F *formule* includes a crêpe with ham or cheese, or a salad with nuts and gruyère, then two pieces of steak which you cook yourself, and for dessert, a crêpe with sugar and lemon, or jam or chocolate. À la carte salads are from 36 to 48F. Drink is extra and expensive, and our spy advises leaving it out: beer is 15F and up, wine comes only in half-bottles with the least expensive at 28F. Service is included in the *formule* and à la carte prices. Open noon to 2:30 p.m., dinner 7:00 to 10:30 p.m., and later on Friday and Saturday nights. Closed Sundays and holidays, and from the beginning of July to the second week in August.

16e arrondissement

Le Jouvenet

1 rue Jouvenet, 16e
Métro: Exelmans-Chardons Lagache

Jonathan Gilbert comments 'I think this is my favourite of all the places I have recently been,' which probably makes it worth trailing all the way out to the Auteuil neighbourhood where otherwise every restaurant is either a) wildly expensive or b) Chinese-Vietnamese. It's tremendous value, as the menu for 60F, including service and all the wine you want to drink, provides a colossal table of hors d'oeuvres from which you can help yourself as many times as you like (Jonathan counted 27 choices, with many fish dishes among them); a rather limited but good selection of main courses which feature steak with various sauces; and admirable desserts such as fresh strawberries, caramel tart, apple pie and so forth. '9 out of 10', and thoroughly recommended. Open noon to 3:00 p.m., 7:00 to 10:00 p.m. Closed Sundays and the last two weeks of August.

Le Paris Passy

3 place de Passy, 16e
Métro: Muette

A Paris friend writes: 'Several people who know the area between the Eiffel Tower and the Trocadéro said that this was the only good restaurant there. Everything else is either wildly expensive, or really no good, or catering to tourists who have little choice. It's about 15 minutes' walk from the Métro to the Eiffel Tower, but worth the trip. It's very busy, and I found it somewhat lacking in friendliness. But you eat at tables in the courtyard, directly on the place Passy where you can watch the chic *habitués* of the neighbourhood go by, and the food is tasty and fresh.' A two-course menu is 56F including service; a good helping of *pâté* or *crudités*, then a *plat du jour* – one summer's day it was scrambled eggs with pipérade, the Basque sauce of red peppers, tomatoes and spices, or chicken or steak with crisp *frites*. If you want a dessert it will cost you 25F for an excellent warm apricot tart, which pushes the price up to 81F – not a great bargain but considered reasonable in this flossy area. Drink is extra, too, and expensive – 14F for a quarter-litre of wine, or a beer. The Passy is open without interruption from 7:00 a.m. to midnight, seven days a week and every day of the year including Christmas.

17e arrondissement

La Bonne Cuisine

17 rue Biot, 17e
Métro: Place de Clichy

Most restaurants in this Montmartre neighbourhood are to be shunned, as the cooking is usually indifferent, the prices nonsensical, the attitude toward travellers almost contemptuous. This one, also known as Jacky Loize, seems to be the exception. The menu at 68F including service is short but very good --green salad or soup to start with, then trout or a *faux filet* steak or lasagne, and *tartes* or cheese. Nominally, it's only served at lunch – evenings à la carte can run into real money – but two of our resident eaters says that they looked sad, asked nicely, and were allowed to have it at dinner. The atmosphere is sweet and nostalgic, you can imagine that the elderly man eating quietly in a corner has been there nightly for the last fifteen years. In décor – linen napkins, a rose on the table, gentle lighting – and conversation – film, music, politics – it's a world away from the sleaze of most Montmartois restaurants. Nice wine at 7F the quarter-litre. Open noon to 2:00 p.m., 7:00 to 9:45 p.m., closed Saturday lunch, Sundays, August and two weeks in February. Sometimes open on holidays, but it depends on the mood of the owners.

18e arrondissement

Un Africain à Paris

9 rue Marcadet, 18e
Métro: Marcadet Poissonière
Tel: 42 23 87 98

This is wonderfully exotic, a real North African restaurant, open only at night – and we have to say that it's near the top of our pauper's price range as everything is à la carte. But it's a real night out, with a 'kora' player to entertain you while you eat. Our friends who discovered it recommend lemon chicken, 49F, or spiced chicken, 60F, with superlative desserts such as iced chocolate mousse on a pool of crème de menthe, 30F. Service is additional at 10 per cent, and the least expensive drink is mineral water at 6F a half-litre, while wine is 15F a quarter-litre. Open 7:30 p.m. to midnight, Mondays through Saturdays. Open on holidays, closed one week in August – telephone first to find out which one.

Les Chauffeurs

11 rue des Portes Blanches, 18e
Métro: Marcardet-Poissonières
Tel: 42 64 04 17

Our reviewer, Gloria Girton, raved over this, probably the last true *restaurant des routiers* in Paris. The clientele are old people, young people, families, market shoppers and truck drivers. The *patron* tends the bar and the customers, his wife does the cooking, the sole waitress is efficient and friendly, and an ancient, well-fed spaniel watches over all. Enormous portions of very good food, served on long, oil-cloth-covered tables, elbow-to-elbow: busy enough to make booking ahead worthwhile. There is no *prix-fixe* menu, but 73F will send you out the door in delirium. To start, a duck-liver *terrine*, 14F, or perfect, fat, white asparagus in vinaigrette, 33F, or a mixed salad of lettuce, tomatoes, beets, onions, black and green olives in a mustardy vinaigrette, 12F. Then, cold roast beef, or steak with shallots, or roast veal with vegetables, in the 43F neighbourhood, or sole *meunière* for 52F. Finally, a choice of fresh fruit – cherries, peaches, bananas, strawberries – when Gloria was there; or homemade ice-cream (peach, with bits of fresh peach), or various *tartes*, all at 14F or less. A very good house red wine is 4F60, and service is included. And the bread, at noon, is still warm from the baker's. Perfect French *cuisine familiale*, and not to be missed. Open noon to 3:00 p.m. and 7:00 to 10:00 p.m., closed Wednesdays, Thursdays, Christmas, Easter, and New Year's Day, and all of July and August.

Restaurant Ephese

58 rue Doudeauville, 18e
Métro: Château-Rouge

As you may have gathered, our young student friends like to wander around unusual neighbourhoods; and David Gaines highly recommends this Franco-Turkish restaurant within walking distance of the boulevard Rochechouart (go there after you've prowled around Tati and the nearby rue Séveste and rue d'Orsel, bargain-hunting). It's small and friendly, and the food is delicious – lentil soup for 14F, or stuffed vine leaves, or taramasalata, then a very good brochette of lamb for 35F accompanied with couscous or rice or bulghur. After lavish helpings, our friends skipped the desserts, but commented that they're the usual rich sweets at about 15F. Service is included, drink extra – beer 10F, wine 11F, so a very satisfying meal was only about 60F or so. Open noon to 3:00 p.m., 7:00 p.m. to midnight, closed Sundays and Christmas, and for two weeks in mid-August.

Le Fait-Tout

4 rue Dancourt, 18e
Métro: Anvers, Pigalle

The rue Dancourt is a short street leading into the peaceful and pretty place Charles-Dullin, and it has several little restaurants. Le Fait-Tout (full name: À Napoli ... On Fait Tout) looks from the outside to be a run-of-the-mill pizzeria; inside it's simple, clean and pretty, with wooden tables and benches, flowers on tables. For 46F you can have a salad with walnuts, or *pâté*, or onion tart to begin, then roast chicken or pork, or lasagne, followed by cheese or a simple dessert. The 59F menu includes *frisée aux lardons* (a distinctive curly lettuce with thin bacon slivers), or fillets of herring, followed by lamb chops, veal, ray in pepper sauce, or superb steak in a choice of sauces – all in enormous helpings. Dessert might be profiteroles or frozen sugared orange stuffed with sorbet. Service is included, but not wine, which is 16F a quarter. Open noon to 2:30 p.m. and from 6:00 to 11:00 p.m. with no weekly or annual closing, and open on holidays.

19e arrondissement

Le Chaumont-Laumière

---

20 avenue Laumière, 19e
Métro: Laumière

This very French and very friendly neighbourhood restaurant is in the street that leads to the beautiful, quiet and relaxing parc des Buttes-Chaumont (p.164), and it's worth seeking out – especially because it serves breakfast from about 8:00 to 10:30 a.m.! The fixed price menu at 51F is extraordinary: *pâté* or garlic sausage or mackerel with potato salad are usually available as starters, then a wonderful dish of pork fillets with mustard sauce and mini-noodles, or rabbit, roast chicken, or an omelette *parmentier* stuffed with potatoes; orange pudding, fresh fruit salad among the dessert choices, or three kinds of cheese. Both wine (or beer or mineral water) and service are *included*, a rarity these days. For 65F the 'house couscous' with lamb, chicken and spicy merguez sausage is a special treat. The new owners have changed the name from Le Petit Laumière, but not the atmosphere or the friendly polite service. Open noon to 2:30 p.m. for lunch, 7:00 to 10 p.m. for dinner, closed Sundays and August. Open on holidays which fall in midweek.

'Le Self' – yes or no?

As the pace of Paris life becomes faster, self-service restaurants are proliferating, and they're a very good bet if you want to eat à la carte, inexpensively, and without the usual hour and a half over lunch. The great advantage of *les Selfs* is that if you have a fancy for making a meal of starters instead of a main dish, it's easy and cheap: ideal for vegetarians. The disadvantage is that if you let yourself go among the rather dazzling choices you can spend as much in a *Self* as in a prettier, more comfortable restaurant with some character.

The best-known *Selfs* in such fashionable venues as the rue de Rivoli and around the Louvre are distinctly *not* good value for money. They are over-praised, overcrowded and over-priced, and especially at lunchtime can be more of an ordeal than a pleasure.

However, there are some lesser-known *Selfs* which can be an agreeable surprise to anyone whose idea of a self-service place is based on McDonald's. Can you believe a meal that begins with avocado stuffed with shrimp (10F), goes on to steak *au poivre* with a heap of crisp *frites* (20F), and ends (if your liver holds out) with a *coupe chantilly* – fruit salad with whipped cream, at 9F. Add a quarter-litre of drinkable wine for 5F50, and a piece of bread, 2F, and the whole really luxurious meal comes to only about 46F. These were the most expensive choices in a really nice *Self*. The quality was higher than many neighbourhood restaurants could have provided on prix-fixe menus. In one good *Self*, a complete meal – starter, main course, salad, bread, dessert and wine, beer or mineral water – was only 42F, in a clean, bright, air-conditioned room.

Les Selfs are, on the whole, quite attractive though without much character in the decoration. At lunchtime, they are lively with chatter and laughter; quiet in the evening when those who eat there tend to be, as in any big city, people who haven't much else to do. Certainly they are worth trying, especially on a day when you are going to be extravagant elsewhere with museum entrance fees, cinema tickets or a spot of shopping. Try these:

Samaritaine

19 rue de la Monnaie, 1er
Métro: Louvre, Pont-Neuf

For lunch or snacks, in the big department store – go early and get a table near the window, for the astounding view across the river and over the city. The food is very good and reasonably priced. A steak with *frites* at 32F was tender and cooked just right, mushrooms in a spicy red sauce for a starter were good and the blueberry pie with whipped cream, 12F, pleased even an American friend in Paris.

Open 11:30 a.m. to 6:30 p.m., but the earlier the better at lunchtime as it gets very crowded and the best choices go early.

La Petite Bouchée

24 rue de la Pépinière, 8e
Métro: St-Lazare

This must be the classiest small 'Self' of Paris, a charming little room up the stairs from the useful snack bar Pomme de Pain. It is wall-to-wall with well-dressed young secretaries and office workers from the *quartier*, who are both value- and figure-conscious – many good salads for about 20 to 25F, well-prepared grills and vegetables. A three-course meal would cost about 48F. Open 11:30 a.m. to 3:00 p.m., closed Sundays.

Take-away – all of rue Huchette, rue de la Harpe, 5e

Métro: St-Michel

The centre of take-away food: almost every restaurant or storefront along these streets will treat you to delicious charcoal-grilled *souvlakia* (skewered lamb and vegetables) or *shawarma* (barbecued, thinly sliced spiced lamb), both in pita pockets. Walk a little further, and you find sweet Mideast pastries to eat from the hand. At various times we've enjoyed *sandwich tunisien*, with tuna, olives, tomatoes, peppers, lettuce drenched in a hot sauce and overstuffed into a hard roll at El Hammamet; and a giant *pan bagna*, a huge roll crammed with *salade Niçoise* at Au Gargantua. They'll cost between 14F and 19F wherever you find them. The names change constantly in these streets but the Mediterranean ambience and the good-natured, slowly meandering crowd are always present. You can eat all day long, from about 10:00 a.m. to midnight, every day except possibly Christmas or New Year's Day.

M. Benvisti

boulevard de Belleville, near rue Ramponeau, 20e
Métro: Belleville

Food in the extraordinary quarter called Belleville – the Arab and old Jewish Paris – is dealt with at greater length in 'Getting around', (pages 54–5). M. Benvisti is a Tunisian-Jewish take-away. You tell the cashier what you want, pay him, and then take a ticket to the counter where they make with great speed huge sandwiches crammed with tuna, olives, capers, cucumber, tomato, and a blazing hot sauce slopped over it for 18F. Ask for *sandwich tunisien* or have an *assiette tunisienne*, same things on a plate for 20F; plus *brik à l'oeuf* which is the delicious Tunisian pastry with fried egg inside, to eat at a sort of stand-up counter. Also available to take away: five kinds of olives, capers, hot peppers, everything to make a great antipasto lunch with a loaf of bread – and beautiful, very sweet Arab pastries. Open from about 10:00 a.m. to 9:00 p.m., closed Saturdays.

Ouvert le dimanche *(Open on Sundays)*

1er arrondissement

Auberge du Palais Royal (lunch only)
Le Galtouse
Le Stado

3e arrondissement

Le Drouot
L'Orée du Marais

4e arrondissement

Le Beautreillis (lunch)
Le Canaille (evenings)
Les Piètons
Le Pot (lunch)
Le Relais St Gervais
Le Trumilou

5e arrondissement

La Brouette (lunch)
La Fontaine St Victoire (lunch)
Le Pavé aux Herbes
La Trattoria (evenings)
Les Dégrés de Notre Dame
Taverne Descartes
All the take-aways of the rue de la Huchette, rue de la Harpe

6e arrondissement

Le Bistro de la Grille
Les Byzantins
Restaurant des Beaux Arts
Polidor

7e arrondissement

Au Ciel de Shanghai

8e arrondissement

Flora Danica
Galérie Point Show

9e arrondissement

L'Auberge du Père Louis
Chartier
Chez Maurice
9 Rue Choron
Pupillin
Picpain
Xavier Gourmet

11e arrondissement

Pho Dong Huong

12e arrondissement

Le Limonaire

13e arrondissement

L'Espérence

14e arrondissement

Crêperie Saint-Malo
Mandarin des Vanves (lunch)
La Moule en Folie

16e arrondissement

Le Paris Passy

18e arrondissement

Les Chauffeurs
Le Fait Tout

19e arrondissement

Most of Belleville

Ouvert en Aôut *(open in August)*

1er arrondissement

Auberge du Palais Royal
Chez Fernand (for two weeks)
Le Galtouse
L'Incroyable
Le Petit Ramoneur (until 20 August)
Relais du Sud Ouest (except for one week)
Le Stado
Au Vieil Ecu

2e arrondissement

Country Life
Le Drouot
La Maisonette (until 23 August)

3e arrondissement

Le Helium

4e arrondissement

Le Bar Cristal
Le Beautreillis (closed one week)
La Canaille (closed one weekend)
Le Chateaubriand (until 12 August)
Les Piétons
L'Orée du Marais
Le Petit Gavroche (dinner only)
Le Pot (lunch)
Relais Saint Gervais
Le Trumilou (closed 'a few days')

5e arrondissement

La Brouette
Les Dégrés de Notre Dame
Taverne Descartes
Le Pavé aux Herbes
La Trattoria
All the take-aways of rue de la Huchette, rue de la Harpe

6e arrondissement

Bistro de la Grille
La Bolée
Les Byzantins
Claude Valentino/Monteverdi
L'Ecaille de PCB
L'Enfance de Lard
Le Jouvenet (open first two weeks)
La Godesse (open first two weeks)
La Macrobiothèque
Marco Polo (open first two weeks)
Osteria del Passe Partout
Orestias
Polidor
Restaurant des Beaux Arts
All of rue de la Huchette, rue de la Harpe

7e arrondissement

Au Ciel de Shanghai

8e arrondissement

Flora Danica
Galérie Point Show

9e arrondissement

Auberge du Père Louis
Chartier
Chez Maurice
Taverne des Dauphins
Picpain
Pupillin
Xavier Gourmet

11e arrondissement

Bois et Charbons
Pho Dong Huong

12e arrondissement

Café Melrose's (until 15 August)

13e arrondissement

L'Espérance

14e arrondissement

Crêperie Saint Malo
Mandarin des Vanves
La Moule en Folie

15e arrondissement

La Pomme de Reinette (open last two weeks)
Le Jouvenet (until 15 August)

16e arrondissement

Le Paris Passy

18e arrondissement

Un Africain à Paris (open three weeks)
Le Fait Tout
Restaurant Ephese (open first and last weeks)

19e arrondissement

Most of Belleville

Les Spectacles
(Sights and Sounds)

The number one attraction in Paris is Paris. A little footwork can provide all the entertainment you need. Parisians have always relied on their feet for diversion – there's a Parisian art of strolling – the city is inexhaustibly explorable. For a few possibilities, see the chapter on 'Getting around' (page 37).

For incomparable theatre, there are the Parisians themselves. They dress distinctively, and carry themselves with a certain air: they have a highly developed vocabulary of gesture; their voices range from a croak to a twitter; they love to see and be seen. Almost any place will do for Paris- and Parisian-watching: park benches, Métro stations, the *zincs* in local cafés, outdoor markets. It's up to you to be receptive.

Should street-life pall, there are other, more organised entertainments – a surprising number of them free, or very cheap.

Paris parks

There are dozens of parks scattered through the city: tiny, intimate parks in the shadow of churches; parks that are 'wild' and rambling in a curiously artificial and very French way; vast, arid, formal parks consisting of gravel and neoclassical sculpture. All are meticulously kept. Here are a few (you'll find many more yourself):

Jardin des Plantes

bounded by the Seine and the rue Geoffrey-St-Hilaire, 5e
Métro: Jussieu, Gare d'Austerlitz or Place Monge

Part formal garden – minimal grass – part botanical station, with some lush peripheral areas. Contains the Natural History Musuem and the Ménagerie. The latter, like every other 'caged' zoo in the world is dismal, smelly, and to be avoided.

Parc de Monceau

boulevard de Courcelles, 8e
Métro: Monçeau

Large, full of artificial waterfalls and ponds, glades, romantic statuary. Like most upper-echelon Paris parks, good nanny territory. Two steps away, at 63 rue de Monceau (southern edge of the park), is the Musée Nissim de Camondo: an 18th-century mansion, preserved inside and out.

Square des Batignolles

directly behind Église Ste-Marie-des Batignolles, 17e
Métro: Brochant, and a fair walk

A charming, unpretentious park in a quiet neighbourhood, with duckponds and a population of elderly park-sitters. The low iron fencing along the paths resembles a lattice of bent twigs – a reminder of the French love for 'natural' artifice.

Parc des Buttes Chaumont

bounded by the rue Manin and the rue Botzaris, 19e
Métro: Buttes-Chaumont

This is a park which most tourists miss because it is so out of the way – a pity, because it is charming. Set on a hillside in the not very fashionable 19e, it was created by Baron Haussmann in response to his monarch's love for anything English. It was once a much more sinister place, where corpses blackened on the gibbet of Montfaucon in the Middle Ages; later a slaughterhouse for horses, finally a general rubbish-heap. Haussmann had the idea of making rock gardens *à l'anglaise*, and there it is, a perfect and peaceful park, only slightly twee.

It's rich in waterfalls, grottoes, rustic chalets, a fake-Greek temple, even fishponds (for which you need a permit from the gendarmerie). It's sixty acres of lovely strolling and picnicking ground, with a fresh breeze always blowing. If you have been in Belleville in the neighbouring 20e, and have collected a sandwich *tunisien* and a bottle of beer for lunch, get on the No. 26 bus heading towards St Lazare, step off at the Botzaris-Buttes-Chaumont stop, and find a sheltered grotto for lunch. Even the local dogs, which run to neatly-clipped poodles and brushed spaniels, have good manners, and despite the English look of the park, people walk lightly, if at all, on the tidy grass.

Bois de Boulogne

from Porte d'Auteuil to Porte Maillot, 16e
Métro: Porte de Neuilly, Porte Dauphine or Les Sablons

When Parisians say 'Le Bois', they are referring to this park. It's a 19th-century creation, roughly modelled on Hyde Park, at the suggestion of that passionate Anglophile Napoleon III. Its history as a green wooded space dates back centuries, to the days when it stood just inside the fortified boundary of Paris. It was a favourite duelling-ground until, and even after, that sport of the court was outlawed by Louis XIV. Now it is 2000 acres of beautiful, varied, country-like terrain: with one museum, two world-famous race courses, a small zoo, a rose garden, a polo ground, a 'Shakespeare Garden' where grow all the plants mentioned in his plays, two lakes, broad avenues for riding, paths for biking. One can literally live in the Bois – there are camping grounds for tents and caravans.

Of the Métros which serve the Bois, Les Sablons takes you closest to the charming Jardin d'Acclimatation with its little zoo and playground. And one of the most delightful of Paris museums is nearby: the Musée des Arts et Traditions Populaires. This is great for a rainy day; a compendium of everything from country crafts (butter moulds, bee-keeping), to games (*boules*, royal tennis) to bagpipes, Breton headdresses, lace, sixteenth-century toys – the list is endless.

Boats in the Bois can be hired by the hour, at an office near the Lac Inférieur, and the pretty little man-made islands can be visited. Take a picnic: and stay away from the restaurants, which are calculated for the rich.

The exquisite park of Bagatelle, within the Bois, is nearly 60 acres surrounding a fairy-tale palace, and in June it is a paradise of roses. Sir Richard Wallace, said to have been the illegitimate son of the Marquis of Hertford (and a passionate lover of Paris), lived here.

In the daytime the Bois is peopled with strollers, dog-walkers, kite-flyers, riders, cyclists, lovers, and dreamers. But at night it's a different story. Stay away. It's not romantic even in moonlight, and it's very, very dangerous. For years it was the pickup place for certain kinds of Paris prostitutes. The latest group of *les girls* turns out to be South American transvestites. Vandalism and violent crime have taken over the Bois at night.

Bateaux-Mouches

Glass-enclosed excursion boats glide up and down the Seine for about an hour, under various names but generically called Bateaux Mouches.

Bateaux-Mouches: from the Pont de l'Alma, right bank (*Métro*: Alma-Marceau), every half hour. From 10:00 a.m. to noon, then from 1:30 p.m. to 7:00 p.m., 20F. From 8:00 p.m. to 11:00 p.m. in the summer, 30F.

Bateaux-Vedettes Pont Neuf: from the Square du Vert-Galant on the Ile de la Cité, (*Métro*: Pont Neuf): every thirty minutes from 10:00 a.m. to noon, then 1:30 to 6:30 p.m. Evening cruises at 8:30 to 10:30 p.m. in the summer, 30F.

Cemeteries

A taste for these is not as macabre as you think (but it does help to go on a rainy day. If you're depressed, they're great places to wallow in despair). There are at least thirteen within the city limits. The best known, and the best for browsing, is **Père Lachaise** (you could win bets as to its real name, which is Cimetière de l'Est).

Bounded on two sides by the avenue Gambetta and the boulevard de Ménilmontant (*Métro*: Père Lachaise) it consists of 19th- and 20th-century tombs and sepulchres: some mouldering and decrepit; some sprucely cared for; some distinctly spooky; others – shiny granite and plastic photographs – very sentimental. Here lie

Colette, Proust, Wilde, Chopin, Hugo, Balzac, Piaf, Gertrude Stein. And Jim Morrison. On sunny days the cats come out to bask on the *tombeaux*. A map of the cemetery is 1F from the gendarme at the gate.

If you haven't exhausted your taste for the illustrious dead, your next stop should be the **Cimetière de Montmartre** in rue Caulaincourt, 18e; *Métro*: Place de Clichy or La Fourche. Contents: Dumas *père* (where is *fils*?), Stendhal, Berlioz, Frangonard, Baudelaire.

Open air markets

As you must have gathered by now, food is an object of worship in Paris. It's appreciated on the plate, and almost as much on the hoof. Paris abounds with open air markets where everything is displayed to perfection: fruits and vegetables placed just so; incredible conglomerations of fish and shellfish; poultry and game hung disconcertingly at eye level. There's nothing antiseptic about the markets, and nothing haphazard – the stall proprietors are there to sell (voices that can be heard streets away), and those who come to buy are determined to get the best. It's hard to know whether to look at the sellers, the clients, or the merchandise.

Street markets are liveliest on Saturday mornings, often open on Sundays before lunch, usually closed Mondays. Some of the best, although not best known:

rue de Lévis, 17e   *Métro*: Villiers
place Monge, 5e   *Métro*: Place Monge
rue de Belleville, 19e   *Métro*: Pyrénées or Belleville
   Sundays, 9:00 to noon
place d'Aligre, 12e   *Métro*: Ledru-Rollin
   A big covered market, with outdoor stalls and a flea market outside.
marché Sécretan, 19e   *Métro*: Jean-Jaurès
   avenue Sécretan, between
    place de Stalingrad and rue
   de Meaux, 19e.
More raucous and infinitely more real and interesting than the better-known ones; especially Sundays from 9:00 a.m. to noon.
rue de Buci, 6e   *Métro*: St-Germain-des-Prés
   Over-photographed, over-publicised, but still a knock-out. Prices tend to be high.

marché de la Madeleine, 8e   *Métro*: Madeleine or St-Lazare
At the bottom of an office building, this enclosed market is
entered from rue de Castellane between rue Tronchet and rue de
l'Arcade, and is a little world in itself. Tuesday to Saturday from
about 9:00 a.m. until about 6:30 p.m.; and a little, inexpensive
Tonkinese counter restaurant for lunch.

Window-shopping

Food

For museum-quality displays, go to Fauchon, *the* de luxe shop which
faces two sides of the place de la Madeleine, 8e (*Métro*: Madeleine).
Early morning is best, when the *terrines* and *pâtés* are arranged in
the window, the crayfish and lobsters set out. Unbelievable *gelées*,
pâtisseries, arrangements of bread, displays of wine, cheeses you
never dreamed of. On the opposite side of the Madeleine is
Hédiard – smaller, more compact, and just as expensive. Michel
Guérard, known for Nouvelle Cuisine, has a glamorous shop
nearby, and, unbelievably, a cafeteria.

Exquisite *pâtisseries* and *charcuteries* can be found all over Paris, in
the most surprising *quartiers*, some that are nearly slums. No one
hesitates to spend five minutes or more peering in the window,
choosing one pastry or a *tranche* of a wild boar *terrine*. One wonders
how all this intricately decorated food ever gets eaten, much less
prepared from day to day. A partial answer is the restaurant trade:
the thousands of restaurants large and small rely on the shops of
their *quartier* for the day's *terrines* and *tartes*. Somehow, Parisians
have overlooked the idea of mass-marketed, prefabricated victuals,
and they do seem to be happy in their ignorance.

Clothes

As you know, they are of vital importance to the French sense of
self-esteem and to their economy. The couturiers' windows are
accordingly magnificent. Whether sedate or outrageous, they
display their wares beautifully, imaginatively, both inside and in the
windows of the great houses. The smaller boutiques, too, have a
fresh and lively approach to display. The department stores,

however, in comparison to almost any American store and some English ones, are a dead loss – frozen in the display techniques of the 1950s. The only worthwhile window among them is the dome of the Galeries Lafayette, and that's spectacular.

Walk up the rue Royale, along the rue du Faubourg-St-Honoré, along the side streets and avenues of St-Germain-des-Prés, along the avenue Matignon, the avenue du Pierre-Premier-de-Serbie, the rue Boissy d'Anglas, and you come away reeling with the great inventive talent and daring of Hermès, Cardin, Chanel, Dior, St-Laurent, Givenchy. It costs nothing to look in the windows of Cartier, Bulgari, Van Cleef and Arpels, and unconsciously you are absorbing what makes for elegance, quality and flair.

Antique shopping

The pleasure of 'antiqueing' in Paris, too, is for the eye only. Prices are high and rising, as the rich take their panic money out of gold and put it into irreplaceable objects of beauty and luxury. So consider the time you dally in front of windows or in shops as part of your education in what constitutes value in craftsmanship and materials.

If you love antiques and want to see an incredible collection all under one roof, an obvious but good answer is Le Louvre des Antiquaires, in the place Palais Royal, 1er. This three-storey building is a mass of showrooms run by some of the best-known dealers of Paris. Unless you are conspicuously well-dressed, don't expect much attention or friendliness from the dealers: they know their customers, and are fairly sure as soon as they set eyes on you that you're not a prospect. (However, a rich friend with one foot in Oklahoma and the other in Eaton Square – in her jeans and ski-jacket – gave them something of a comeuppance one year when she bought an art deco table for 30,000F in cash, after having been ignored by the dealer for an hour and a half as she wandered around the room. Being wealthy and secure in herself, she bargained him down from 35,000F. It just shows.)

The back streets of the Marais, around the rue des Francs-Bourgeois, are beginning to be lined with elegant small antique shops, but here again you will find few if any bargains. Look, too, at the new Village St-Paul, in the rue St-Paul near the Seine (4e), a beautifully reconstructed cluster of grey stone mansions now housing some lovely shops. Then cross to the Left Bank, and wander around the side streets that make up the St-Germain-des-Prés area: rue Jacob, rue Furstenberg, rue du Bac, rue des Beaux Arts, rue de l'Université.

In the more rarefied reaches of the 7e, you'll find the Village Suisse – a collection of rather expensive dealers – at 78 avenue de Suffren (*Métro*: La Motte-Picquet), open Thursday to Monday, 11:00 a.m. to 7:00 p.m.

What is conspicuously missing in Paris is fine antique silver: much of the best table silver and decorative pieces owned by the aristocracy and the rich bourgeoisie were melted down to pay for the wars of Louis XIV, and most of what remained went into the fires of the Revolution. The few pieces that escaped are now in museums. You will now find that the best silver on offer is elaborate late-nineteenth-century work, a few fine Art Nouveau pieces – and more available – some of the chic, stark creations of the 1930s, at prices about one-third *more* than a London or New York dealer would charge. You may be lucky in a flea market or a small semi-junk shop, but don't bet on it.

Again, all this comes under the general heading of education. Remember, too, that if you find anything you like and can afford, and it's too big to go in your luggage, you will have to deal with shipping, insurance, customs, and collection at the other end, which can easily double the original price.

The flower markets

If it's not food, clothes, paintings that separate Parisians from the rest of the world, maybe it's their intoxication with flowers. The flower shops and stalls are fantasies of scent, colour, life, and the sort of instinctive flair for arrangement of even quite humble flowers that is absolutely French. The markets are found on the Ile de la Cité, at the back of the Madeleine (8e, *Métro*: Madeleine), and at the place des Ternes. The first two are thick with tourists in high summer, but don't let that deter you. The place des Ternes is well off the tourist beat and has a fine street-market as well as flower stalls. A few blossoms in a water glass or Perrier bottle will cheer up your hotel room.

Plants: walk along the quai de la Mégisserie, 1er (*Métro*: Pont Neuf), if you want to see how the French approach the whole question of gardening, with an emphasis on window-box plants, kitchen and herb gardens, small-scale city adornment. One of the great seedsmen of Europe, Vilmorin, has a big shop here. A packet of real French basil grown from their seed seems to have a special flavour which may be more in the imagination than in reality (but check to see if your country allows you to import seeds). A Paris-wise pauper bought a little pot of chives and kept it in her very humble hotel room for two weeks, using it to liven up salad lunches and cream cheeses when she was having a more than usually broke period. Weekdays only.

Ducks, deer, swans: also on the quai de le Mégisserie are the caged animals, birds, tortoises, domestic and wild fowls – which can break your heart. Two swans in a cage; a miniature deer for some rich child's private zoo; even the chickens are pitiable..Don't look.

Museums

Paris glories in the existence of nearly a hundred museums: from the largest in the world (the Louvre) to one of the most specialised which displays only the crystal of Baccarat. Many are in the area of central Paris (see museum map, pages 274–5), others within half an hour's travel on the Métro, bus or RER express lines. Some are small and exquisite and so highly specialised that in their best week they get no more than a dozen visitors. Some are great private houses now open to the public, worth seeing even if you didn't look at the contents. One of the most extraordinary, the Musée Nissim de Camondo, is a frozen slice of eighteenth-century France, created by the grieving parents of a First World War hero. Still another has an enticing collection of mechanical toys and clockwork gadgets. There are not one but *two* modern museums in Paris, while poor London struggles on without any.

Many of the major Paris museums are free or half-price on Sunday. Some give discounts to students (an International Student Identity Card helps) and to those under or over a certain age. Details under each museum mentioned. If you're under 18 or over 60 (women) or 65 (men), show your passport and ask for *demi-tarif* which cuts museum charges in half. Two elderly friends of ours were admitted free to the Petit Palais on production of passports.

It's true that almost every museum charges an entrance fee, and if you are a conscientious pauper used to the generous free musuems of Britain, this comes as a shock. Brace yourself, do without lunch if you must, but either pay the sum asked or wear yourself out on Sundays. You will be rewarded in every sense by the thrill of the beautiful, the odd, the heart-warming or the blood-chilling.

Most museums close on Tuesdays, a few on Mondays, some both days. A few are open on public holidays but most are closed. All are near a Métro stop or within five minutes' walk. All have free cloak-rooms (obligatory) for carrier bags, umbrellas, briefcases, but they won't take anything that holds money, jewellery, passport or camera. Some let you take photographs, some forbid flash equipment. Check for rules when you go, as they change from time to time.

Most Paris museums, as one would expect from the general French attitude towards civilised comfort, have benches or chairs on which to fall when your feet, eyes and mind give out. The attend-ants on the whole give good directions as to what's where, and will do their best to answer questions in English. They have eyes in the backs of their heads and voices that when raised can cut like a laser beam. Don't touch, don't breathe on, don't put a finger near the surface of a painting or a sculpture unless you are prepared for a loud metallic French shout.

Be prepared to queue for admission to the Louvre, and to the Musée d'Orsay (Impressionists, Post-Impressionists), and to any major exhibitions which may be open. For these, take along a thermos of coffee and sandwiches to sustain you: for the Manet exhibition at the Grand Palais in 1983 and the Renoir show of 1985, people stood for three hours in cold, rain or heat before they could even get to the ticket window. This can leave you too exhausted to enjoy what you came to see. Sometimes queues are shorter at lunchtime, or when an exhibition has just opened and is not yet highly publicised.

One way to beat the queues is the fairly new *Carte Musées et Monuments* which gives you free entry to the dozens of museums and historical sites in Paris. It costs 50F for one day, 100F for three days, 150F for five days – these last two must be used on consecutive days. You'd get your money's worth if you are a real museum buff and can cope with three or four a day; and it allows you to bypass queues, enter by 'group admission' doors, and sail past the ticket offices. At the Louvre, for example, you don't stand in the endless line inching toward the new Pyramid, but go to the escalator in the arcade leading from the Palais Royal Métro, normally reserved for groups. Work out for yourself whether the convenience is worth the money. We think the three- or five-day investment is a better buy. Our thanks to Howard Rye of London, who used the *Carte Musée* with pleasure and profit.

The museums listed and described in this section include our own personal guide to the lesser-known ones as well as the more popular leaders.

1e arrondissement

The Louvre

Métro: Palais Royal, Louvre

Hours: 9:00 a.m. to 6:00 p.m. Wednesdays to 9:45 p.m. Closed on Tuesdays.

Admission: 25F; 13F for 18-25s and over-60s; under 18 free.

The Pyramid! It's been called 'an architect's megalomania', 'a magical machine', 'violation of the historic Louvre', 'a triumph of the imagination', and a litany of phrases ranging from violent denunciation to ecstatic praise. Go and see for yourself. It is now the main entrance to the museum, and is attracting queues of the curious. This elegant airy structure is 71 feet high, surrounded by three baby likenesses. It has freed many of the superb rooms from the clutter of ticket-windows, postcard racks, gift shops and whatnot. Access to the museum's unbelievable treasures is now astonishingly easy, and you could spend half a day playing with the computerised information service below the pyramid.

Perhaps the best thing is that as you move out of the high-tech underground entrance hall, you find the great crypt, revealed during the excavations, which now displays the original walls of palaces of past centuries. Beyond that, the Louvre stretches for ever. It's still in process of being transformed, and in the years to come more rooms will be opened, more wonder revealed. At the moment, so many things are going on in what Mary Blume of the *International Herald Tribune* once called 'the uncomfortable, dingy, distinctly user-unfriendly Louvre' that it's almost impossible to sum it up here.

Obviously, if you had but one day in Paris (or one lifetime), the Louvre would be the one indispensable museum. The Big Three (Winged Victory of Samothrace, Venus de Milo, Mona Lisa) may have been over-exposed, but you must see them, at least on your first visit. A guided tour, booked in the entrance hall, could be a good way to learn your way around: after that you'll find your own personal treasures, the Poussins, the Chardins, the Rembrandts, the Egyptian hoard, the Italian primitives.

A sophisticated Parisian recommends sauntering around the Pyramid, hoping to see the daring Alpinistes who abseil around it to clean its glittering panes (apparently little account was taken in the planning for the ravages of rain, dirt, city pollution and seagulls); but says that after your first visit, if you're in a hurry to get into the Louvre, make for the Pavillon de Flore, westward of the main block (Métro: Tuileries), or for the entrance on the Quai du Louvre. And be wary of a very hot or very cold day at the Pyramid: there is neither shade nor shelter as you wait for security checks and single-filing into the entrance, and in summer the sun beats down relentlessly on the entry-level platform before you descend to the gloriously-lit *sous-sol*. Apparently, the great central pillar in the Pyramid was meant as a base for the Winged Victory, but cooler heads prevailed.

The Louvre itself is set on the site of royal palaces that date back to the twelfth century, and stretches over acres along the Seine. Much of the present structure is 'new', as things Parisian go. Both the great Napoleon and the later, lesser Louis-Napoleon had a hand in building or reconstructing. François I was the first royal collector – or looter – in the sixteenth century. He picked up trifles like Giottos, Leonardos, Veroneses on his way through Italy and Spain.

The incredible Egyptian collections owe their existence to the Napoleonic campaigns. Louis XIV housed most of his 'finds' at Versailles, but after his death they were dispersed, some to the Luxembourg Palace but most to the royal palace of the Louvre. After 1798, the Louvre became the Central Museum of the Arts of the infant republic, and was almost at once opened to the public.

This is a sketchy description of what may be the world's greatest museum: to do it justice the rest of this book would have to be dropped. Go early in the morning, go often, leave before you develop visual fatigue. Remember that if you are lucky you will return to it many times in the future.

The Jeu de Paume

place de la Concorde, 1er
Métro: Concorde or Tuileries

By the time you read this book, the lovely little Jeu de Paume may have reopened – redecorated and re-planned – with new treasures to show. In recent years it had become intolerably crowded, almost impossible to see its matchless collections.

The treasures of the Jeu de Paume have migrated to the sumptuous new Musée d'Orsay, and for the moment the old tennis court is empty. After renovation – possibly by the end of 1989 – the Jeu will house major temporary exhibitions.

The Orangerie

place de la Concorde, 1er
Métro: Concorde

Hours: 9:45 a.m. to 5:15 p.m., every day except Tuesday and major holidays.

Admission: 15F; 8F on Sundays.

A hundred yards closer to the Seine from the Jeu de Paume, this is a museum with (so far) no queues. It houses the Guillaume-Walter collection, mostly early 20th-century paintings, reflecting the highly personal choices of Mme Walter and her two husbands (Paul Guillaume and Jean Walter). There are fourteen ravishing Cézannes, some fine Picassos, many Derains and Soutines, some unusual Douanier Rousseaus – and areas of creamy, satiny, plushy Renoirs. Certainly worth seeing – many critics hated it; those who find out about it seem to love it. The great Monet water-lily paintings in the Salle des Nymphéas are not to be missed.

The Museum of Decorative Art

107 rue de Rivoli, 1er
Métro: Palais Royal

Hours: 12:30 p.m. to 6:30 p.m., Wednesday to Saturday; closed Mondays and Tuesdays. Sundays 11:00 a.m. to 6:00 p.m.

Admission: 20F; 14F reduced price for students.

A magnificent collection of furniture, tapestries, arts and crafts, books about the decorative arts. It often has fine special exhibitions (early 1981, for example, a show that started with the Middle Ages, took in Art Nouveau and Deco, and ended with modern furniture).

3e arrondissement

Musée Carnavelet

23 rue de Sévigné, 3e
Métro: St-Paul or Chemın-Vert

Hours: 10:00 a.m. to 5:40 p.m. Closed Mondays.

Admission: 15F, free on Sundays. Half-price for students. Free for over-65s. These prices may change for special exhibitions here.

The Bicentenary year of 1989 saw a long-overdue renovation of this exquisite 17th-century building which houses the museum of the City of Paris. Once the home of Madame de Sévigné, it has been extended and joined to its next-door neighbour, the Hôtel Le Peletier de Saint-Fargeau. All the history and beauty of Paris right back to Roman times is beautifully displayed here – with a most remarkable feeling that it has all been assembled by one ardent collector. A fantastic collection of revolutionary artefacts is in the Le Peletier house – fans, buckles, proclamations, warrants for arrests and executions; drums, flags, Louis XVI's razors, Napoleon's travelling toilette set, the little notebooks of the imprisoned Dauphin. Beautiful period rooms have been reconstructed throughout both buildings; don't miss the Art Nouveau room from the old Café de Paris, and a 1920s ballroom.

4e arrondissement

The Conciergerie

1 quai de l'Horloge, 4e
Métro: Hôtel-de-Ville

Hours: 10:00 a.m. to 5:30 p.m., every day.

Admission: 22F weekdays, 12F Sundays, holidays.

Don't go unless you feel fairly strong. Deep in the huge and pretty formidable Palais de Justice, the Conciergerie puts the Terror of 1789 right at your throat. No matter how you feel about the pre-revolutionary aristos, the sight of Marie Antoinette's cell, and the rooms where philosophers, writers, artists and the nobility waited for death, cannot leave you unaffected.

Beaubourg: Musée National d'Art Moderne

Centre National de l'Art et de Culture George Pompidou, 4e (this mouth-filling title is usually shortened to *Beaubourg*)
Métro: Hôtel-de-Ville, Rambuteau

Hours: Noon to 10:00 p.m. weekdays, 10:00 a.m. to 10:00 p.m. Saturdays and Sundays, closed Tuesdays.

Admission: 33F; 17F for 18-25 years, and over-65s. Sundays free. A pass for the entire Beaubourg centre for the day is 45F and lets you enter the museum and all the other shows that otherwise charge separate fees. An annual pass to Beaubourg is 90F, reduced to 65F for those under 18 and over 65 years of age.

A dazzling collection of every important modern painter of the twentieth century. Sit down from time to time to rest and stare, because these paintings aren't meant to soothe the eye or the spirit. Beaubourg itself is like a great museum on its own, and much of it is *free*, including the escalator that snakes up the front of the building and gives you an unmatchable view of the city. But the *small* escalator that leads to the big one is narrow, short, and often jammed with queues that even crowd the huge entrance courtyard.

5e arrondissement

Musée de Cluny

6 rue Paul-Painlevé, 5e
Métro: St-Michel

Hours: 9:45 a.m. to 12:30 p.m., 2:00 to 5:15 p.m. Closed Tuesdays.

Admission: 15F weekdays, 8F Sundays.

Utterly fascinating medieval monastery buildings which now house one of the world's great collections of arts and crafts of the Middle Ages. Spurs, chastity belts, sculpture, ivories, bronzes – and, except in the high summer months, almost empty of visitors. Often you find yourself in a small dark room staring at some endearing little object that no one has bothered to document or catalogue. And of course, the high point is the haunting tapestry series called, collectively, La Dame Aux Licornes. Bonus: when your feet finally give out, you can hobble a hundred yards to any of twenty inexpensive and good restaurants on and around the boulevard St-Michel.

7e arrondissement

The Invalides

Esplanade des Invalides, 7e
Métro: Invalides, Latour-Maubourg, École Militaire

Hours: 10:00 a.m. to 6:00 p.m.

Admission: 23F; 11F50 for students and *Carte Vermeil* holders. This ticket entitles you to all three of the museums and to Napoleon's tomb, and can be used on two consecutive days.

The Invalides is a catch-all name for the complex of museums which deal primarily with Napoleon, but also with everything to do with French armies from the shot-torn battle flags of Louis XIV to more modern armour. Napoleon's tomb, under the dome of the Invalides, is majestic, solemn, and always surrounded by a silent, circling group. In summer there's usually a son-et-lumière production. Two performances a night, in English 9:30 p.m. and 11:15 p.m., 23F

Musée d'Orsay

1 rue Bellechasse, 7e (at the quai Anatole France)
Métro: Chambres des Deputés or Solférino

Hours: 10:30 a.m. to 6:00 p.m. except Thursday, 10:30 a.m. to 9:45 p.m. Closed Mondays.

Admission: 23F; 12F for students and seniors; 12F for everyone on Sundays; under-18s free.

Built for the Great Exhibition of 1900, the old, derelict Gare d'Orsay has been joyously transformed into a palace of 19th- and early 20th-century French art: Ingres and Delacroix, Daumier, Moreau and Degas; Manet, Monet, Renoir; Seurat, Redon, Toulouse Lautrec; Bonnard, Vuillard and Vallotton . . . the entire contents of the Jeu de Paume, with generous helpings of the Louvre and the Palais de Tokyo, are ranged among three floors of galleries and halls. The light is for the most part natural – filtered through the glass roof – and the internal architecture has a curious King Tut's Tomb effect – at once airy and monumental, in muted tones of grey. It's a stunning success.
Hang onto your ticket, you can go in and out of the museum as often as you like in the course of one day.

Musée Rodin

77 rue de Varenne, 7e
Métro: Varenne

Hours: 10:00 a.m. to 5:00 p.m. Closed Mondays and Tuesdays.

Admission: 16F; 8F on Sundays.

This old and beautiful house in a rather pompous part of Paris holds many of Rodin's most superb works – their power and vigour fairly bursts the walls. More sculpture in the remarkably beautiful garden. And a place to eat in the museum. A nice Paris touch: on the Métro platform at Varenne, life-size reproductions of the greatest Rodins, and some small ones in a dramatic spotlit glass cage.

8e arrondissement

Musée Nissim de Camondo

63 rue de Monceau, 8e
Métro: Villiers

Hours: 10:00 a.m. to noon and 2:00 to 5:00 p.m. Closed Mondays, Tuesdays and holidays.

Admission: 15F; 10F for under-18s and over 60s; 10F on Sundays.

Very quiet: most tourists pass it by, which is their loss. A museum dedicated to the memory of a young aviator shot down in the First World War, which sounds both dull and depressing. Not so. His father, a wealthy art collector, recreated the interior of a house as it would have been done by an 18th-century tycoon. French furniture, *objets d'art*, then were of a luxury and perfection seen nowhere else in the world, and there they are, gleaming with care, love, and polishing, and waiting for the minuet to begin.

Musée du Petit Palais

avenue Winston-Churchill, 8e
Métro: Champs-Élysées-Clemenceau

Hours: 9:45 a.m. to 5:00 p.m., closed Mondays.

Admission: 15F; free for under-18s and over-60s. 8F on Sundays.

This museum, also often neglected by Paris visitors, has some fine works bequeathed by private collectors – beautiful Manet pastels, Berthe Morisot, Mary Cassatt, Toulouse-Lautrec pastels, Bonnard, Vuillard, Cézanne – and historic French furniture, bibelots, clocks and so forth. The peaceful, flowering circular garden is usually deserted; a good place to rest, read, meditate. However, they courteously discourage picnicking so don't try it. Often there are fine temporary exhibitions: check *Pariscope* or street posters.

10e arrondissement

Musée de la Publicité

18 rue de Paradis, 10e
Métro: Château d'Eau

Hours: Noon to 6:00 p.m. Closed Tuesdays.

Admission: 18F; 10F for the unemployed, for students and *Carte Vermeil* holders or over-65s with passport. The ticket admits you to their little *cinémathèque*.

The poster museum has now widened its scope to include all forms of advertising (signs, prints and cinema and TV ads). It sells reproductions of historic French advertising posters, and good postcards. Its own *affiches* are well worth buying for the pure pleasure of the graphic design – something the French have been doing with wit, flair and irony for decades. The admission charge is steep, and the museum is small, so don't go unless you're really interested. The building itself is interesting and you can see *that* free of charge!

12e arrondissement

Musée des Arts Africains et Océaniens

293 avenue Daumesnil, 12e
Métro: Porte Dorée

Hours: 10:00 a.m. to 12:30 pm., 1:30 to 5:30 p.m. every day.

Admission: 22F; free for under-18s. 13F Sundays.

It's worth trailing all the way out to this fairly remote part of Paris to find an almost unknown treasure. The arts of black Africa – bold statements in wood, bone, leather, brass – the delicate beauty of carvings and leather from Muslim North Africa – and some gem-like artefacts from the Pacific islands colonised by the French. Poster collectors: don't miss the museum's own magnificent *affiche*.

Musée Guimet

6 place d'Iéna, 16e
Métro: Iéna

Hours: 9:45 a.m. to noon, 1:30 to 5:15 p.m. Closed Tuesdays.

Admission: 15F weekdays, 8F on Sundays.

The exact opposite of the Beaubourg Modern Museum: calm, soothing Far Eastern art. The Asiatic Art Collection of the Louvre, and worth return visits if you can afford it – save money with picnic lunches on these days. Japanese and Chinese masterworks, irrep-laceable sculpture from parts of Cambodia that have vanished for ever in wars, art of India and Pakistan, and an important exhibition on Japanese Buddhism. All rooms open Monday, Wednesday, Friday, but some are closed other days.

Musée Marmottan

2 rue Louis-Boilly, 16e
Métro: La Muette, and about ten minutes' walk through a park

Hours: 10:00 a.m. to 5:30 p.m. Closed Mondays.

Admission: 25F; 10F for students and over-60s.

Worth the high price only if you are a Monet fan. Beautifully organised permanent collection, plus many paintings by his artist friends and contemporaries. Often there is an additional exhibition of great interest – check *Pariscope*. Don't miss the touching collec-tion of letters and postcards to friends and patrons, a haunting record of difficulties, illness, lack of money.

Musée Moderne de la Ville de Paris

11 avenue du Président-Wilson, 16e
Métro: Iéna

Hours: 10:00 a.m. to 5:30 p.m., closed Mondays. Open until 8:30 p.m. Wednesdays.

Admission: 35F; 20F for students and over-65s. Prices may change for special exhibitions.

Much of the Musée Moderne's contents have been moved to the Musée d'Orsay, across the river on the quai Anatole France, and to Beaubourg – but there is still an impressive permanent collection on exhibit, and it installs great temporary shows: retrospectives, private collections, and thematic exhibits. This is the place to find cubist, fauve and École de Paris paintings. Check *L'Officiel des Spectacles* for current events.

18e arrondissement

Musée de Montmartre

12 rue Cortot, 18e
Métro: Lamarck-Caulaincourt
Montmartrobus

Hours: 2:00 to 6:00 p.m. weekdays, 11:00 a.m. to 6:00 p.m. on Sundays. Closed Mondays.

Admission: 20F; 10F for students and over-65s.

An 18th-century house crammed with souvenirs of the legendary artists' quarter. The Toulouse-Lautrec posters may have been reproduced on cheap paper a million times, but the originals can still stop you in your tracks. Many drawings, relics, and costumes of the days when Montmartre was a place to be enjoyed, not where one is ripped off as at present.

This list of museums, of course, is the merest scratching of the surface. We have missed out (but you don't have to) such esoteric delights as the Musée Bricard (locks and keys from Roman times to the 1950s), some as fine and intricate as jewellery), the Delacroix and Balzac houses, the Victor Hugo Museum in the place des Vosges, the Grévin (waxworks to make Mme Tussaud melt with envy), and a great crazy one devoted entirely to the art of the counterfeiter. If you can read French and want details of every museum in Paris and the surrounding area, get the brochure *Musées, Expositions, Monuments de Paris et de l'Ile de France,* published every two months by CNHMS, Hôtel de Sully, 62 rue St-Antoine, 4e (*Métro:* St-Pual), and often available from the Tourist Office at 127 Champs-Élysées.

Galleries ·

Welcoming and forbidding, worthwhile and not to be bothered with. One of the best ways to refresh the eyes without paying entrance fees to museums, or trying to get to all the main museums in the one inexpensive day (Sunday).

Most of Paris's galleries are to be found in the avenue de Matignon, the boulevard Haussmann, the rue Miromesnil (establishment art, for the most part, in the 8e), and near Beaubourg and the area around St-Germain (progressive, experimental). Most galleries hibernate in August. Check *Pariscope* or *L'Officiel des Spectacles* for specifics. A few possiblities:

Daniel Templon

30 rue Beaubourg, 3e
Métro: Arts-et-Métiers

Contemporary abstractionists, with emphasis on big American names.

Beaubourg

23 rue du Renard, 4e
Métro: Hôtel-de-Ville

Contemporary European realist painters and sculptors.

Zabriskie

37 rue Quincampoix, 4e
Métro: Rambuteau

Pioneer photography gallery: Arbus, Brassai, Steichen, Strand, Weston, and newer work.

Claude Bernard

5-9 rue des Beaux Arts, 6e
Métro: St-Germain-des-Prés

Contemporary realists, including Bacon, Hockney, Wyeth; and a strong collection of twentieth-century greats.

Dragon

19 rue du Dragon, 6e
Métro: Odéon

Surrealists, current and traditional.

Galerie de Seine

18 rue de Seine, 6e
Métro: Odéon

Contemporary surrealists and abstractionists.

Denise René

196 boulevard St-Germain, 7e
Métro: Bac

Contemporary abstractionists, kinetic art.

Artcurial

9 avenue Matignon, 8e
Métro: Franklin-D.-Roosevelt

Huge complex of galleries: established artists from Max Ernst to David Hockney.

Galerie Maeght

13-14 rue de Téhéran, 8e
Métro: Miromesnil

Large and *very* prestigious.

Cultural centres

You can take advantage of nationalistic self-promotion by attending free, or almost free, events at various cultural centres. Some are dull beyond belief; others – among them the ones listed here – are full of life, even explosive.

Centre Culturel Américain

261 boulevard Raspail, 14e
Tel: 43 21 42 20
Métro: Raspail

Concerts, courses and spectacles, exciting and well organised, with emphasis on the contemporary.

Centre Culturel Britannique

9-11 rue de Constantine, 7e
Tel: 45 55 54 99
Métro: Invalides

Lectures, films and concerts, and a good library. Closed Saturdays and Sundays.

Centre Culturel Canadien

5 rue de Constantine, 7e
Tel: 45 51 35 75
Métro: Invalides

Art galleries, a sculpture garden, a library, and an auditorium for concerts. Monthly children's concerts. Admission free. Closed Sundays.

Centre Culturel de la Communauté Française de Belgique

7 rue de Vénise, 4e
Tel: 42 71 26 16
Métro: Les Halles, Rambuteau

Theatre, films, concerts, art shows and dance -- burgeoning activity, from 5F to 30F.

Centre Culturel Latino-Américain

6 rue des Fossés-Saint-Marcel, 5e
Tel: 43 36 56 04
Métro: St-Marcel

Exhibitions, concerts and conferences.

Institut Néerlandais

121 rue de Lille, 7e
Tel: 47 05 85 99
Métro: Bac

Classical music concerts, and Dutch jazz and contemporary music. Free. Closed Mondays.

Centre Culturel Portugais

51 avenue d'Iéna, 16e
Tel: 47 20 86 84 and 47 20 85 94
Métro: Étoile

Classical music concerts.

Centre Culturel Suédois

11 rue Payenne, 3e
Tel: 42 71 82 20
Métro: St-Paul

Exhibitions, concerts, theatre, film – usually free

Goethe-Institut

17 avenue d'Iéna, 16e
Tel: 47 23 61 21
Métro: Iéna

German music, film, and art.

   Check also (if your interests run in these directions) the cultural centres of Yugoslavia, Egypt, Mexico, Spain, Italy, and Brazil. They're all in the phone book.

Concerts

The French are not the most musical nation on earth, and the dearth of classical music in Paris seems to be worrying quite a lot of people. Compared to London, New York, Manchester, Chicago, Cleveland, it's a bit of a desert. The 'major' composers rank as minor compared to Germans, Austrians, Italians. French popular music is unoriginal, not even a good copy of American or English. But there is music to be found, and more of it every year. Much of it is vastly overpriced, but we've tracked down a number of concerts that are either free or very nearly so.

In churches

You can hear some of the finest organ music in the world, played in the incomparable settings of Paris churches, often on Sunday afternoons, and it's free. For current listings, check the magazine *Pariscope*, published every Wednesday (3F).

Maison de la Radio

An orchestra organised by the French National Radio Service (ORTF) often gives free, or very inexpensive, concerts. For details, send a self-addressed stamped envelope to Radio France, 116 avenue du Président-Kennedy, 16e. Or drop in and see what you can find out. *Métro*: Ranelagh or Passy.

Métro music

Classical music students at the Conservatoire National are encouraged by their teachers to learn to perform, not just to practise, and a very good way for them to do so is to pick a spot in a Métro corridor and play for the passers-by. It's a neat way to pick up some change, too. The quality is often exceptionally good, although the acoustics may leave something to be desired. Some fairly good Irish bands, accordionists, provincial flute-and-drum ensembles, and even expatriate American blues and jazz singers also make use of the Métro, and are not to be sneezed at (they're impossible to ignore, anyway).

Beaubourg

The cobblestoned vastness in front of the Georges Pompidou Centre, 3e (*Métro*: Hôtel-de-Ville or Rambuteau) often plays host to musicians of very good standard, mixed in with the mimes and fire-eaters.

Rue de Provence, 9e

Of all unlikely places, a pedestrian square between Au Printemps, the department store, and Prisunic frequently has chamber groups, soloists, or blues or pop singers performing to people sitting on the steps of the nearby church. *Métro*: Havre-Caumartin.

Discounts

Student discounts: reduction in ticket prices for classical music in the big concert halls is usually available. Check listings in *Pariscope*, or apply with student card to COPAR, 39 avenue Georges-Bernanos, 5e (*Métro*: Port-Royal).

Senior citizens: with the *Carte Vermeil*, which the French generously provide for women over 60 and men over 65 of any nationality, discounts for musical events are given. See page 230 for details of this marvellous card. Look for the initials 'CV' in the price listing of any event. Or show your passport at the box office.

Free music – a typical week's offerings*

Festival of the Golden Muses of Paris: young, talented musicians in the parc de Choisy

Music at the Louvre: soprano and piano in the new Louvre Auditorium

Fête de Musique à l'Hôtel de Sully: a whole afternoon of concerts in one of the historic mansions of the Marais

Jacqueline and Jean-Pierre Carrière, pianists, playing two-piano classics at the Institut Hongrois

The Rosamonde Quartet at the Grand Théâtre, boulevard Jourdan

The American Boys' Choir, American Church, quai d'Orsay

Music of the Middle Ages, at the Église Saint-Merri

Festival de la Butte Montmartre, Musée Montmartre

---

* *Pariscope* and *L'Officiel des Spectacles de Paris*, out every Wednesday, list all the musical events of the week. Look for the words *Entrée Libre* or *Gratuit*, which means you.

Spectator Sports

Racing

If you can resist betting, a day at a French track with the sun shining, the crowd shrieking and stamping on losing tickets, is an experience not to be missed. You'll also see some very classy animals, hot competition, and a mix of people from working class to the truly elegant racehorse owners and followers.

The two racecourses at the southern end of the bois de Boulogne are enchanting. **Longchamps** is by all odds the smartest and most modern. It's the world's longest track, and said by horsey people to be one of the most difficult. The Prix de l'Arc de Triomphe and the Grand Prix are the great social events – go very early if you hope to get in. However, on other days, go for the fun, and the beauty, and try to refrain from betting as, unless you really understand the monumentally complicated French system, you may find that in the end you didn't have your money on the horse you chose at all.

To get to Longchamps, take the Métro to Porte d'Auteuil, then the special bus which costs 9F (*Paris Visite* and RATP tickets not valid). Inside the Bois, on the bus route, you will see several gates marked *Pelouse*; entrance here is to the infield, standing among the crowd, and costs 5F. If you stay on to the gate marked *Pesage*, you enter the grandstand which costs 20F weekdays, 35F Sundays and holidays, for unreserved seats on wide bare stone steps. Take a newspaper to sit on, they're dirty.

Here, we recommend splurging on a 20F entrance fee, as the surroundings are beautiful and comfortable, and you can follow the knowledgeable to watch the horses from above the saddling enclosure behind the stands. Take the lift to one of the towers marked 'Restaurant Panoramique' for a most lovely view over the course and the park, and some extremely posh lavatories, free.

Racing at Longchamps goes on from early April to October.

Auteuil, the other racecourse in the Bois, is for steeplechasing, and gets a very mixed crowd (i.e. pickpockets). If you can get there for the Prix des Draggs in early summer, it's one of the best almost-free sights of the world. Admission to the *pelouse* is 5F. Grandstand admission is 15F on weekdays, 25F on Sundays, special prices for big races.

Vincennes, in the Bois de Vincennes at the other end of Paris, is another city track, this time for trotters, which look like something out of Degas. There's daytime racing all year around; night racing from the end of March to the first week in December – a great way to spend a spring or summer evening. Don't believe anyone who tells you it is a ten-minute walk from the Château; it's fifty minutes dusty or muddy foot-slogging. Get there by RER to Joinville-le-Pont (free with your *Paris Visite*, or a 4F ticket), then about fifteen minutes' walk.

The **Hippodrome** at St-Cloud is reachable in either of two ways: quickly by RER to Rueil station, then by bus 431 to the stop 'Laboratoire Débat' for the *pesage*, or 'Champ des Courses' for the *pelouse*; more slowly, the Métro to Pont de Sèvres, then bus 431 to the stops as above. St-Cloud is the place for flat-racing, a lovely track which attracts lots of fashionable people and famous horses at certain classic races. Last week in February to end of July, then from late September to the end of November.

Tennis

Tennis generates immense interest in Paris: quite a lot of tournaments with some of the world's great players competing. The scene changes so fast that it is impossible to make an accurate listing here, so check the newspapers if you are really that interested (or bored with what Paris itself is offering). The Stade Roland-Garros (*Métro*: Porte d'Auteuil then – during major tournaments – special buses to the stadium) is world famous, but the prices are high, especially for big events, so don't say you weren't warned.

Cinema

For many film buffs, France leads the world in appreciation of the cinema, and Paris leads France. No matter what your taste in films – recent release, art-house, cult movie, retrospectives, Third World – some cinema in Paris will be showing it. *Pariscope* and *Officiel des Spectacles* have complete listings. 'V. O.' means the film is shown with its original sound-track (and so its original language). 'V. F' means a French sound-track has been dubbed in.

A big difference in cinema-going is that in France, the usher who shows you to your seat should get a tip – 1F or so per person.

Circus

The circus is having something of a revival in Paris – a great place to take the kids when walking around Paris palls. One of them actually offers a whole day with the circus artists who will show you rehearsals in the morning, then sit with you at lunch, and perform the full spectacle in the afternoon.

The listing below is necessarily provisional, as places, times, and dates change with the seasons and circuses come and circuses go. Check with *Pariscope* or *Le Figaro* for up-to-date listings. Fortunately, you don't need to understand or speak French to enjoy these spectacles.

Circus Alexandra Franconi

parc de Saint-Cloud
Tel: 46 02 84 14

Tickets 50F and 60F for grown-ups, children 30F and 40F. Performances Wednesdays, Saturdays, Sundays, and holidays at 3:00 p.m.

Cirque de Paris

corner of avenue Commune-de-Paris and avenue Hoche, Nanterre (it's in the suburbs, and you get there by RER to Nanterre)
Tel: 47 24 11 70

Here's where you can spend the day with the circus people, if you telephone first. Performances Wednesdays and Sundays, 3:00 p.m.

Cirque Pauwels

square du Serment de Kouffra, 14e
Métro: Porte d'Orléans

Performances Wednesdays, Saturdays, Sundays and holidays at 3:00 p.m. Tickets from 40F to 80F.

Puppets

Marionetterie, if there is such a word, is a very old French art, and although the shows are nominally for *les jeunes*, parents and hangers-on love them too. These are a few current at the time of writing: have a look at *Pariscope* for up-to-the-minute listings.

Marionettes des Champs-Élysées
Rond-Point des Champs-Élysées, at the corner of avenue Gabriel and avenue Matignon.
Métro: Champs-Élysées-Clémceau, Franklin D. Roosevelt

The guignol horror show that has entranced kids for ever. Tickets 9F. Wednesdays, Saturdays, Sundays, holidays at 3:00, 4:00 and 5:00 p.m.

Marionnettes du Ranelagh
Jardins de Ranelagh, avenue Ingres, 16e
Métro: Muette.

Wednesdays, Saturdays, and Sundays, 3:15, 4:15 p.m. Tickets 7F50.

Marionettes de Montsouris
avenue Reilles-rue Gazan, near the lake
Métro: Cité Universitaire, Glacière

Tickets 10F. Wednesdays, Saturdays, Sundays, 3:00 and 4:00 p.m.

Théâtre Guignol Anatole
parc des Buttes Chaumont, 19e
Métro: Laumière

Tickets 7F. Wednesdays, Saturdays, Sundays, holidays, 3:00 and 4:00 p.m.

Théâtre de la Petite Ourse
Tuileries Gardens, 8e
Métro: Concorde
Tel: 42 64 05 19

Wednesdays, Saturdays, Sundays, about eight different shows from 3:30 to 5:15 p.m.

Note: Paris is extremely rich in children's theatres which do magic shows, straight plays and pageants. Often there are extra perform-ances during Christmas and Easter holidays. Some theatres close for five to eight weeks during the period mid-July to mid-September, so it's best to refer to the current *Pariscope* for last-minute information. Two of the best which usually have something going the whole year:

Cité des Sciences et de l'Industrie
30 avenue Corentin-Cariou, 19e
Métro: Porte de la Villette.

Closed Mondays.

Musée en l'Herbe
Jardin d'Acclimatation in the Bois de Boulogne, 16e
Métro: Sablons

Wednesdays, Saturdays, Sundays at 3:00 p.m. Tickets 30F which gives you entry to a theatre performance and the museum itself.

Television

French TV is *very* French. If your hotel has a set in the office, breakfast room or lobby, linger and look. When a big soccer match, race or (best of all) the Tour de France, is on, make for the nearest TV dealer and join the crowd which will stand there for ever with boos, whistles, groans and some racy French language. The TV news *speakerines* are chosen for intelligence and wit – they sparkle – eyes, teeth, lipstick and intellect – in the hard brilliant studio lights.

Paris, plus

Versailles

Some of the most alluring places to visit are within an hour or two of Paris by public transport or by fast train. It would be almost illegal to be in Paris and not to see Versailles. This vast complex of parks, palace, and the pavilions known as Les Trianons, is almost impossible to comprehend when you are on the spot. It's wise to collect and study a good small guidebook before you go. The *Blue Guide* has a very good, succinct and easily followed section on the château, the park and gardens, and if you have already invested in it you really won't need another book. Versailles is easy to reach, and if you have the time to do it, go for a few hours three or four times, rather than wearing yourself out mentally and physically by one long visit.

You can reach Versailles free with your *Paris Visite* (outer zone only), Métro to Pont de Sèvres, then bus 171, but it takes about an hour. RER line C5; every fifteen minutes and takes about half an hour, but be prepared for long queues at the ticket windows, and make sure you go to Versailles Rive Gauche (RG), nowhere else. *Aller-retour* (return) tickets cost 22F; make sure you get both tickets when you buy.

Half-day all-inclusive tours, by coach, including transport, entrance to major attractions, and guide, are 165F from many ticket agencies, but in our view to be avoided. You are shoved through at a brisk trot, told where to look, never allowed to lag or sit down, and returned to Paris more dead than alive. You can do the whole thing at your own pace for half the price.

The main treasures of Versailles – the Chapel, the State Apartments of the King and Queen, and the Hall of Mirrors – must be seen by every visitor. The fee for them is 16F, reducing to 8F if you are between 18 and 25 or over 60. Under 18, it's free. On Sundays, everyone gets in for 8F – but NEVER go then, as queues for tickets can stretch half a mile.

The King's Private Bedroom and the Royal Opera can be seen only by guided tour, for 25F, lasting an hour and a half ... the guides are wonderful. After the tour, you can see the State Apartments, the Chapel and the Hall of Mirrors by yourself without paying more.

The Queen's Private Rooms and Madame de Maintenon's Apartment are guided tours too, one hour for 20F, after which you can see the rest, as above.

The Grand Trianon costs 12F, but combined with the Petit Trianon it's 15F.

The Lenôtre gardens carved out of the swamp, and the Mansart fountains, a marvel of hydraulic engineering, are 'musts'. If you can visit more than once, don't miss two of the smaller delights: the Musée des Voitures, with its perfectly preserved state coaches, wedding carriages and hunting calèches; and the extraordinary Hameau, the rustic village where Marie Antoinette went on playing at being a country wife up to 1789.

Guided tours of the Versailles Park and Grounds are available; information from the Versailles Tourist Office, telephone 49 50 36 22.

The Château and the Grand Trianon are open Tuesday through Saturday from 9:45 a.m. to 5:00 p.m., the Petit Trianon 2:00 to 5:00 p.m. only. Everything is closed on Mondays and public holidays.

Chartres

Again, it can be done by taking a fairly pricey tour bus, which gives you cosy shepherding; or, cheaper, more fun, and infinitely more flexible – take the train from Gare de Montparnasse as early as you can and wander round on your own. They run about every 45 minutes from 6:26 in the morning, with the last train back at 10:53 at night. Return fare is 100F.

Wander around the town, which is a delight in itself, and absorb the miracle of the cathedral by yourself, through your own eyes, and not blurred by tour-guide patter. Then find a small neighbourhood restaurant, which will be half the price and twice the pleasure of any suggested by an organised group, and eat what you want at a price you want to pay. Or take a picnic. Get a small, good guidebook to Chartres before you leave Paris, and read it on the train. Henry Adams, the 19th-century American writer, did rather a good job on both Chartres and Mont-St-Michel.

A coach tour to Chartres costs about £23, takes 5 hours (and since it's 88 miles from Paris, travelling time eats into Chartres time); it gives you a view of Rambouillet and Maintenon châteaux on the way, and a guided tour of the cathedral. Various companies do tours on different days, so check with a travel agent for details.

The Monet Gardens – Giverny

A coach tour to the famous water-lily gardens of Monet costs about 125F from Paris for half a day – don't do it, as the bus trip out is intensely boring and the commentary more so, with piped music all the way back. Instead, take the train from St Lazare to Vernon for 70F, and bus to Giverny, pay about 15 to 20F for admission to the house and gardens, wander freely, picnic, and come back when you choose. The ponds and bridges and flowers are *exactly* as they were painted.

Mont-St-Michel

Once a month, the RATP (Paris Transport) runs a day trip to this dream-like mountain village rising from the sea. It's not very expensive, it's all in French, and it's an experience you'll never forget. Coaches leave at 7:00 a.m., and it's a long day. Get brochures about this and other day trips from RATP, 52 quai des Grands Augustins, 6e (*Métro*: St Michel).

Malmaison

A curiously neglected side trip from Paris, except among those who are passionate about Napoleon. This is the château bought and furnished by him for Josephine, set in most lovely grounds. Nearby is a museum crammed with Bonaparte memorabilia. Take the RER from Charles-de-Gaulle-Étoile to La Défense, five minutes away, then the 158a bus to the Malmaison-Château stop. Buses run about every fifteen minutes and take about 25 minutes to the bus stop nearest the château, then it's about an eight-minute walk.

The RER station at the Charles-de-Gaulle-Étoile *Métro* stop is huge, eerie, depopulated, and if you get lost you'll find yourself asking directions from a weary flower-seller. If you have a *Paris Visite* (outer zone), travel on the RER and the suburban bus line is free. Otherwise, take a ticket from the automatic dispenser (one way). Follow signs marked "St-Germain-en-Laye" for trains to La Défense. On the 158A bus, the fare is one ticket.

Entrance to the château is 12F (6F for *Carte Vermeil* and under 18, free on Wednesdays), and you can't wander around: when a little group has collected, a guide appears. The tour takes about an hour and a quarter, it's all in French, so if you are a true Napoleon fan, read the very good entry in the *Blue Guide*. At the end of the tour (which tells you more than you want to know about the history of the porcelain plates and the very banal paintings), give the guide one or two francs. The château is unexpectedly small for such a great man (and the beds are tiny); but for those who expect Napoleon to rise from the dead and take over France, it's very touching. Open 10:00 a.m. to 12:30 p.m., 1:30 to 5:30 p.m. (last visits noon and 5:00 p.m.), closed Tuesdays, public holidays.

À bon marché
(The shops)

What are paupers doing shopping anyhow? Generally speaking, you've got a much better chance of picking up bargains in your home territory. Still, there are things that the French and French shops do better than almost anyone else. And if we have to put a label on what that *je ne sais quoi* is, we'd say it was attention to detail. So you'll find it in the cut of clothes, or the choice and display of foods, or in accessories for you or your home. With space and weight of your luggage in mind, we'd suggest small things that show individuality – if you wear specs, look at French frames; or think about replacing your watch, or buying a new fountain pen, or finding just the right piece of jewellery, or tie or belt. If you're a seamstress, look at the vast range of buttons. If you're houseproud, this could be your chance to buy the door-knobs or finger plates that will make the difference to your home.

Shopping is distinct from window-shopping, though you can combine the two. What you crave in Lanvin or Kenzo can be duplicated or approximated elsewhere at a discount; or found 'once-worn'. You can use Paris to stock up on often outlandish items of food: pickles and conserves that would cost a mint in Soho, available for next to nothing at the Prisunic. Second-hand books, cheap but thrilling gifts, museum prints, and every kind of flea-market hand-me-down. But remember, you've got to fit it all into your luggage and get it home.

Manners: as everywhere, you can go farther and faster on a few elements of *la politesse* and a smile. In some situations, however, no amount of manners will do you the least bit of good. Salespeople in large establishments tend to be more abrupt than in small ones, less willing to help. Solution: know what you're looking for; find out the correct terms (the name of the article, the colour, the size, the brand); do not be browbeaten into buying something you don't want; if one person won't tell you where to find it, try another.

Avoid paying with anything but cash. A bank will always give you a better exchange rate than a shop (or for that matter, a hotel or restaurant) for traveller's cheques or foreign currency. Credit cards are billed at the going rate on the date of billing, not the day you used the card, so you'll have only a rough idea of what you spend.

Bargains

Here we include cheap shops – not resale. Paris is a mine of good clothes at less than Paris prices – if you know where to look. The rue St-Placide in the 6e is lined with shops plastered with signs: *Dégriffés, Soldes Permanents, Les Prix Dingues*. The rue St-Dominique, in the 7e, is a magnet for bargain hunters. However, be warned that shops in both these streets have a mushroom growth and disappear just as fast. A big vacant shop can be stocked up with clothes for men, women and children, from various sources, do a roaring trade and vanish in six months or less. Le Clef des Soldes was a biggish place in the rue St-Dominique a few years ago, specialising in deluxe ready-to-wear for men and women (Cardin, Hechter, etc). Then it went completely over to sports and ski-wear, the next year it was gone, and now it's back, full of racks and bins.

This listing is the current crop of good cheapies, all over Paris. Don't write us a letter of reprimand if they've disappeared. We would rather have a letter from you telling us of *your* discoveries, so that we can look them over ourselves and possibly include them in a future edition.

These shops can be fun to fish around in. They often have bins of oddments, or racks of clothes that can be just what you are looking for (equally good chance of nothing but monster coats and dwarf dresses). With patience you can turn up something.

6e arrondissement

rue St-Placide

Métro: St-Placide, Sèvres-Babylone
Bus: No. 96

Hours: mostly Mondays through Saturdays, 10:00 a.m. to 7:00 p.m.

Antoinette: no. 7

Noted only because on our latest look, there were racks of pretty Liberty print blouses for 199F. What might they have now?

Mouton à Cinq Pattes: nos. 8, 10 and 16

Once a single 'rummaging' shop, this has spread in recent years. No. 8 at the top of the road now has the more expensive designer-label clothes, though some of the clothes were cheap enough – T-shirts 69F, jackets 199F, sleeveless T-shirts 45F. No. 10 has children's clothes, some with the Mouton's own label; and No. 16 has the bins and racks and boxes in which the dedicated bargain-hunter might just find the buy of the season. Suits were 399F, raincoats 299F, Katharine Hamnett sun-dresses 199F and jackets 350F. There were big cardboard boxes with everything – skirts and trousers – for 50F. Open 10:00 a.m. to 7:00 p.m., Tuesdays to Saturdays, closed Mondays (these hours can change, so be patient).

Bali Balo: no. 12

Perhaps not a bargain shop, but if you're in the street anyhow, look in for Hermès-style bags for 299F, as well as a range of back-packs and shopping bags.

Mission Impossible: no. 14

On our latest visit, the shop had almost nothing but suede and leather-wear – leather mini-skirts in all sorts of colours were 99F. But there were also T-shirts and shorts suits at 59F, and vest-type T-shirts at 39F.

King Soldes: no. 24

Another small shop, but with pricier and smarter suits and jackets.

IULE: no. 31

A new arrival on the street. A small shop which had French Connection T-shirts at 40F and jackets at 125F.

Philomème: no. 34

This is one of the few shops in this super-shopping street that has survived under its own name for years. Once it specialised in women's raincoats, but on our last visit the stock was more general. Best value were shirts and skirts at 99F.

La Braderie: no. 36

La Braderie seems to be able to find the unusual. Our shopper fell for some silk-and-cotton mix blouses, beautifully tailored in the prettiest pastel colours, for 129F. And they also had French Connection T-shirts for 29F and 39F, and sun-dresses for 159F.

Moda Soldes: no. 45

A shoe shop lined with boxes of men's and women's shoes, including Yves St-Laurent and other designer styles, all at discount.

L'Annexe: no. 48

Inexpensive and for the most part fairly well-made men's casual clothes: jackets from 69F, shirts 119F. VISA, Mastercard and American Express cards accepted. Open 10:00 a.m. to 7:30 p.m. Monday through Saturday, but sometimes inexplicably closed.

Au Train Bleu: no. 55

A big shop with several floors of toys and games and models, but the only place our shopper has come across that sold a hexagonal chess set (three sets of chessmen play on a hexagonal board).

Magic Soldes: no. 60

Mostly cheap kids' clothes, but some good oddments for women such as a rack of French Connection cotton casual dresses for 69F.

Jock Soldes: no. 62

Another shop worth looking at if you're mooching down the street. They usually have at least one good thing on offer. Currently cotton short-sleeve shirts at 180F for two.

7e arrondissement

rue St-Dominique
Métro: Latour-Maubourg
Bus: No. 69

Once a centre of bargain shopping, the rue St-Dominique has been 'gentrified' in the last few years. A few old favourites are still there, and it is a busy, cheerful street. So:

Toutes Griffes Dehors: no. 76

No longer a 'rack and bin' shop, the stock is now pretty up-market. Ted Lapidus, Pierre Balmain, Ng, Gaston Jaunet, neatly arranged, some at half price, others only 10% off.

Le Clef des Soldes: no. 99

This is the hardy perennial of the rue St-Dominique. It may move from one side of the road to the other, but it's still in business. Full of racks and bins of men's, women's and children's clothes. Bathing suits in the latest cuts and colours were 79F, women's trousers (by Pierre Cardin) were 149F, men's polo shirts 79F. Upstairs they have sports clothes. Nike running shorts and vests, for instance; or tennis shorts for 99F. They have a notice board for personal ads in the entrance, worth a look if you need a baby-sitter, or just for the fun of seeing what's what.

Centrale des Griffe Couture: no. 101

A discount store for men's clothes, end-of-line and overstock designer clothes by Yves St-Laurent, Daniel Hechter, and Ted Lapidus for example. And shirts, ties, polo shirts, trousers, blazers . . .

Stock Sacs: no. 109

Not a big shop, seen from the street, but the inside is packed with all sorts of small leather goods, handbags and luggage. They don't mind browsers, but if you are looking for something specific, they'll tell you if they have it, or if they expect other colours in that style.

9e arrondissement

boulevard Haussmann
Métro: Havre-Caumartin

If you're a serious shopper, this would be a good area to get your bearings. There's Galeries Lafayette, Au Printemps, Prisunic, Monoprix and even Marks and Spencer – all within one fair-sized block. And there are discount and specialist shops tucked away behind and between these giants.

Au Printemps

no. 64, at rue du Havre

Go on a Saturday and enjoy the fun of the stalls outside this elegant department store – but go inside as well to admire the vast range of goods and the building's architecture. If for any reason you should want a lampshade for a candle (it fits over the top and sinks as the candle burns), here is where you will find it. But you'll also find a set of six cocktail glasses for 39F, and see a very good selection of what's in fashion. Men have their own shop, Brummel, just behind the main store.

Parallèle

rue Joubert, corner of rue de Caumartin

Behind Au Printemps, there's a pedestrianised area facing the Église St-Louis. Parallèle is one of the discount shops lining these streets, selling Naf-Naf jumpsuits for 199F and jackets for 399F.

Jigger

58 rue Caumartin, and 56 and 66 bis rue de la Chaussée d'Antin

And while you're in the pedestrian area, see what's on offer at Jigger, from T-shirts for women at 39F, shirts from 50F up, and ever-changing stock of inexpensive and fashionable clothes, even dresses for about 100F. Around the corner in the rue Chaussée d'Antin, there's more to select from in two more Jiggers. All open 10:00 a.m. to 7:00 p.m., Mondays through Saturdays.

Prisunic

rue de Provence

The enterprising Prisunic chain is the French, very French equivalent of what Woolworths once was – but there the resemblance ends. You can buy a light-bulb, saucepans in high-fashion colours, food-processors and waffle makers; and smartly dressed Parisian girls and young men have been known to find 'the' wildly-coloured striped jersey, or a reasonable copy of a couturier silk scarf done in a silk-look polyester for only 42F, and shoes from trainers to velvet espadrilles.

Check out the food department for herbs, mustards, wines, olive oil flavoured with basil – eighty-five kinds of cheese – and pâtisseries. The cafeteria serves quick snacks, pastries, coffee or wine at half the price a brasserie would charge. Open 9:00 a.m. to 7:30 p.m., closed Sundays.

Tissus Bouchara

corner of rue Charras

Next door to Printemps, this huge shop sells fabrics. When we were last there, they had Indian cottons in summer colours at 50F a metre, and silks at 70F! Linens were 165F a metre, and cheerful ginghams only 16F. They also sell buttons, zips, threads, paper patterns – everything you need.

12e arrondissement

Square: 26 rue Charles Baudelaire, 12e
Métro: Ledru-Rollin

Not far from the market in the place d'Aligre. A funny little shop with a window sign 'T'as la Fripe Chic! T'as le Look Choc!' which translates roughly, as 'Get cheap rags for the look of chic-shock'. If you are a 'Retro' fan – clothes from the 1950s and 60s - this is the place to find a stiffly-boned ball dress for 150 to 500F, or a man's dinner jacket from 250F, real sailor tops for women, 80F, a lot of new or very slightly used cheapies. A good place for leisurely shopping, then take a picnic from the nearby market to the charming park across the street. Open Tuesdays to Saturdays from 10:30 a.m. to 1:00 p.m., 3:00 to 7:00 p.m., and Sundays 10:00 a.m. to 1:00 p.m. Closed Mondays.

18e arrondissement

Childebert: 14 rue Custine, 18e
Métro: Château-Rouge

This is an astounding place. Its walls are lined with *closed* shoeboxes, set up according to size in narrow aisles. Each box is labelled by type of shoe and colour, and you'd be surprised at how quickly you pick up the code. 'TB' means low heels (*talon bas*), 'TH' means high heels (*talon haut*), 'moc-marron' means 'moccasin-type, chestnut brown', and so on. One quarter of the shop is for men, one quarter for handbags, the rest for women's shoes. It's jammed, uncomfortable, and fun. To give you an idea: Charles Jourdan shoes were 400F, roughly one-third the London price. Open Mondays 2:00 to 7:00 p.m., Tuesdays through Fridays 10:00 a.m. to 1:00 p.m. and 2:00 to 7:00 p.m., and Saturdays 10:00 a.m. to 7:00 p.m. without lunchtime closing. Closed the middle two weeks in August.

Rue Séveste – Rue de Steinkerque

Métro: Anvers or Barbès-Rochechouart

Between the boulevard Rochechouart and the Butte Montmartre there's a warren of streets given over to discount clothes, shoes, luggage, fabrics. Many of the goods are Third World imports, but if cheap and cheerful is what you want, the choice here is vast. The rue Séveste is a street market, with stalls along the road.

Tati

4-28 boulevard Rochechouart, 18e

At the Barbes-Rochechouart end of the road, this complex of big, untidy and very cheap shops deserves a small book of its own. One of a chain, this Tati is heaven for those who have the time and the knack of picking through racks, shelves, and bins of clothes at prices so low you think they've misplaced a decimal point. Divided into several shops: **Tati Hommes** for men, **Tati Femmes** for women, and especially good value, the children's shop.

Jordy

36 boulevard Rochechouart, 18e

Up-market (compared to the rest of the neighbourhood), but still inexpensive. Men's shirts and suits, sometimes very convincing fake-leather jackets, what you find here depends on the season – some are good buys and others very questionable quality, so use your common sense. Open 9:30 a.m. to 5:00 p.m., Mondays to Saturdays.

Club Rochechouart

50 boulevard Rochechouart, 18e

Unexpected, in this very raffish street which is lined with cheaper than cheap shops. A fashion editor told us about the Club a number of years ago. It has some very smart clothes for women, few of a kind, and you may have to go back several times to find what you want. A striking black 'kite-shape' dress, probably a quick copy of something in the current couture world, was 345F, less than you'd pay for a run-of-the-mill dress in a chain store. And there were summer suits in flowery fabrics for 299F, or in plain colours, 199F. Open Monday noon to 7:00 p.m., Tuesdays through Saturdays 10:00a.m. to 5:00 p.m. Open in August, and VISA cards accepted.

Sympa

corner of rue de Steinkerque and boulevard Rochechouart, and on rue d'Orsel

Every spare inch is taken up by rails or series of bins through which you have to sort to find clothes at ridiculous prices. Kookai T-shirts, Lycra swimsuits, cotton leggings, cycling shorts, underclothes, children's wear. This is for those who have the time and patience to have a leisurely browse through. Around the corner, the next Sympa shop had briefcases, bolsters, pillows, shoes of all kinds, and tacky kitchen knicknacks. You could find a pair of plastic sandals for 10F, shoes for about 50F, a suitcase to carry home all those impulse purchases for 100F. Open 10:00 a.m. to 7:30 p.m., Monday through Saturday, open in August.

Dalya

rue de Steinkerque

Worth having a rummage around for inexpensive casual clothes which will last you a summer, a skirt for 60F for example, or a thin T-shirt for 35 to 40F. Open 9:30 a.m. to 7:00 p.m., Mondays through Saturdays, and open in August.

Paname

rue de Steinkerque

A small shop, but have a look. Best buy last time were Naf-Naf cotton T-shirts and leggings for 199F.

Bonnes Éstoffes

rue de Steinkerque

Less crowded than Sympa or Tati, and with a more sober range of clothes (for men, women and children) but still at bargain prices. Raincoats, suits, jackets, swimsuits. A fully-lined Madras cotton jacket was 240F.

Tissus Laik

1 bis rue de Steinkerque

Start here at the shop with the sign T.A.M. and work your way around the neighbourhood – rue d'Orsel, rue Briquet, rue Séves-tre – you'll find some good French fabrics. Stock changes rapidly, but last time we saw linen at 99F a metre, and all colours of Lycra, and fun fabrics like net with flock motifs. And there are upholstery and curtain fabrics capable of being transformed into clothes. M. Laik, like many others, keeps his shop open 9:30 a.m. to about 6.45 p.m., Tuesdays through Saturdays, and closes in August.

Second hand

If you think all the pretty girls of Paris who carry Vuitton bags and wear Charles Jourdan shoes buy them on their salaries, you've missed one of the great features of Paris: the many shops that sell slightly used couture clothes, expensive bags, and such telling accessories as silk scarves and art deco jewellery. The rich women who buy at the couturiers often wear their clothes only five or six times before turning them over to a resale shop – and this is Paris, not in the least like Madame's Dress Agency in the high street: no timid little coats with tired rabbit collars.

If you're lucky, you can find a timeless black wool Chanel suit (last year's model, but who's to know) for about 2500F, roughly one third its original price, lined with pure silk, trimmed in classic Chanel style. Or a fine polished leather handbag for 250 to 450F, instantly recognisable as having started life on the rue St-Honoré.

More rarely, you can find superb men's clothes and beautiful, expensive children's clothes.

Some of these shops have been going on for years, and have well-established connections not only with the elegant women of the *quartier*, but with the couturiers themselves: often you will find evening dresses that have been worn only in the seasonal collections, or shoes that have only walked on carpeted runways. They are almost always model sizes (for which read tall and thin), and the shoes are apt to be narrow. If your taste runs to the extreme of fashion, these shops can be a joy. But it takes time and the patience to return several times if you don't find your little Yves St Laurent treasure at first visit. Most of the shops are closed on Mondays, have a clearly posted sign (in French) about their policy on returns or exchanges, and some of them have salespeople who speak English of a sort. Many close in August.

Almost all clothes are legibly labelled with price (and sometimes with original price). In the few that we found where each garment did not have a price tag, we had the feeling that the owner of the shop matched the price to the customer: in which case, feel free to raise your eyebrows, say something like *'Un peu trop cher'* (a bit too expensive), and put the garment back on the rack. This tip was passed on by a friend who brought the price of a Christian Aujard dress down from the (oral) asking price of 420F to a bargain level of 330F. Keep a steady nerve and be prepared to leave the shop without buying anything. Check seams, hem, buttons, linings in men's suits and coats, insides of shoes and handbags, and point out any weak spots which might bring the price down. In every resale shop we checked, the merchandise was in superb condition – having been cleaned, brushed or polished before being put on view.

These vendors of de luxe merchandise sometimes have a few rails of women's and men's clothes that come from the better French ready-to-wear manufacturers at the end of a season – special purchases in small quantities. They're often worth going through carefully, as the colours, fabrics, and general air of Parisian smartness – masculine as well as feminine – will delight you when your Paris visit is only a memory.

Some 'resale' shops spring up hopefully in fashionable parts of Paris, buying fairly ephemeral clothes from the young and capricious. By their nature, these rather tentative shops may not be very long lived, as their survival hangs on their supply of customers to bring in clothes as well as to buy them. It is hoped that all the addresses below will still be in business for a while: they are the best-established and most trusted by the more fashion-minded of our Paris friends. But don't lose your cool if you find they have moved or gone out of business. Most of the neighbourhoods in which they are located are worth a visit for local colour; and if one shop is gone, another one a hundred yards away may catch your eye.

8e arrondissement

Anna Lowe

35 avenue Matignon, 8e
Métro: St-Phillipe-du-Roule

Investment clothes, according to our Paris shop spy, sell for a fraction of the price they might command around the corner in the rue du Faubourg St-Honoré. Anna Lowe was a model and has connections with the couture houses, from which she gets end-of-season clothes, and with the best ready-to-wear lines, from which she gets fashions only two months after they go on sale. At various times, you'll find Yves St Laurent Rive Gauche suits, Comme des Garçons skirts, and such designer labels as Kenzo, Guy Laroche, Hermès. Ms Lowe also has handsome clothes made especially for her shop, and to *her* taste which is perfect. Simple alterations are free! Open Mondays to Saturdays, 10:30 a.m. to 7:00 p.m. Closed the first two weeks in August.

Le Troc des Trucs

50 rue Colisée, 8e
Métro: St-Philippe-du-Roule

This is a 'dépot-vente' where well-heeled women leave their last season's clothes to be resold. You'll find superb quality women's fashions for as little as one-quarter of their original price. Open 3:00 to 7:30 p.m., Mondays through Saturdays.

16e arrondissement

Catherine Baril

14-16 and 25 rue de la Tour, 16e
Métro: Passy

These two long-established resale shops are well-stocked with designer clothes, some quite clearly recognisable even with the labels cut out, others still labelled. Whatever we mention now will have gone by the time you read this, but there will be more – like the Chanel boutique suit for 1100F, an Azzadine Alaia skirt (unlabelled) at 720F, and so forth. Have a look at the bargain rails of last year's model clothes from 320F up. Open Mondays 2:00 to 7:00 p.m., Tuesdays through Saturdays 10:00 a.m. to 7:00 p.m. Usually closed the first three weeks in August. Major credit cards acceptable.

Réciproque

95, 101, and 123 rue de la Pompe, 16e
Métro: Pompe

Huge and with a tremendously wide selection, worth spending a morning wandering around these three shops. At 95, there are well-arranged racks of good couture clothes worn a few times by private clients or at fashion shows, and a lot of well-made ready-to-wear things. At 101, excellent men's clothes and gifts. At 123, jewellery, scarves and miscellaneous clothes even including hats! Open Tuesdays through Saturdays 10:00 a.m. to 6:45 p.m., usually closed for the last week in August

Maguy

30 rue de la Pompe, 16e
Métro: Pompe

Charming little bibelots (the best ones are in the window it seems) as well as women's fashions and men's clothes too. Open Mondays through Fridays 10:30 a.m. to 12:30 p.m., Saturdays, 3:00 to 6:30 p.m. Closed usually from the second week in July to the first of September.

Gift shopping

The shops of Paris are crammed with perfect gifts – at a price. Wander along the rue du Faubourg St-Honoré, or the rue de Rivoli, or rue Royale, or among the boutiques of the Left Bank, and you will begin to feel like a poor relation outside a rich man's door. But once you get your eye in, you can with some perseverance find an enticing selection of small portable presents at a fraction of the big-name shop prices.

Note: many shops close during August for the annual holiday; and hours can change, from time to time. If a shop has closed, or even disappeared entirely, it's not a disaster, you'll wander the neighbourhood and find places of your own.

Monoprix, Prisunic, Uniprix

These have turned up frequently in these pages as perfect hunting grounds for food, clothes, household gadgets. Consider them for gifts, too: make for the larger shops, in the more fashionable areas of the Right Bank, which quickly seize upon the year's fashionable ideas and copy them down to a price. Monoprix at 21 avenue de l'Opéra, 1er, *Métro*: Opéra, usually has silk-look scarves in subtle colours, with a very 'designer' look, for as little as 25F. Their scarves and mufflers for men, in wool or wool and acrylic, are elegantly designed in stripes, patterns or muted plaids, and look much better than their price of about 42 to 45F.

Look in Prisunic for traditional French earthenware plates and cups; a big café-au-lait bowl for breakfast, in a shape that dates back to the eighteenth century, is 11F50.

1er arrondissement

FNAC

1 rue Pierre Lescot, Forum des Halles, 1er *Métro*: Les Halles
136 rue de Rennes, 6e *Métro*: Montparnasse
26 avenue Wagram, 8e *Métro*: Étoile

These are big, crowded, incredibly well-stocked shops with books, magazines, records, cassettes, small gifts and gadgets. Great for last-minute buys. Open from 10:00 a.m. to 7:30 p.m., closed Sundays and Mondays.

Madame Bijoux

13 rue Jean-Jacques Rousseau, 1er
Métro: Palais Royal, Louvre

A very small shop which specialises in 'retro' clothes and theatrical fantasies from the 1930s and 40s. Masks, beads, 1920s shoes, costume jewellery, boas, buttons. Some junk, some gems. Open, usually, 11:00 a.m. to 7:00 p.m., Mondays to Saturdays, but phone first (42 36 98 68) to make sure.

2e arrondissement

Centre Franco-Americain

47 rue d'Aboukir, 2e
Métro: Sentier

It has been found that the duty-free shops at Paris airports are the second most expensive in Europe, so you might do better checking out this small place where perfumes etc. are tax free, and 25 per cent off the marked prices: for example, Givenchy eau de toilette, 240 ml, list price 420F, less 25 per cent here. They also offer Dior, Chanel, Cartier, Yves St Laurent, Hermès scents and a good line of skin and body treatment products and make-up. Open 9:00 a.m. to 6:30 p.m. Mondays through Fridays, closed 'most of August' (but this varies). We have found that their prices are keener than the more well-known, very crowded shops under the arches of the rue de Rivoli near the Louvre.

3e and 4e arrondissements

rue des Franc-Bourgeois (odd nos. are 4e, even 3e)
Métro: Rambuteau, St-Paul

Jean-Pierre de Castro: no. 17

Silver, silver, silver. Napkin rings at 40F, bracelets made from forks and spoons 50F, repro art deco frames from 60F, tea strainers 120F, and old silver (spoons, knives, forks) sold by the kilo, about 15 pieces, for 400F! Open Mondays 2:00 to 7:00 p.m., Tuesdays through Saturdays 10:30 a.m. to 7:00 p.m., Sundays 11:00 a.m. to 7:30 p.m.

La Charrue et Les Étoiles: no. 19

The name translates as The Plough and the Stars. There's everything here for the collector of animalia; miniatures, paintings, jewellery, chess sets, and at the moment a delectable set of Viennese bronze cats playing fiddles, posing before mirrors, and so forth. Open 10:30 a.m. to 7:00 p.m., Mondays through Saturdays, and on Sundays from 11:30 a.m. to 7:30 p.m.

La Licorne

38 rue de Sévigné, near rue des Francs-Bourgeois

The shops in the Marais change almost overnight, and if this is still there it's a delightful place to find not very expensive costume jewellery. VISA, Eurocheques. Open 9:30 a.m. to 6:30 p.m., Mondays through Saturdays.

La Maison Rouge: no. 45

It's worth looking here for 1900s–1930s curios and trinkets, and sometimes you'll find some choice bits of jewellery. Open 10:00 a.m. to 7:00 p.m., closed Tuesdays; open Saturdays and Sundays from 2:30 to 7:00 p.m. Usually closed the last week in August but this can vary.

À L'Olivier

25 rue de Rivoli, 4e.
Métro: St-Paul, Hôtel-de-Ville

The traditional place to find cold-pressed extra-virgin olive oil as well as walnut and avocado oils and a range of most unusual olives and olive-based soap. Open 11:00 a.m. to 7:00 p.m., Mondays to Fridays. In August, 11:00 a.m. to 1:00 p.m., 3:00 to 7:00 p.m. Major credit cards accepted.

Izrael, Epicerie du Monde

30 rue François-Miron, 4e
Métro: St-Paul, Hôtel-de-Ville

Spices, herbs, delicious goodies from all over the world in a very crowded neighbourhood shop. Try a few ounces of their olives with lime, coriander and sesame seeds, (48F a kilo). Open Tuesdays to Fridays 9:30 a.m. to 1:00 p.m., and 2:30 to 7:00 p.m. Saturdays, 9:00 a.m. to 7:00 p.m., closed Sundays and August.

Au Grenier du Marais

7 rue François-Miron, 4e
Métro: St-Paul, Hôtel-de-Ville

A friend describes its stock as 'delicious antique jewellery', with gold earrings for about 200F unlike anything else you find in Paris for under 500F. And, on our last visit, a collection of spectacle frames to put Dame Edna Everage to shame. The owner is cheerful, friendly, happy to bargain, and accepts VISA, American Express and Eurocheques. Hours 9:30 a.m. to 7:00 p.m., Mondays to Saturdays. Closed in August.

Kazé

11 rue François-Miron, 4e
Métro: St-Paul, Hôtel-de-Ville

A wonderful little shop which sells Japanese pottery, cooking knives, wooden implements, paper, ink, brushes, and clothes – and best of all, traditional Japanese fabrics by the metre at 60F. (Be warned, Japanese looms are very narrow, so you'll need more than you think).

5e arrondissement

La Tuile à Loup

35 rue Daubenton, 5e
Métro: Censier-Daubenton

A shop scented with herbs, filled with beautifully designed, rather rustic gifts: wicker, wood, earthenware casseroles, baskets and cookbooks (in French). Old-fashioned wicker heart-shaped *coeur à la crème* baskets, classic glazed earthenware wine pitchers, breadboards. Open 10:30 a.m. to 1:00 p.m., 3:00 to 7:30 p.m., Tuesdays to Saturdays, Sundays from 10:30 a.m. to 1:00 p.m. Open in August.

6e arrondissement

Au Chat Dormant

13 rue du Cherche-Midi, 6e
Métro: St-Sulpice, Sèvres-Babylone

A miniscule paradise for cat lovers, with gifts ranging from postcards to antique silver boxes, everything saluting cats. Figures of cats in marble, metal, porcelain, plastic. Umbrellas whose handles are heads of cats. Paintings, prints, posters. Open Mondays 2:30 to 7:00 p.m., Tuesdays to Saturdays 11:00 a.m. to 7:00 p.m.

10e arrondissement

rue de Paradis, 10e
Walk down this street between the rue d'Hauteville and rue de Fidélité, and you will find a nexus of attractive shops with an infinite variety of porcelain and crystal, not all that extraordinarily cheap but of great beauty. At that, prices seem slightly lower than in the Galeries Lafayette or the pricier gift shops of the Left Bank. Such

names as Daum Cristal and Havilland are everywhere; almost everything available is small, portable and desirable, although breakable. At Au Paradis, 55 rue de Paradis, look for exquisite porcelain handmade vases and jugs in subtle colours. Most shops seem to open around 10:00 a.m. and almost everything is closed on Saturdays.

14e arrondissement

La Salle des Ventes

123 rue d'Alésia, 14e
Métro: Alésia

In this lively, very untouristy area, a real discovery: one big sale-room which specialises in huge pieces of furniture, and another with old jewellery, china, glass, silver. A wonderful place to browse – and you might find some delightful very French *objet* to take home: a pretty watch for about 200F up, a 1920s crystal-and-plastic waist-length necklace, a cheese plate from the Auvergne for 90F, or a set of silver serving spoons for 800F. Open 10:00 a.m. to 7:30 p.m., Mondays to Saturdays.

Flea markets

Les Marchés aux Puces – one of those romantic conceptions of Paris, whose faded glamour lingers somewhat past its prime. As there are now 'flea markets' of sorts all over the world, your chance of finding a nice little precious object for almost nothing is probably as good in a Sunday morning sale in Salford, as in the most famous flea market in Paris. However, if you think you want the fun of scrabbling through bins and tables, or just watching Parisians striking bargains in rapid-fire slangy French – and you still hope to find something everyone else has missed – so be it. Here is the latest, most realistic information, from French sources.

The flea market at St-Oeun

Métro: Porte de Clignancourt and a fair walk

Acres of sprawling market-stalls, crammed with people on the hunt for bargains or for 'the picturesque', which these days means German tourists photographing American tourists. It is the best known, and the most expensive. Much of the stuff you see is pure and simple junk, brought in to unload on the unwary. For the rest – the dealers know where the good buys are, and by the time you have reached here by public transport they have come and gone. Most of the best-looking stalls are owned by merchants who also do business from flossier premises, in the 1er, 8e and 16e *arrondissements*. The prices you see in the flea market will be no lower than in the rue du Bac. However, it's an experience, and if you are willing to make the longish journey, rummage and enjoy the bargaining, it could be fun. Saturdays, Sundays and Mondays from dawn to about 1:00 p.m. *Please watch out for pickpockets!*

Despite the apparent haphazardness of the market, it is actually laid out in a fairly comprehensible and sensible fashion. Outside, on the fringe, are the inevitable buses, station wagons and hand-carts spilling over with second-hand jeans, Indian blouses, 'Afghan' rugs, damaged transistors, and such-like. Inside, you will find a number of individual markets, well sign-posted. Most interesting:

Marché Vernaison, 136 avenue Michelet. Everything from gilt buttons of Napoleonic tunics, to small walnut prayer-stools, toys, jewellery, lamps, glassware. Forget about any art nouveau *trouvailles* – the Paris, London and New York dealers got there five years ago. Go for the small pieces of the thirties, forties, fifties, even the sixties now, and hope that fashion catches up with you.

Marché Malik, rue Jules-Vallès. Mostly old clothes, umbrellas, walking-sticks, tatty fake-sheepskin coats, scratched records, bins of lace, twenties-style dresses, earthenware, glass, tin, perfume bottles – sometimes these are fun, smelling in a ghostly way of scents no longer made. The clothes may need washing or dry cleaning.

Marché Biron, rue des Rosiers. Expensive, elegant furniture and bibelots, on stands run by professionals who know precisely the worth of everything they stock. You might beat them down ten to twenty per cent, but as the original price is usually astronomical to begin with, you'll still end by spending a lot, if you buy at all. However, everything is good value, and backed by reputable names in the business.

Marché Paul Bert, rue Paul Bert. Some really exquisite crystal, modern gilt, bronze, polished wood furniture, ornaments, mirrors. They could easily fetch double the asking price if put up at Christie's – that is, if you could afford to pay what the vendors are asking in the first place.

Marché Jules-Vallès, rue Jules-Vallès. The most fun, and the most promising for finding something unusual and not too expensive, if you feel your stay in Paris isn't complete without something from the flea market. Look for small bisque-headed dolls, theatrical costumes, 1930s shoes, decorative glassware, candlesticks, ashtrays, doll trunks. Bargain if you can, most of the dealers speak some kind of English, but don't be disappointed if the final price is not really rock-bottom.

The other flea markets

These are where the knowledgeable Parisians find their bargains. As they become better known, the quality of merchandise brought to them goes up, and prices are rising fast. A few years ago, these were true junk stalls, set up along the edge of an established street market. Some still qualify, just, for this status, but foreign dealers are moving in to buy, smart young stallholders are setting up their stands, and the time to go is *now*.

Place d'Aligre, 11e

Métro: Ledru-Rollin

Look for signs to 'Marché Beauvau'. The surrounding market of fruit, vegetables, meat and seafood is one of the lesser-known and most delightful in Paris, and worth a visit for itself. In the square, about twenty tables of odds and ends are set up. Boxes of the most astounding old clothes – cracked leather shoes, a furry bowler hat, a pair of striped trousers, a stack of fourth-hand handbags. But look for old postcards, small pieces of silver or silverplate, glassware, cooking utensils of every age and condition, books, odd boxes of jewellery – mostly Woolworth stuff, but occasionally a piece of once-expensive jewellery turns up. There's a table of buttons old and new that will send button-collectors wild. Everything quite cheap, the atmosphere quiet, the dealers pleasant.

A few years ago, it shrank by about twenty stalls, as the Mayor of Paris apparently decreed that it was bringing too much traffic to the surrounding streets, but by the end of the summer many of the long-established vendors had crept back. The street market around it is a wonderful place to shop for fruit, flowers, North African olives and hot peppers, good breads, and the corkscrew you forgot to bring. Plenty of picnicking material, for a snack in the square bounded by rue Vollon and rue Trousseau. Every day but Monday, from about 9:30 a.m. to about 1:00 p.m.

Porte de Vanves, 14e

avenue Marc Sangnier, 14e
Métro: Porte de Vanves

A very good small flea market is held here on Saturday and Sunday mornings – mostly junk, but if you have a quick eye you can spot some real bargains. Look for oldish Dinky toys; copper jelly moulds; old glass lamps; costume jewellery of the 40s and 50s, comics, postcards, pots, bottles. A few small (rather pricey) antiques. After lunch on Sunday it becomes a 'Marché au Fripes' – real trash.

The grander end of this market in avenue Georges-Lefenestre, around the corner, is described below.

Marché aux Puces de la Porte Didot

Take the *Métro* to Porte-de-Vanves, walk through the tatty part, and in the avenue Georges-Lefenestre you find 'the real market of grandpapa'. This means delectable junk and little treasures but not rock-bottom cheap. You have to be able to bargain in French if you want to get prices down. Good for pretty china, glass, silver, ornate little picture frames, small antique furniture. Not many (foreign) tourists yet, but a lot of beady-eyed young French couples decorating their houses cheaply. Photographers come here for props. On a summer weekend, it is an agreeable stroll under the trees and through the good-natured, ambling crowd. You can even find places to sit and have a picnic while your feet recover; or find a café in the nearby rue Raymond Losserand. Saturdays and Sundays, from 8:00 a.m. to about 6:00 p.m., but best before lunchtime as by mid-afternoon most of the best stallholders have begun to pack it in. The Porte de Vanves/Porte Didot market has been under threat of closure for the last few years, as local shopkeepers complain that it takes away trade from them and sometimes brings undesirable characters into the *quartier*. Police show up regularly to chase away the unlicensed who spread their odds and ends on newspapers on the pavement. But the market still goes on, at this writing at least.

Paris pratique
(Staying afloat)

The quality of your stay in Paris – reverie or nightmare – is going to depend on some very basic circumstances: the state of your digestion, your feet, your French. The amount of time you spend looking for a post office is stolen from the time you spend looking at paintings. The confusion you encounter when dealing with telephones, tipping and traffic detracts from your pleasure in everything else Parisian. The information that follows, alphabetically arranged, is simple and practical – it can make the difference between two weeks of fretting about mechanical details and ten minutes of dealing intelligently with them.

Animals

Parisians are unsentimental about animals, but they like to have them around. Small dogs of peculiar breed on leads trail every other person – on the Métro, in restaurants, everywhere. The sidewalks are consequently treacherous. You can get entangled, or step in something, but you'll rarely be snapped or barked at.

Cats run wild in certain areas, notably the cemeteries, and are not to be petted. This goes for all animals in France, except those personally known to you. See Animal bites, page 268.

Live animals for food are closely caged and brusquely treated. If this puts you off your feed, avert your eyes.

Babysitters

Association Générale des Étudiants en Médecine

105 boulevard de l'Hôpital, 13e
Tel: 45 86 52 02 from noon to 7:00 p.m.

Especially recommended for children 18 months or younger. Medical students are called *carabins*. You must pay a *frais* or subscription to this association, plus 25F per hour; after midnight, taxi fare home.

American College in Paris

31 avenue Bosquet, 7e
Tel: 45 55 91 73, extension 19 or 24

The cost is 25F per hour. Give the sitter something to eat if the evening begins before 6:00; provide two Métro tickets, or, after midnight, either take the student home or offer taxi fare.

Baby Sitting Actif

34 rue Delambre, 14e
Tel: 43 27 82 38

Their rate is 22F per hour, but it goes down to 15F an hour from 8:00 p.m. to midnight, with an agency fee of 35F.

Centre Regional des Oeuvres Universitaires et Scolaires

Faculté Orsay
Tel: 49 41 70 56

Ask for someone who speaks English, and inquire about the current hourly rate, which when last checked was 25F, but may have gone up.

Baths, public

If your hotel doesn't provide a shower – or if it's too expensive – try the Bains-Douches Municipaux. Bring a towel, soap, shampoo, and slippers (the flip-flop variety). More about this on page 64. Cost 5F. Open Thursday, noon to 7:00 p.m., Friday and Saturday, 7:00 a.m. to 7:00 p.m., Sunday, 8:00 a.m. to noon.

8 rue des Deux Ponts, 4e
18 rue Renard, 4e
38 rue du Rocher, 8e
40 rue Oberkampf, 11e
188 rue de Charenton, 12e
34 rue Castagnary, 15e

18 rue de Meaux, 19e
place des Fêtes, 19e
27 rue de la Bidassoa, 20e
66 rue de Buzenval, 20e
148 avenue Gambetta, 20e
296 rue des Pyrénées, 20e

There are also 64 fountains donated to Paris by Richard Wallace (he tried to give Paris his furniture collection, too; it was turned down and wound up in London). The fountains are scattered throughout the city, contain clean water, and are good for a *toilette de chat* ('a lick and a promise').

Books (in English)

When French newspapers begin to give you indigestion, revert to English. Remember, though, that imported books are expensive – about double their home price.

Brentano's

37 avenue de l'Opéra, 1er
Tel: 42 61 52 50
Métro: Pyramides

Galignani

224 rue de Rivoli, 1er
Tel: 42 60 76 07
Métro: Tuileries

Nouveau Quartier Latin

78 boulevard St-Michel, 6e
Tel: 43 26 42 70
Métro: St-Michel

An eclectic international bookshop, with plenty of mixed fiction for the browser, and well-stocked academic bookshelves. Their true speciality, though, is in textbooks for foreign language teachers. Open 10:00 a.m. to 7:00 p.m. every day of the week.

Shakespeare and Company

37 rue de la Bûcherie, 5e
Métro: St-Michel

This little shop has earned its place as one of the sights of Paris. It sells old and new paperback and hardcover English books, has chairs outside for browsers, is next to a charming little park, and has a splendid view of Notre-Dame. And there are notices of flats to let, poetry readings . . .

W. H. Smith & Son

248 rue de Rivoli, 1er
Tel: 42 60 37 97
Métro: Concorde

Village Voice

rue Princesse, 6e
Métro: Mabillon, Odéon

Librairie Albion

13 rue Charles IV, 4e

Closed in August. Sells and *lends* English and American books.

Clothing sizes

Women:
Dresses/Suits

British	10	12	14	16	18	20
American	8	10	12	14	16	18
French	38	40	42	44	46	48

Stockings/Tights

British/American	small		medium		large	
French	0	1	2	3	4	5

Shoes

British	4½	5½	6½	7½
American	6	7	8	9
French	37	38	40	41

Men
Suits/Overcoats

British/American	35	36	37	38	39	40
French	36	38	40	42	44	46

Shirts

British/American	15	16	17	18
French	38	40	42	44

Shoes

British	7	8	8½	9½	10½
American	7½	8½	9	10	11
French	41	42	43	44	45

Discounts—*for students*

Carte Jeune

A nifty little item for those between 18 and 25. Entitles you to a 50 per cent reduction on all French railways, and free couchette. It's valid only between 1 June and 30 September. Get it from main railways or travel agents. Cost: 125F

Council for International Educational Exchange (CIEE)

49 rue Pierre-Charron, 8e
Tel: 43 59 23 69
Métro: Alma-Marceau

Provides International Student Identity Cards, useful for discounts on museum and film entrances, Eurail-passes, and much more. You must have proof of full-time student status, a passport-sized photo, and 30F. Using the card: Look for prices under *Tarif spécial pour étudiants'*.

Ligue Française des Auberges de Jeunesse (LFAJ)

38 boulevard Raspail, 7e
Tel: 45 48 69 84
Métro: Bac

For Youth Hostel card-holders. Hostels are cheap (15 to 25F per night) but offer little privacy. Not for long stays. See 'Au lit', page 59, for more information.

Student restaurants *(les restos U.)*

About 18F per meal

Albert Châtelet
10 rue Jean-Calvin, 5e
Métro: Censier-Daubenton

Assas
92 rue d'Assas, 6e
Métro: Notre-Dame-des-Champs

Bullier
39 avenue Georges-Bernanos, 5e
Métro: Port-Royal

Censier
3 rue Censier, 5e
Métro: Censier-Daubenton

Cuvier
8 bis, rue Cuvier, 5e
Métro: Jussieu

Mabillon
3 rue Mabillon, 6e
Métro: Mabillon

Mazet
5 rue Mazet, 6e
Métro: Odéon

Discounts—*for those over 60*

Carte Vermeil

With great generosity, the French provide this discount card for those of 'the third age' – a much nicer phrase than the unctuous Anglo-American 'senior citizens' – available to anyone, of any nationality, who is over 60 years of age (women) or 65 (men). Take proof of your age – your passport – to the Abonnement office in any major railway station, or to the SNCF (French Railways) office in the lower ground floor of the Office de Tourisme at 127 Champs-Élysées, 8e (*Métro*: Georges-V). Pay them 65F, and get in return the *Carte Vermeil*, which is valid from 1 June to the next 31 May; during that time it entitles you to manifold discounts on entertainment, travel, and many museums.

The office at the Gare St-Lazare is an easy one to deal with, as the station is served by several Métro and many bus lines, and is not so crowded as the one at the big Gare du Nord or at the SNCF-Champs-Élysées. Don't expect anyone to speak English, but you won't need much French to communicate your wishes, as they are used to dealing with foreigners who have cottoned on to this very useful offer.

As you look through *Pariscope* for theatres, music, cinemas, etc., note the price reductions available for holders of the *CV*; it can be 40 per cent or more. Most museums and special exhibitions (such as those at the Grand Palais and Petit Palais) give half-price admission to holders of the *CV*.

Even without this card, production of your passport will almost always get you into museums for half price, sometimes free.

Holders of the British Senior Citizen Railcard should note that they will need the £5 Rail-Europ supplement card for discounts on rail/boat/hovercraft: check British Rail, in England, or at 55 rue St. Roch, 1er (*Métro*: Pyramides), for details of specific offers. Dates and hours may be restricted; read the small print to make sure you can get back from your holiday when you want to.

Dry cleaning

It's called *Nettoyage à sec* or *Le Pressing*. Sample prices:

Trousers – 28F
Jacket – 35F
Dress – 40 to 55F

Le Pressing (your clothes are brushed and pressed) is also available everywhere for a touch-up.

Electricity

Although the current, in most modernised hotels, is 220 volts, as in the UK (in older hotels it may still be 110 volts, so inquire before using any appliance), you must fit a *European* two-round-pin plug to the flex of electrical gadgets. Many hardware shops and iron-mongers sell these (or get one in Paris). If you have an appliance with a three-cord flex, make sure the earth wire (green and yellow) is securely bound and covered with electricians' tape, so that it cannot touch the other wires nor the wall socket. Or buy one of the pricey but safe adaptors sold in ironmongers. Also do be considerate: you might check with the concierge about using a hair-dryer, which draws a lot of current.

Embassies

See 'Au secours', pages 259-269

Emergencies

See 'Au secours', pages 259–269

Entrances and exits

French doors open inward. This takes a while to get used to.

Entré = Entrance
Sortie = Exit
Tirez = Pull
Poussez = Push
Passage Interdit = No Admittance

Guidebooks and Phrasebooks

The only ones worth having, to our knowledge, are:

Blue Guide to Paris

In English, detailed information on museums and areas of historical interest.

Michelin Green Guide

In English, good overview, and excellent maps.

Gault-Millau: 'Le Nouveau Guide' magazine

In French, published monthly – 30F. About £3 in the UK, $6 in the
US.

An invaluable source of inside information on restaurants, hotels,
travel, holidays. However, most of its restaurant recommendations
are well above our price limits. Gault-Millau are utterly frank about

the places they write about, and they write wittily and often colloquially. In one of their issues they actually had a feature called 'Restaurants to Flee From'.

Le Nouveau Guide is almost too much of a country-wide or world-wide magazine to be of use to those staying in Paris, but you might have a look at the cover of the magazine of the month, and buy it only if it is featuring something inexpensive and Parisian.

Survive in French

Longman's 'Survive' Travel Pack gives you a 90-minute cassette which helps you accustom yourself before you go to how people actually speak. It has a lot of useful key sentence patterns which can be put together to cope with almost every situation. In addition, the 'Survive' book in the pack is crammed with information on telephoning, tipping, how to order from a menu, how to find out about opening and closing hours, etc. Get it well before you go, and practise. £9.95

Linguaphone Travel Pack. Here you get two 90-minute cassettes, one specifically for travel and full of hints and information, the other a general language cassette of fairly basic French, with phrases for most of the situations you'll encounter. In addition, there's a mini-dictionary, and a pack of 52 Panic Cards which give you instant phrases for emergencies ... you could use them on a rainy day to construct some really gruesome games. £9.95

Penguin French Phrase Book. Very comprehensive indeed, the writer has covered almost anything that can happen to you and a lot of things you hope will not. £2.95

Pan Travellers' French. Small, thin, truly pocket-size, and packed with useful words, phrases and pronunciation. Particularly strong on medical emergencies, chemists, hotels. £2.50

BBC 'Get By In French'. A quick course for beginners about meeting people, booking a hotel room, shopping, getting around in a French city – practical, short information. £2.95

Paris Pas Cher. Available in Paris, and in French, better for bargains and consumer information than for more mundane things like hotels and restaurants, but a good read. 95F.

Hairdressers

Le training – a first-class example of *Franglais* – offers you a chance to get a free or reduced rate haircut or styling in some very good salons. These sessions are popular with the young and broke of Paris, so you may have to wait or return another day. For women only (as far as is known now): although the trendier unisex salons may by now have 'training' sessions, too. You are sure of getting something smart and professional, as the cutter who works on your hair is actually employed in the salon at normal times, not just a learner-driver, so to speak; and there is always one of the top stylists of the establishment hovering near to criticise or comment or direct. Don't mind if you are treated as an object rather than a client to be flattered and soothed. And you probably will find that your own wishes are not paramount. Don't go in with long straight hair and expect to come out with just a trim. Get an idea beforehand of the general attitude of the salon before you put your head in their hands.

Note that although prices were accurate at the time of going to press, they may have risen by the time you read this book.

Bruno

15 rue des Saints-Pères, 6e
Tel: 42 61 45 15
Métro: St-Germain-des-Prés

Tuesdays, 6:00 p.m. Shampoo, cut, blow-dry 30F. No appointment necessary. Not July and August.

Jean-Jacques Maniatis

35 rue de Sèvres, 6e
Tel: 45 44 17 37
Métro: Vaneau

Tuesdays and Thursdays, 5:00 to 10:00 p.m. Free – but you must stay for the whole session.

Marianne Gray

52 rue Saint-André-des-Arts, 6e
Tel: 43 26 58 21
Métro: St-Michel

Training sessions are once a week, telephone for current information. Not July or August. If a first-year student does your hair under the eye of a senior stylist, it's free. Work by an advanced student is at half the normal salon cost, or about 40F for a complete restyle. Tip the *coiffeuse* about 4F, even if the treatment is free.

For an non-training (paid) coiffure, expect to pay about 45F for a cut, 22F for a shampoo, and blow-drying or setting about 28 to 30F, all plus 15 per cent.

Health

See 'Au secours', pages 259–269

Holidays

1 January
Easter Sunday and Monday (Pâques)
1 May (French Labour Day)
Ascension Day
Whit Monday
14 July (Bastille Day)
15 August (Feast of the Assumption)
1 November (All Saints' Day – Toussaint)
11 November (Remembrance Day) and
Christmas.

The entire month of August is high season for tourists, low season for Parisians. The city trades its population in for a flock of provincials and foreigners. Stay out of town unless you don't mind being asked directions by passers-by.

Information sources

For basic information, consult the Offices de Tourisme. The Hôtesses speak English, and will provide information on hotels, transportation, sightseeing, travel in France, and such.

Office de Tourisme:Main office

127 avenue des Champs-Élysées, 8e
Tel: 47 23 61 72
Métro: Georges-V
Hours: Monday to Saturday, 9:00 a.m. to 8:00 p.m.; Sundays and holidays, 9:00 a.m. to 6:00 p.m.

Branch offices:

Gare de Lyon

Hours: 8:00 a.m. to 1:00 p.m. and 5:00 to 10:00 p.m., Easter to 1 November. Other months to 8:00 p.m., Monday to Saturday.

Gare de l'Est

Hours: 8:00 a.m. to 1:00 p.m. and 5:00 to 10:00 p.m., Easter to 1 November. Other months to 8:00 p.m., Monday to Saturday.

Gare du Nord

Hours: 8:00 a.m. to 10:00 p.m., Easter to 1 November. Other months to 8:00 p.m., Monday to Saturday.

Gare d'Austerlitz

Hours: 8:00 a.m. to 10:00 p.m., Easter to 1 November. Other months to 8:00 p.m., Monday to Saturday.

The Yellow Pages are known as *Le Professionel* in Paris

Language courses

Berlitz

29 rue de la Michodière, 1er
Métro: Opéra

Alliance Française

101 boulevard Raspail, 6e
Tel: 45 44 38 38
Métro: Notre-Dame-des-Champs

Office National des Universités et Écoles Françaises

96 boulevard Raspail, 6e
Tel: 42 22 50 20
Métro: Notre-Dame-des-Champs

Offers information on French language courses from French Universities.

Lavatories, public

There are still a few *vespasiennes* in Paris, but don't count on stumbling across one. Métro stations frequently (but not always) have lavatories (marked WC-Dames, WC-Hommes); for once, correct vocabulary is *essential*. The attendant expects ½-franc in the saucer. Superb new automatic lavatories are being sited at many street corners: a 2F piece gets you up to ten minutes in an immaculate white cubicle.

Café and brasserie toilets offer various states of hygiene and civilisation – about half the time, you'll find the 'à la Turque' kind, which can be very clean or very dirty, especially in the smaller out-of-the-way places which as a pauper you will frequent. *Never* leave home without a pack of humane loo-paper, as advised on page 19.

If your need for a lavatory doesn't quite coincide with your desire for a cup of coffee, you might try the *Jeton* Trick. Find a café or brasserie and ask to use the phone. Buy a *jeton* (phone token – 2F) if you must, at the bar. The phone and lavatory, if you're lucky, will be found next to each other. Don't use the phone. On your return to the *caisse*, sell the *jeton* back to the management. Your party didn't answer.

Libraries

If you expect to be able to use one of the great French libraries (the Bibliothèque Nationale or the Bibliothèque Ste-Geneviève) you will need some authoritative support: a letter from your university describing your research, or from your corporation. The more official the better. Count on bureaucratic resistance.

Lost and found

We have found the Lost and Found charming and helpful, and they have at least one person who speaks good English.

Bureau des Objets Trouvés
36 rue des Morillons, 15e
Métro: Convention
Hours: Mondays, Tuesdays, Wednesdays and Fridays, 8:30 a.m. to 5:00 p.m. Thursdays, 8:30 a.m. to 8:00 p.m.

Lost or stolen passport: see 'Au secours', page 259–269.

Maps

The best we know is the *Plan de Paris*, edition A. Leconte, red cover, 59F, and worth it. For details, see 'Aux alentours', page 37.

Mental Health

SOS Amitié (in English)

Tel: 47 23 80 80
Hours: 7:00 a.m. to 11:00 p.m.

For pouring out your troubles by phone. No advice given, no sides taken, but they lend a sympathetic ear and can recommend other sources of specific help or refuge.

Metric system

To convert centimetres into inches, multiply by .39
To convert inches into centimetres, multiply by 2.54

1 cm = 0.39 in
1 m = 39.4 in = 3.28 ft = 1.09 yd

1 in = 2.54 cm
1 ft = 30.48 cm = 0.304 m
1 yd = 91.44 cm = 0.914 m

1 kilogram (kg) = 2.205 lb
2 kg = 4.409 lb
5 kg = 11.023 lb
10 kg = 22.046 lb

1 lb = 0.45 kg
2 lb = 0.90 kg
5 lb = 2.25 kg
10 lb = 4.50 kg

To convert degrees Centigrade into degrees Fahrenheit, multiply Centigrade by 1.8 and add 32.

To convert degrees Fahrenheit into degrees Centigrade, subtract 32 and divide by 1.8

Money

See also 'Preliminaries', page 14, for an idea of how much to bring with you.

The denominations	Will get you
5 centimes	nothing
10 centimes	nothing
20 centimes	nothing
1½F (50 centimes)	nothing
1F	a phone call
2F	admission to the *pelouse* at race-tracks; *or* a paperback thriller in a flea market.
5F	coffee, drunk at the 'zinc'
50F	a good lunch
100F	a day in Chartres: *or* two good lunches; *or* a real splurge meal for one.

French paper currency is whimsical. The portraits on the bills are not of politicians but of artists: Berlioz (on the now defunct 10F note), Racine (50F), Corneille (100F), Pascal (500F). This is conclusive proof that the French value philosophy above literature, and literature vastly above music.

If knowing exactly what you are spending is important to you, consider the X-Changer, a gadget that instantly computes foreign exchange rates. £4.99 from larger branches of Boots, Underwoods, Debenhams in London. (However, there is such a thing as carrying too many gadgets and worrying too much about whether the meal cost £6.50 or £7.00 when you should be concentrating on the *ris de veau*).

Bureaux de change

Despite our wise words about sleeping cheap and eating well, within certain sets of limits, money does seem to drip through the fingers in Paris. And when you need it most – on weekends, or just before dinner – where do you go to get it? Even during banking hours on weekdays you can find yourself walking miles, past bank after bank of busy money-changing citizens, but barred to *you* by the inflexible sign *no change, no wechsel*. Most banks and bureaux de change will not cash personal cheques on English or American banks, even backed by bank or Visa cards and passports: traveller's cheques and cash only. In our experience it's wise to carry a mixture of Eurocheques which can be cashed at face value in francs at banks and bureaux de change which display the EC sign; traveller's cheques and some notes. Every guidebook lists the exchange facilities in the railway stations: but we can only say that they are a foretaste of hell. Fearsomely crowded, jostling with impatient travellers barging themselves and their rucksacks past you to get to ticket offices and trains. But fear nothing, here are the life-saving addresses, many open on Saturday and some even on Sunday:

CCF (Crédit Commercial de France)

115 Champs-Élysées, 8e
Métro: George-V
Hours: Mondays to Saturdays, 8:30 a.m. to 8:00 p.m., and in July, August and September on Sundays from 10:15 a.m. to 6:00 p.m.

Cash or traveller's cheques only; no personal cheques on English or American banks cashed. Minimum charge for each transaction: 20F.

UBP

154 Champs-Élysées, 8e
Métro: Charles de Gaulle-Étoile
Hours: Mondays to Fridays 9:00 a.m. to 5:00 p.m., Saturdays, Sundays and holidays, 10:30 to 6:00 p.m.

But watch out – this is the Mug's Bank. No English cheques cashed; one per cent fee for traveller's cheques with a minimum charge of 20F; and two sets of formalities to undergo. Use ONLY on Sundays or holidays when desperate.

BNP

Place de l'Opéra at rue 4 Septembre
Métro: Opéra
24-hour VISA automatic cash machine, and an automatic changer for foreign notes.

But beware! Their *Change* around the corner in rue 4 Septembre, hits you with a commission of 24F for changing notes, and 29F65 for traveller's cheques!

Barclays Bank

33 rue 4 Septembre, 2e
Métro: Opéra
Hours: 9:30 a.m. to 4:00 p.m., Mondays to Fridays.
and
Rond-Point des Champs-Élysées, 8e
Métro: Champs-Élysées-Clemenceau
Hours: as above

Barclay cheques only, and traveller's cheques: only 7F50 commission on cheques up to £100 a day.

Beaubourg

Centre Pompidou, 3e
Métro: Les Halles, Rambuteau

A Bureau de Change has been opened on the ground floor of Beaubourg – open during the Centre's daytime hours and on Saturdays and Sundays. The exchange rate is fairly standard, but note that a fee of 12F50 is charged on each transaction.

Citibank

30 Champs-Élysées, 8e
Métro: George-V, Franklin D. Roosevelt

A small, busy and newish bank in this very convenient location, with good exchange rates and useful opening hours: Mondays to Fridays, 9:00 a.m. to 6:45 p.m., Saturdays 10:30 a.m. to 1:15 p.m., 2:30 to 6:30 p.m.

Banco Borges

30 rue du 4 Septembre, 2e
Métro: Opéra, 4 Septembre
Hours: Mondays to Fridays, 9:30 a.m. to 6:30 p.m., Saturdays 9:00 a.m. to 5:00 p.m.

Bureau de Change

9 rue Scribe, 9e
Métro: Opéra
Hours: Mondays to Fridays, 9:00 a.m. to 5:15 p.m. No exchange fee charged.

Melia Travel Agency

31 avenue de l'Opéra, 1er
Métro: Opéra
Hours: Mondays to Fridays 9:30 a.m. to 6:30 p.m., Saturdays 9:30 a.m. to 6:00 p.m. Days before holidays (e.g., 24 and 31 December): 9:00 a.m. to 4:00 p.m.
Always closed from 12:30 to 2:00 p.m.

Banque Portugaise

5 rue Auber, 9e
Métro: Opéra
Hours: Tuesdays to Fridays 9:30 a.m. to 6:15 p.m., Saturdays 9:00 a.m. to 7:00 p.m.

Banks and bureaux de change have varying charges for cashing traveller's cheques or Eurocheques, so shop around. At Barclays', you can cash a personal cheque for up to £100 per day, backed with a bank card and your passport, for a single fee of 7F50.

American Express traveller's cheques are best cashed (no fee) at their office, otherwise you pay at least one per cent. Barclays' traveller's cheques cost you nothing to cash at their branches.

Cheques, Credit Cards

Traveller's Cheques, of course, are the safest way to carry money, as if lost or stolen they will be replaced with varying degrees of speed. However, you pay in advance, and you pay a commission when you buy them, and sometimes when you cash them abroad. Most English banks, and major travel agencies like Thomas Cook, charge 1 per cent commission for sterling traveller's cheques, and 1.25 per cent for foreign currency traveller's cheques. Be a little wary of taking a lot of money in these last, as you'll lose on the exchange if you bring them back unspent and want to cash them. American Express and Barclays in Paris charge no fee for cashing their own traveller's cheques. Incidentally, keep a record of the cheque numbers, denominations, when and where cashed, separate from the cheques themselves – this is a chore to do, but if they're pinched you know what to tell the issuers.

Eurocheques seem, on the face of it, a very good alternative to carrying cash which lost, stolen or mislaid is gone for ever, or paying in advance for traveller's cheques. You pay your bank a yearly fee (£4 at NatWest, £6 at Barclays), and get books of ten cheques each and a Eurocheque card, and write them out in local currency as needed. This saves you the petty annoyance of queueing at banks or bureaux de change. BUT: many small hotels, restaurants and shops will either courteously refuse to accept Eurocheques, or will add on a fee which can range from 5 per cent to 10 per cent, because *their* banks levy a surcharge on Eurocheques from English banks. One French bank charges its account-holders a flat fee of 100F (more than £9) for every Eurocheque, no matter how small. In addition, you pay about 1.6 per cent of the sterling value of the cheque when it clears through your account here, plus about 30p handling charge for each. Is it all worth it?

National Giro will furnish its account holders with Post Cheques, which can be cashed at any post office in francs – and this can be a tremendous convenience for out-of-banking-hours emergencies. These Post Cheques must be ordered in advance, take about a week to ten days to get, and come in books of ten each worth up to £50. *And* – a real plus – you keep the money in your account until you actually cash the cheque, unlike traveller's cheques which are bought in advance. However, no shops or hotels or restaurants will accept them, and French banks on the whole are baffled by them. A charge of 50 pence is added here when the cheque clears.

Credit cards can be used to draw cash from French banks displaying the appropriate symbol; the amount varies from year to year, but you will be charged interest at the current rate – at this writing, between 1.8 per cent and 2 per cent *per month* – from the moment you get the money. No interest-free grace period here. American Express charge-card holders can cash personal cheques, backed by the AMEX card, for up to £500 every 21 days. Diners' Club will advance up to 8250F to its card-holders every two weeks, but as these are charge-cards, not a credit card, a sizeable interest charge will be added if the account is not settled promptly when the bill comes in.

When it comes to using credit cards to pay for meals, hotels, and purchases, opinions differ. More and more restaurants – even some brasseries and cafés in such working-class districts as the rue de Charonne – will accept plastic. With Visa and Access, you'll have up to six weeks' free credit before you have to pay up. Diners' Club and AMEX like their accounts settled promptly. In all cases, you will be billed at the exchange rate on the date when the voucher meets the computer, not as it was on the date you used the card. This can hurt, as we found out in the summer of 1989 when the pound was behaving rather erratically.

Protect the Plastic: for about £6 a year, you can insure all your charge and credit cards against loss or theft. Credit Card Sentinel (0705-472234), CPP (071-351 4400), and CardWise (0702-362999) all run identical schemes. You report your loss with one phone call, they notify every organisation you have specified, and get replacement cards under way. All have reverse-charge facilities for overseas calls. All will advance cash, interest-free for a limited period, if your money has gone with your cards (£400 from Sentinel, £500 from CPP and CardWise). If you call in within 24 hours of discovering your loss, you're covered against any fraudster using your card. But make sure you keep your PIN (personal identification number) separate from your Cashpoint withdrawal card; if it's used before you notify the card protection company you're out the cash.

If you don't use this insurance, then note down the numbers, expiration date, and loss-notification number of the company. Call them right away and tell them exactly when you discovered the loss, so they can issue a stop-order which protects you against someone booking a round-the-world flight on your VISA card. Each company has a slightly different policy on covering losses on credit cards, so be sure you know your rights when you make your call. If you get an automatic answering service, at night, Sundays, or holidays, say your piece slowly, and include the phrase, 'As of this moment, X a.m. or Y p.m., of reporting the loss, I am no longer responsible for any charges incurred on this card number: 0000 0000 0000.'

Newspapers

In French: *Le Monde*, marginally left of centre, is the most serious and well-informed; *Figaro* veers right. Either will give you a morning's occupation if your French is slow. *France-Soir* leans toward the sensational, a good source of crime and scandal stories; *Libération* (*Libé* for short) is thoroughly 'in', very pointed, truly biased; *Le Canard Enchâiné* is a sort of French *Private Eye*, and requires a firm grip on French politics and argot to make any sense at all; *Paris-Match* is the *Life* of France. A couple of hundred others, of all sorts and persuasions.

In English: the *International Herald Tribune* (daily) for comprehensive stock quotations, news, and American 'Op-Ed' features. Columnists recruited from the *New York Times*, the *Washington Post* and elsewhere. *Guardian, Times, Telegraph, Independent*, available daily near the Hôtel Crillon, place de la Concorde, at Palais Royal, Opéra, and other central news kiosks. And discover *Passion*, the monthly English-language magazine for intellectual news, views and reviews, personal ads, fashion, beautiful photographic essays.

Nuisances

Noise: hotel regulations specify quiet before 10:00 a.m. and after 10:00 p.m. Bang on the wall or call the manager if you have noisy neighbours. Try 'Il y a du bruit' (It's noisy), or 'C'est trop bruyant'.

Other complaints

Mosquitoes: *Moustiques*
Fleas: *Puces*
Lice: *Poux* (don't complain, leave the hotel)
Inedible: (mild) *Cela ne me plaît pas*
         (strong) *C'est dégôutant, ça*
Odour (extreme): *ça pue!*
Unwelcome advances: *Laissez-moi tranquille. Fiche-moi le camp!*

Beggars: if you're unwilling or unable to give handouts, the best defence is not to understand what they want. *Parle pas* will do in most cases – but Parisian beggars have been known to beg in English!

Thieves: see page 267

Smoking: if the smell of Gauloises and Gitanes bothers you, leave the country. It's true that smoking is forbidden in post offices, Métros (but only in the trains), buses, and certain other public places, but you can't spend all your time in these. The rule (*défense de fumer*) is generally adhered to, although Parisians will often light up just as the Métro doors open.

Numbers

It's absolutely necessary to understand the difference between, say, *quatorze* and *quarante*; between *cinq* and *cent*. When you can tell in an instant what *quatre-vingt dix-neuf* means, you've arrived. Memorise the following:

1	un	vingt-et-un	21
2	deux	trente-et-un	31
3	trois	quarante-et-un	41
4	quatre	cinquante-et-un	51
5	cinq	soixante-et-un	61
6	six	soixante-et-onze	71
7	sept	quatre-vingt-un	81
8	huit	quatre-vingt-onze	91
9	neuf	cent	100
10	dix	deux cent	200
11	onze	mille	1000
12	douze		
13	treize		
14	quatorze		
15	quinze		
16	seize		
17	dix-sept		
18	dix-huit		
19	dix-neuf		
20	vingt		

premier (ière)	first
deuxième	second
troisième	third
quatrième	fourth
cinquième	fifth

Without understanding the numbers, you won't be able to ask information about bus routes; pay for a meal or a minor purchase without getting it in writing; figure out what the gendarme means when he says the Métro is *deux-cent cinquante* metres away.

Open and closed: abbreviations

TLJ – every day (*tous les jours*)
Sauf lundi – except Monday
S, D & F – Saturdays, Sundays and holidays (*samedis, dimanches et fêtes*)

Periodicals

Pariscope and *Officiel des Spectacles*, for weekly listings of cinemas, theatre, concerts, dance, music, cabaret, races and other sports, and art galleries. 3F, every Wednesday.

Police (see also 'Au secours', pages 259–269)

Paris police come in different guises. The everyday cop, the gendarme (*le flic*), travels on foot, usually in pairs. He is to be addressed thus:

   '*Pardon, Monsieur l'agent . . .*'

Any other means of getting his attention, short of falling in front of a bus, will get a chilly reception.

The CSP are a special anti-terrorist force who guard embassies, certain banks, agencies such as Aeroflot (the Russian airline) and the like. They wear blue windcheaters, carry guns, and look like thugs. Do not ask them what time it is.

If you are a foreigner, and are asked, for whatever reason, to show your *papiers* – your passport – to a gendarme, do so. If you don't have it on you, it's a fast trip downtown for you.

In general it would be unwise to break any laws while in Paris.

La politesse

Without which you might as well stay at home. Parisians – if you'll permit the generalisation – are formal creatures. What they lack in rigid class distinctions they make up for in the personal carapace of manners that each carries around. It's unlikely that any Parisian will adopt you into the bosom of his family, or spill his innermost secrets to you, but with the right approach you can at least penetrate the first line of defence.

The trick is to use the standard forms of *politesse: Excusez-moi, monsieur*; *s'il vous plaît, madame*; *pardon, mademoiselle* ... and use the honorific – never the *tu* form unless a) you're a member of the family; b) you're a bitter enemy; or c) you're among the more casual student generation, who seem to have given up the second person plural. And say the words as if you mean them. As a rule, Parisians prefer to be spoken to directly; they are all for eye-contact; they enjoy shaking hands (brief – up-and-down only – but firm) on all occasions, once a relationship has been established.

And as a means of establishing relationships – even purely commercial ones – we suggest that you cultivate certain people and places throughout your stay. Even if you spend most of your days in the hinterland of the city, there should be a few characters – the concierge of your hotel, the owner of your neighbourhood café, the woman who sells you the newspaper, the staff of a restaurant or two where you return several times – who will get to recognise you, know you however slightly, welcome your appearance, bid you good appetite or good day. If you make the effort to communicate – in however stumbling French – it will be appreciated. If you enjoy their food, their accommodation, their city, don't feel shy about showing it.

Post

Another exercise in bureaucracy: receiving parcels through the post office is said to be Kafkaesque.

Stamps (*timbres*) are available at post offices (*bureaux de poste*) and at tobacco shops (*tabacs*) for French destinations only. Postboxes are oblong, about two feet by three feet, a pale, Dijon-mustard colour, generally attached to walls, and virtually invisible. In post offices you have a choice of three slots: Paris only, *Avion* (airmail), and *départment étrangers* (anywhere outside Paris).

The French produce some of the prettiest (and biggest) commemorative stamps in the world. They're called *timbres de collection*, and are available at a special window in the post office.

A 24-hour post office is open at 52 rue du Louvre, 1er, but never go on Saturday afternoon or Sunday unless you can face an hour's queuing. At 71 avenue des Champs Élysées, 8e, a post office is open Sundays and holidays, for stamps, telephones and telegrams only – also very crowded.

Letters from Paris to the United Kingdom cost 2F20 for 20 grams (airmail envelope and two thin sheets of paper); postcards are 2F. Airmail letters to the US and Canada are 3F40 for 10 grams.

Post codes: the postal code for Paris is 75, then 0, and then the number of the *arrondissement*. Most of the Marais is thus 75004. It's always written 75004 Paris, postal code first and town name second.

Telegrams: via the telegram counter at any post office, or call 42 33 21 11. Seven word minimum; the address counts as part of the message.

Telex: public telex offices at 7 rue Feydeau, 2e. Tel: 42 33 20 12 or 42 33 20 13. *Métro*: Bourse. Open daily, 8:00 a.m. to 8:00 p.m.

Railway information

The great source of all knowledge about how to get from anywhere to anywhere in France is in the Information Bureau at Gare St-Lazare, near the entrance closest to the rue de Rome. It takes a few minutes to crack the code of how to work the timetables, which are mounted on rollers behind glass, but once you've done that you're in clover. Also available: a certain number of printed time-tables from a central stand in this office, each section labelled by the name of the station from which the train leaves. No one here speaks English, so equip yourself with your pocket dictionary to make sure you understand all the footnotes. And don't leave this planning until the last minute before a journey.

Shoe repair

cordonnerie – cobblers
chaussures – shoes
lace de soulier – shoe lace

cuir – leather
semelle – sole
talon – heel

Slang

The current argot runs to Franglais, which you should have no trouble with (although it does change: jogging, a few years ago, was known as *le footing*, now it's *le jogging*). And abbreviation: you can go to *un resto très sympa* and possibly finish your meal with a liqueur or *un cogna*.

Anyone in deep trouble is said to be *dans le chocolat* which is a delicate way to avoid saying *dans la merde*.

For a complete and very funny read, get Miles Kington's *Let's Parler Franglais!* published by Penguin – he may have invented some of the words, but they sound authentic.

Taxis

In Central Paris, the area bounded by the Boulevard Périphérique, taxis are a real bargain – fares have gone up only fractionally since 1988. All prices are for up to three people in the taxi.

Tarif A, 7:00 a.m. to 8:00 p.m.:
Pick-up charge   9F50
Price per kilometre   2F85

Tarif B, 8:00 p.m. to 7:00 a.m.
Pick-up charge   9F50
Price per kilometre   4F02

Sundays and holidays, Tarif B.

Waiting time, or if the taxi is crawling very slowly in heavy traffic, 85F per hour.

To go to Charles de Gaulle/Roissy or Orly airports, 4.02 per kilometre from 7:00 a.m. to 8:00 p.m., 5F39 per kilometre from 8:00 p.m. to 7:00 a.m. – these higher prices begin at the Boulevard

Périphérique, up to that point you pay normal Paris prices as above.

Luggage heavier than 5 kg or for big heavy bags, supplement 3F50.

Telephones

A subsidiary of the Post Office. In public places, such as airports, phones are frequently found with post offices and telegraph offices under the sign PTT (Poste, Téléphone, Télégraphe). Otherwise, there are many kiosks on the streets, cubicles in hotels, restaurants, bars, brasseries.

Pay phones: as in any big city, you will find that a certain number of public phones are unusable, but it must be said that the French are rapidly making pay phones vandal-proof, and you have quite a good chance of finding a kiosk when you need one. Very often, queues are shorter at 'Télécarte' points and it may be useful to buy the 40F *carte*, from post offices and many shops, including Le Drugstore at the Étoile. If you don't find a pay phone when you need one, you may have to do a bit of travelling – here's a list of peaceful venues.

The *sous-sol* (lower ground floor) of Galerie Rond-Point, 12 avenue des Champs-Élysées (*Métro*: Franklin D. Roosevelt), has three good working phones, all with numbers where you can be called back.

Galerie Claridges at no. 74 has two phones, and wonder of wonders, complete telephone directories.

The Galerie des Champs, 84 Champs-Élysées, has three phones (free loos too, unlike other public places).

Most luxury hotels have public telephones, and a place to sit down, but they do not welcome callers with backpacks or shabby clothes.

After you have put in your Télécarte, or coin, and dialled the number, you will hear a jumble of noise and then a 'ring' tone which sounds like the British 'number engaged' sound. Don't hang up – this is the French 'number ringing' noise.

You can often phone from cafés, *tabacs* and bars, although some have a notice over the bar telling you that telephones and toilets are reserved for the clientele. You may be asked to buy a *jeton* from the cashier, which will probably cost about 2F; or the time of the call will be registered on a meter at the bar and you pay later. *Jetons* are not transferable from café to café, so if your party doesn't answer, get your money back. *Jeton* phones require you to press a rectangular button to the right of the phone when your party answers.

Long distance: outside the eight-digit area, time and distance come into play. In phone kiosks, there is a table listing the correct amount to pay for a call lasting a specified number of minutes. Consult the table, dial, wait for an answer, insert the money. When your time is almost up you'll be warned by a tone. Put in more change only then.

International: the cheapest way to call the UK is to amass a pocket-ful of 50-centime and 1F coins and dial direct from any unvan-dalised coin-fed telephone kiosk. The instructions (in French) are clearly set out on a panel near the phone.

Don't use British Telecom's much-touted 'UK Direct' service unless you're in dire need. When they advertise it, they don't tell you the cost: it's astronomical. Here's how the system works:

From France, you dial 19 (toll-free number), wait for a second dial tone, then dial 00 44. This connects you to a London operator, who then makes a transferred-charge call to any UK number, or alterna-tively will put the charge on your BT credit card.

This is all very swift and convenient, but be warned that calls of even the shortest duration (Hello, I'll be home Thursday at lunch-time, how's the weather, goodbye) are charged at the flat rate for three minutes. That's £2.25. On top of that, you're charged £2 for 'operator service', PLUS VAT on the whole transaction. That's close to £5 for the briefest call.

Travelling paupers should call home the hard way: either through Paris PTT locations where an operator will put in the call for you and give you the charge when you're finished; or direct, with a handful of change. A one-minute call costs about 5F – roughly 55 pence at the moment. Why make British Telecom richer than it is?

We thank the *Independent* newspaper for calling our attention to this costly UK gimmick, and reader John Gallery for writing to us after he too discovered the cost of convenience calls.

Time

The French use the twelve-hour clock, but run on 24-hour time. Hence, 5:00 p.m. is 17:00 (*dix-sept heures*); midnight is 24:00 (*minuit*); and so forth. It takes practice.

The days of the week, starting with Monday, are *lundi, mardi, mercredi, jeudi, vendredi, samedi,* and *dimanche.* The months of the year are easier to deal with: *janvier, février, mars, avril, mai, juin, juillet, août, septembre, octobre, novembre* and *decembre.* We narrowly escaped Napoleon's idea of *Germinal, Thermidor, Brumaire,* which, from 1793 to 1806, replaced the more familiar Gregorian Calendar.

And France is one hour ahead of the UK; six hours later than the US (East Coast time). You should be aware of this before you call your friends at 3:00 a.m., *their* time.

Tipping

The rules are clear-cut. Try not to deviate if you want to stay on good terms with your hosts.

Taxis: 10 to 15 per cent.

Lavatory attendants: 1F.

Waiters: 15 per cent is almost always included (you'll note the words *servis compris* on the menu). When service is *non-compris*, your expenses will be itemised, with 15 per cent (rounded off either way) tacked on at the bottom of your bill, and the whole thing totalled.

Cafés: 15 per cent is included (as for waiters) for table service. At the counter, leave some change.

Hotels: Service is added into the bill – but if the concierge or any other personnel have done you special favours (calling theatres, getting taxis), they should be rewarded.

Porters and Left Luggage: Set price, 7F50 per piece of luggage. No tip needed.

Hairdressers: 10 to 20 per cent.

Theatre and cinema ushers: 1F for the cinema and theatre, per person.

Traffic

Since we assume you're not suicidal, we won't deal with traffic regulations from a driver's viewpoint here. As a *piéton* – a pedestrian – you should know a few rules of the game.

If you're English, Scottish, Welsh, Irish or Japanese, you should know that traffic in France travels on the *right*. Therefore, when you step off the kerb, do not look to your right. *Look left.* Then look right, left again, and in all directions as quickly as possible before you head out, or you'll be mowed down. Many Paris streets, though not all, are one-way.

For pedestrians, a green light is a little green man in the traffic signal; sometimes a pinpoint of green or white light; sometimes nothing at all. A red light is a little red man. But in either case, it's very difficult to see the lights in bright sunshine. Your best bet is to wait for all traffic to stop, and ride on someone else's coat-tails across the street. All traffic lights, red or green, are called *feux rouges*.

Zebra crossings exist, but may be ignored by all concerned. Traffic tends to edge into them even when stopped.

Paris streets are either incredibly wide (the *grands boulevards*) and hence impossible to cross without feeling totally naked; or incredibly narrow, with cars parked halfway up the kerb, pedestrians walking with one foot in the gutter, single file, or face to the wall. Either way it's risky, so watch your step.

Wheelchair access

Paris for the less mobile. To be perfectly plain about it, Paris isn't the ideal city for anyone in a wheelchair or with serious walking difficulties. The Métro and the buses are only for those with a certain degree of mobility on their own two feet. The major museums are out of reach because they are reached by flights of steps. The Louvre is said to have a special entrance for those in wheelchairs, but *Which?* magazine, June 1981, reported absolute frustration when attempted by one of their researchers.

That said, one must in all fairness add that Paris itself – its streets, its squares, its buildings, its illumination at night – is infinitely accessible and always rewarding.

In the government-produced *Guide des Hôtels*, there is a 'wheel-chair' symbol which seems to promise much in the way of facilities for the disabled. Sadly, it has been impossible to establish any norm of exactly what the facilities are: many hoteliers who offer such conveniences as lifts or bedrooms on the ground floor forget that access to the hotel is up several steps, or through a narrow door. And far too many lifts, because of space restrictions in lobbies, are actually approached by two or three steps which make manoeuvering impossible. Other hotels listed with the 'wheelchair' symbol have split-level lobbies impossible for wheelchairs, and tricky even for those who use crutches or canes.

A useful series of guides for France is published under the titles of *Access*, from 68B Castlebar Road, Ealing, London W5. Two or three of the hotels their group has vetted still come within our price and comfort range:

Véronèse, 5 rue Véronèse, 13e. Tel: 43 31 20 90. *Métro*: Place d'Italie.
Good-sized lift; some bedrooms on ground floor.

Aviator, 20 rue Louis-Blanc, 10e. Tel: 46 07 79 24. *Métro*: Louis-Blanc.
Easy access from street; moderate-sized lift.

Grand Hôtel du Septième, 13 rue Chevert, 7e. Tel: 45 51 10 48. *Métro*: École-Militaire.
Easy access from street; moderate-sized lift.

More specific information is available from an excellent publication called *Voyager Quand Même* (Travel Anyway), in French and in English, published by Le Comité National Français de Liaison pour la Réadaptation des Handicapés (CNFLRH), 38 boulevard Raspail, 75007 Paris.

Association des Paralysés de France (APF), 17 boulevard Auguste-Blanqui, 75013 Paris, will furnish information about services and help available, and has representatives in various areas to help, as well as a magazine called *Faire Face* (in French) which often contains useful information.

Women on their own

Word has it that women alone do just fine in Paris (the reverse has also been mentioned). Our sources say that women can eat alone in almost any restaurant (except in an obviously raffish neighbourhood), drink alone in most bars, stay alone in hotels, walk alone in most parks and *quartiers* without being disturbed or made to feel uncomfortable. But use your head; don't walk in parks or lonely dark streets at night – either alone or in company.

Au secours *(emergencies)*

Dealing with real trouble at home is bad enough. In a foreign country, and in a foreign language, it can be devastating. But there are resources.

Medical emergencies

If it's more than a minor ailment, you need an English-speaking doctor or nurse, or a supply of medicine dispensed by someone who can understand you and your problem without the aid of faltering French or a translator. Here are the numbers to note. Write them down in your pocket notebook for the times (we hope rare) when you don't have this book in your hand.

SOS Dentists

87 boulevard Port-Royal, 13e
Tel: 43 37 51 00
RER: Port-Royal

An English-speaking dentist is almost always at hand. Ask for a receipt, as you may be able to claim emergency treatment on your medical insurance.

SOS Médecins

87 boulevard Port-Royal, 13e
Tel: 43 37 77 77 or 43 07 77 77
RER: Port-Royal

As above.

Hospitals:

British Hospital

3 rue Barbés, Levallois-Perret (in a suburb of Paris, but easily reached)
Tel: 47 58 13 12
Métro: Anatole-France

24 hours, 365 days a year. Telephone first for an appointment. Medical only; no dental facilities.

American Hospital

63 boulevard Victor-Hugo, Neuilly
Tel: 47 47 53 00
Métro: Porte-Maillot, then bus 82 to last stop.

Telephone first for an appointment. Hours: 9:00 a.m. to noon, 2:00 to 6:00 p.m. Sundays, emergency treatment only, no fixed appointments. Dental as well as medical.

Pharmacists

Pharmacie Anglaise des Champs-Élysées
62 avenue des Champs-Élysées, 8e
Tel: 43 59 22 52 and 42 25 25 13
Métro: George-V
Hours: 8:30 a.m. to 10:30 p.m., Mondays to Saturdays. Closed Sundays.

Well-stocked with familiar English and American brands of medicines, or their French equivalents, and attended by professional people who speak English. They will fill a prescription from a doctor, or can give you advice about a proprietary product for minor ills (headache, diarrhoea, streaming cold, strains and sprains, rheumatic pain).

British-American Pharmacy

1 rue Auber, 9e
Métro: Opéra
Hours: 8:30 a.m. to 8:00 p.m., Mondays to Saturdays. Closed Sundays.

Very much like the one mentioned above, staffed with bright, English-speaking people.

Pharmacie des Arts

106 boulevard Montparnasse, 14e
Tel: 43 25 44 88
Métro: Vavin
Hours: 8:00 a.m. to midnight, Mondays to Saturdays; 9:00 a.m. to 1:00 p.m., Sundays and public holidays.

Another late-night refuge. They have been dealing with English and American tourists for years, and can produce an over-the-counter remedy for almost anything, as well as quickly filling medical prescriptions. Prices tend to be high but the extraordinary opening hours make it worth it if you are in real need.

Pharmacie des Champs-Élysées

84 avenue des Champs-Élysées, 8e
Tel: 45 62 02 41
Métro: Franklin D. Roosevelt, George-V

Open 24 hours a day, seven days a week – very small, but useful in extreme emergency, and they speak about eighteen languages.

Pharmacie Le Drugstore

boulevard St-Germain (corner of rue de Rennes)
Tel: 45 48 04 55
Métro: St-Germain

Open 10:00 a.m. to 2:00 a.m. seven days a week. English spoken, and English and American remedies stocked.

Poison Centre

Hôpital de l'Assistance Publique Fernand Widal,
200 rue du Faubourg St-Denis, 10e
Tel: 42 05 63 29
Métro: La Chapelle

Burn Centre

Hôpital de l'Assistance Publique Trousseau,
26 avenue Dr Arnold Netter, 12e
Tel: 43 46 13 90
Métro: Porte de Vincennes

Drug Crisis Centre

Hôpital Marmottan,
19 rue d'Armaillé, 17e
Tel: 45 74 00 04
Métro: Argentine

Alcoholics Anonymous in English

Tel: 48 06 43 68

VD Clinic

Ligue de Préservation Sociale
29 rue Falguiere, 15e
Tel: 43 20 63 74
Métro: Pasteur

Open Mondays to Fridays, 2:00 to 4:30 p.m. and 5:00 to 6:45 p.m. Closed weekends.

Medical bills

English travellers in France get a pretty good deal. Partially free, medical care is available through the reciprocal scheme of the EEC. Good news: this now applies to the self-employed (barristers and such) and the unemployed, as well as to full-time employees; and if you're going abroad as a family, a single form covers all of you.

At least thirty days before departure get Form CM-1 from your local Department of Health and Social Security office, or by mail from the DHSS Leaflets Unit, Stanmore, Middlesex HA7 1AY. Fill it in at once and you are rewarded with Form E-111. If you need a doctor or hospital treatment in France, pay the bill, get a receipt, and present it for repayment (70 to 80 per cent of the charges) to the French Sickness Insurance Office. Full details accompany form E-111. Guard your E-111 with your life, as it cannot be replaced by post if lost, and the British Embassy can do nothing about reissuing it for you.

House calls by a doctor will cost from 100F, depending on the neighbourhood. Office calls are about 75F.

First Aid

At night, Sundays, or holidays, your concierge can telephone the nearest Commissariat of Police to get you the name of an emergency doctor. In case of a street accident or emergency, look for the automatic callbox marked *Services Médicaux*, at the nearest intersection of major streets.

Insurance

Medical: Don't assume that because you are a citizen of an EEC country, you'll get free medical care for the asking in France. Begin by getting the indispensable Form E-111, and hang on to it like grim death. This provides rather minimal coverages, and you'll still have to pay 20 per cent of the total cost. If you're unlucky enough to need a private ambulance to a private hospital or clinic, you pay the full whack. If you are sick enough to need bringing home by an air ambulance, or by a regular flight with someone to care for you, this can cost up to £5000. So take out insurance (through your travel agent, if you like, but even then read through before paying for the policy). Don't buy the first policy you are offered, and *check for exclusions*.

EuropAssistance is one of the best-known *au secours* systems, offering emergency help 24 hours a day, every day of the year. Their Medical Emergency Service *plus* Personal Travel Insurance covers practically every contingency you can think of. For 5 days, it costs £12.30, for 6 to 12 days £15.60, up to 23 days £18.30.

For this you are offered up to £1 million in medical expenses, unlimited cost of getting you home to the UK for urgent medical care, up to £1000 if your journey is called off for reasons beyond your control, up to £1000 for luggage lost or stolen, and so forth.

You pay the first £25 for any medical claim, for cancellation, or for loss of luggage or money. If you know there's a strike coming up on a certain day – as in the nerve-racking summer of 1989 – if you're delayed by riot, war or civil commotion, your policy won't shell out. But if your travel plans are wrecked by an unforeseen wildcat strike, you are covered, which is a great comfort. Policies from travel agents, or direct from EuropAssistance, 252 High Street, Croydon, Surrey CR0 1NF. Telephone: 081-680 1234.

Private Patients Plan (PPP) subscribers now get International Emergency Medical Cover at no extra cost. Their SOS Alarm Centres are manned 24 hours a day, and provide instant advice for anyone sick or injured, and if necessary, a medically-supervised flight back to the UK, with costs of up to £35,000 covered. In France, they will put you in touch with an English-speaking doctor. For full details, write to PPP House, Upperton Road, Eastbourne, East Sussex BN21 1LH, or telephone 0323-410505.

BUPA subscribers get up to £100,000 in medical care, including the cost of bringing you home if necessary, and non-medical care which includes up to £1500 for cancellation or curtailment charges due to circumstances beyond your control, up to £1500 for loss of luggage, travel tickets, passports or whatever, and a £250 allowance if you lose your money. These two policies will cost you £10.10 for the first 8 days, £13.60 for up to 16 days. You pay the first £20 of any non-medical claim. There are no age limits on this policy for BUPA members. You must get your policy seven days before travelling. Telephone: 071-352 5212

VISA and Access card-holders are protected by free death and injury insurance if travel is charged on these cards. But if you've taken out one of the all-purpose policies mentioned above, remember that you can't claim on two different policies if anything goes wrong.

Fine print department: As it is almost impossible to find a policy that will give you instant money to replace clothes, camera, luggage, etc., or pay urgent medical bills, one veteran traveller advises charging *everything* on credit cards. Save the receipts, photocopy them, send the originals to your insurance company within 48 hours of returning home, and hope that the payout arrives before you have to fork over to the credit card company. If medical or hospital bills are very high, the Emergency Number on your policy will guarantee payment.

Contact lens wearers must make sure their policy includes travel coverage.

Travel insurance

Everything you travel with – clothes, radio, watch, money, luggage, specs – can be covered by comprehensive travel insurance. This should, ideally, include cancellation insurance for plane, train, or boat tickets that may not be usable because of illness or accident. Try to get the kind of policy that provides you with instant money to get replacement clothes, luggage, camera, etc., without waiting months for reimbursement; or follow the advice in 'Fine print department' above. Check the policy very carefully. One friend who thought her fur coat was covered by her household policy had it pinched in a restaurant, and too late found that said coat was only covered in the house – not while being worn. Ask your travel agent for the best deals going.

Robbery, attack, rape

Or any other crime of which you are a victim – use the automatic callbox, marked *Police Secours*. Ask for someone who speaks English. We are advised by feminist friends in Paris that the police are notably unsympathetic to to anyone claiming rape, as they seem to take the attitude that women who wear anything more provocative than an anorak are asking for trouble.

Lost passport

Wise words from a travel adviser in Paris who has helped bail out the unlucky, the feckless, the forgetful: photocopy the first few pages of your passport which show your vital details, when and where the document was issued, the French visa (if necessary), and keep it either with your travel tickets or in your wallet. If you lose the passport, report at once to the nearest police station (ask a policeman or a *pervenche*, the blue-clad meter maid), then go to your embassy (addresses below). They can issue you a new passport, or a travel document which will get you home or allow you to go on your way. In some parts of the Continent, this can mean at best a sour look and some questioning at immigration points; at worst a few hours of cooling your heels in airport or train station while they check up on you. Remember that your Travel Insurance policy will help pay the cost of replacing your passport (photos, embassy fees, etc.) which will at least ease the pain.

Lost money

Report it to the police, as for passports, then forget it. See Travel insurance (p. 265).

Traveller's cheques

You *do* keep a record of those numbers in that notebook, don't you? Cross off each as you cash the cheques. If you lose the remaining ones, get in touch with the issuing company right away (their European addresses and telephone numbers are in the fine print that comes with the cheques). With varying degrees of speed, they will provide duplicate ones. Report this loss, too, to the Paris police.

Lost or stolen jewellery, camera, clothing, luggage

Report to the nearest police station (ask someone who speaks French, if you can, to write out a brief description of the lost item in French). Last resort: the Lost and Found Office (Bureau des Objets Trouvés), 36 rue des Morillons, 15e, *Métro*: Convention (see page 238). File a report of what you lost and where you think you lost it. The chances of recovering anything are almost nil, but in dealing with such an emergency you'll be surprised at how your French improves, and you'll get to see the inside of offices and police stations that are right out of Maigret. French functionaries are not noted for their ability to speak English – that's not what they're paid for – so if you can chase up a French-speaking friend to go with you, it will help. And of course, claim on your travel insurance.

Theft

Street theft

You can protect your serious money with an old-fashioned money belt, available from Youth Hostel and camping shops among others: or a more modern 'Hide-a-Pocket' in thin soft leather, on a short strap, to be looped over a belt and worn beneath trousers or skirt. It's about £5.95 from several mail-order houses (Barclaycard among them), and at 7" x 4", it's big enough for passport, credit cards, traveller's cheques and cash. While this may sound fussy and grandmotherish, it is a neat inconspicuous way to make sure that no alien hands are laid on your valuables.

The Child Thieves of Paris

If you find yourself surrounded by a posse of charming, laughing, appealing urchins jumping up and down and patting and pawing you, *strike out with anything at hand*: rolled-up newspaper, magazine, umbrella, your fists. These pretty little fiends are carefully trained by local Fagins to surround the unwary tourist, and with small lightning darts at jacket and handbag, take *everything*. Passports, money, credit cards, tickets can go in a flash while you're wondering what hit you. Favourite venues are Notre Dame, the Tuileries, crowded Métro platforms, queues anywhere. The kids race away laughing and jeering. Even if police pick them up, they cannot be held for more than an hour or two because of their ages, and in the meantime their '*Controleur*' has received all the goodies. An American couple sat on a park bench to rest, and within two minutes were picked clean by kids who made a screen of newspapers around them while two of their bandit band rifled pockets and handbag, and ended by snatching a gold chain from the woman's neck. If it happens to you, yell loud and harsh: *Fiche-moi le camp! Voleurs! Va t'en!* and lay about you with vigour. Forget about dignity. Get rid of these vicious kids.

Animal bites

Cat scratches, dog bites, a nip from a horse or a squirrel – don't shrug them off. The best we can advise is *not* to fool around with any animal, tame or wild, on the continent. Rabies is at large in Europe, no joke. The French call it *la rage*, and you will see warning posters in many places. If you are scratched or bitten, get a doctor at once, and report the incident to the police quickly. They will pick up the animal and hold it until it is proved to be either safe or rabid. And they will keep you under observation until your condition has been thoroughly checked. You may need a series of painful, costly, and time-consuming injections which can wreck your holiday: so don't feed squirrels or stray cats, and unless you know an animal and its owner personally, keep your hands to yourself.

Stranded

If you are without passport, money, traveller's cheques, or transport because of loss, theft, or other damage, call on your embassy. If they are convinced that you are a genuine victim without resources, they can arrange for your transportation home (the slowest and cheapest way). You must agree to pay them back as soon as you reach a source of funds. Each embassy has a different policy, so check with yours. To get a temporary passport, remember you'll need photographs.

British Embassy

35 rue du Faubourg St-Honoré, 8e
Tel: 42 66 91 42
Métro: Concorde

It's a beautiful, historic house and worth taking a look at if you have legitimate reason to call. Nicer manners than at the American Embassy, and not so many guns in evidence, but the same basic approach.

British Consulate
2 Cité du Rétiro, 8e
Tel: 42 66 91 42
Métro: Concorde

American Embassy

2 avenue Gabriel, 8e
Tel: 42 96 12 02
Métro: Concorde

Brusque but helpful. Don't expect much sympathy or offers of extra money, as they have had to deal with too many feckless tourists in the sixties and seventies who thought they were a soft touch for Uncle Sam's largesse.

American Consulate
2 rue St-Florentin, 1er
Tel: 42 96 14 88
Métro: Concorde

Canadian Embassy

35 avenue Montaigne, 8e
Tel: 47 23 52 50
Métro: Alma Marceau

Australian Embassy and Consulate

4 rue Jean-Rey, 15e
Tel: 45 75 62 00
Métro: Bir-Hakeim

New Zealand Embassy and Consulate

7 rue Leonardo-da-Vinci, 16e
Tel: 45 00 24 11
Métro: Victor-Hugo

Maps

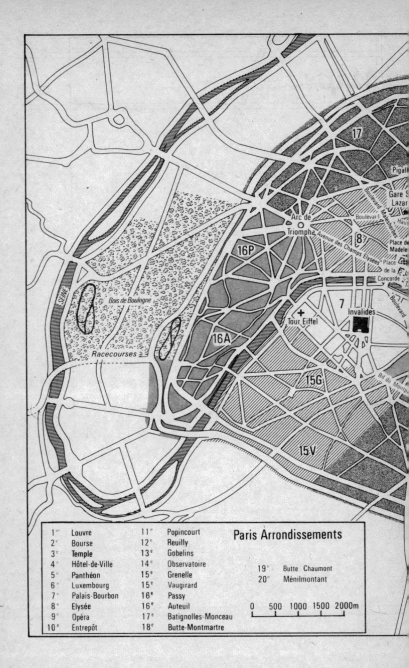

Paris Arrondissements

1er	Louvre	11e	Popincourt
2e	Bourse	12e	Reuilly
3e	Temple	13e	Gobelins
4e	Hôtel-de-Ville	14e	Observatoire
5e	Panthéon	15e	Grenelle
6e	Luxembourg	15e	Vaugirard
7e	Palais-Bourbon	16e	Passy
8e	Elysée	16e	Auteuil
9e	Opéra	17e	Batignolles-Monceau
10e	Entrepôt	18e	Butte-Montmartre

19e   Butte Chaumont
20e   Ménilmontant

0   500   1000   1500   2000m

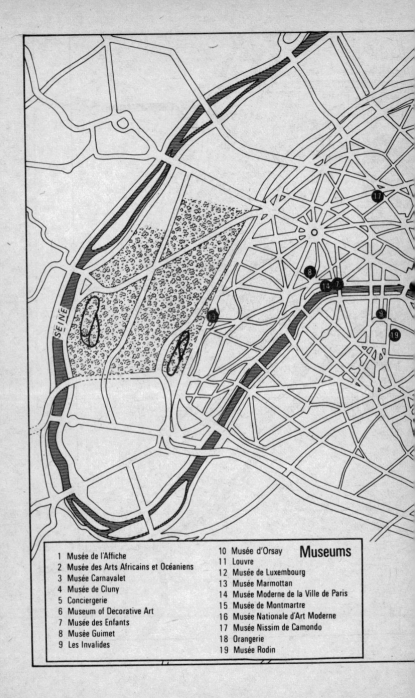

Museums

1 Musée de l'Affiche
2 Musée des Arts Africains et Océaniens
3 Musée Carnavalet
4 Musée de Cluny
5 Conciergerie
6 Museum of Decorative Art
7 Musée des Enfants
8 Musée Guimet
9 Les Invalides
10 Musée d'Orsay
11 Louvre
12 Musée de Luxembourg
13 Musée Marmottan
14 Musée Moderne de la Ville de Paris
15 Musée de Montmartre
16 Musée Nationale d'Art Moderne
17 Musée Nissim de Camondo
18 Orangerie
19 Musée Rodin

Index

Index compiled by Peva Keane